PEARSON CUSTOM LIBRARY

ENGLISH
MERCURY READER

PEARSON

ISBN 10: 1-256-59194-7
ISBN 13: 978-1-256-59194-8

General Editors

Janice Neuleib
Illinois State University

Kathleen Shine Cain
Merrimack College

Stephen Ruffus
Salt Lake Community College

Table of Contents

Whatsizface

David Rakoff

David Rakoff (1964–) was born in Montreal, Quebec, and grew up in Toronto. He is the youngest of three children. Both parents were M.D.s, his mother being a psychiatrist. He earned his B.A. (1986) from Columbia University in New York. He contributes essays to Public Radio's This American Life *and to the* New York Times Magazine. *He has worked in theater with good friends David and Amy Sedaris on their plays* Stitches, The Little Freida Mysteries, The Book of Liz, *and the Obie award-winning* One Woman Shoe. *He has published essays in* Vogue, Salon, The New York Observer, *and* Wired, *among others. He has twice received the Lambda Book Award for Humor, won the 2010 Academy Award for Best Live Action Short Film,* The New Tenants, *and appeared on* The Daily Show. *His books include* Don't Get Too Comfortable *(2005) and* Half Empty *(2010).*

I am not a handsome man. All that means is that my face has never been my fortune. Luckily for me, it hasn't been my punch line, either. I have some pretty eyes and, like everyone, I have my moments. I may even be thought attractive by those who love me, but that is emphatically not the same as the irrefutable mathematics of plane and placement that make for true beauty.

As a teenager reading *Death in Venice*, I understood the world to be divided between the Aschenbachs and the Tadzios. There are those who gaze, and those who are gazed upon. I am not talking about the natural inequity of attention that the old bestow upon the young— we are all hardwired to respond to babies, for example, but it would take the rare and deeply odd child to singsong to a grown-up, "Who's got a cute receding hairline? Oh yes it is." I am talking about within one's own cohort: some are destined to promenade the Lido in Venice, blooming like flowers under the heat of appreciative stares, while the rest of us are born to watch, sweating through our grimy collars and eating our musty strawberries while the plague rolls in.

Inveterate Aschenbach that I have always been, we are at peace, my face and I, although it can be a tenuous cease-fire. A certain degree of dissatisfaction with my features is part of my cultural birthright. In my largely Jewish high school scores of girls got new noses for their birthdays, replacing their fantastic Litvak schnozes with "the Mindy," as Paul Rudnick has dubbed that shiny-skinned, characterless lump. Despite the prevalence and remarkable timing of these operations, coinciding as they so often did with upcoming Sweet Sixteens, they were always framed as life-or-death necessities— emergency procedures to repair lethally deviated septa and restore imperiled breathing. Even then, we knew enough to lie. Elective cosmetic surgery was the province of the irretrievably shallow. It was also a largely female pursuit. For most boys, failing the unlikely scenario wherein you infiltrated the mob, turned state's evidence, and got a new set of features thanks to the good doctors at the witness protection program, your face was an irreducible fact.

Still, without benefit of a mirror I can easily reel off all of the things I might change, given the opportunity. Starting at the top, they include a permanent red spot on the left side of my forehead; a brow pleated by worry: a furrow between my eyebrows so deep that at times it could be a coin slot; purple hollows underneath my eyes that I've had since infancy, and, also since childhood, lines like surveyors marks on my cheeks— placeholders for the inevitable eye bags I will have; a nose more fleshy and wide than prototypically Semitic, graced with a bouquet of tiny gin blossoms resulting from years of using neither sunscreen nor moisturizer; a set of those Fred Flintstone nasal creases down to the corners of my mouth; a permanent acne scar on my right cheek; a planklike expanse of filtrum between the bottom of my nose and the top of my too-thin upper lip; and, in profile, a double chin.

None of which is really a problem in New York City. Being a little goofy looking suits the supposed literary life-of-the-mind I lead here. (What a paper-thin lie. There are days when I'd throw out every book I own for the chance to be beautiful just once. Reading is hard, to paraphrase that discontinued Barbie.) Seriously contemplating the erasure or repair of any of these is inconceivable within the city limits. It's too small a town. There is a place, though, where the sunny notion of physical perfection and its achievement by any means necessary is carried unashamedly on the smoggy, orange-scented air: swimming pools, movie stars. Cue the banjo music.

I make consultations with two Beverly Hills surgeons. I want them to tell me what they might do, as though I had limitless inclination and resources, with no input from me. The reason for my silence is that I'd like outside confirmation of those things that are true flaws and those that are dysmorphic delusions on my part. There is also the vain hope that it is all dysmorphic delusion. That if I fail to bring it to their attention, somehow it will turn out that I've had the nose of a Greek statue all along. Primarily, though, I am hoping to catch them out in a moment of unchecked avarice; instead of proposing the unnecessary pinning back of my ears, I imagine them letting slip with their true purpose, as in, "I recommend the Italian ceramic back-splashes in my country house kitchen." Or "You'd look much better if my toxic punishing bitch of an ex-wife didn't insist on sending our eight-year-old daughter, Caitlin, to riding lessons in Malibu for $300 an hour."

Garth Fisher's practice is decorated with a grandeur disproportionate to the space, like a studio apartment tricked out with pieces from the set of *Intolerance*. The waiting area has overstuffed sofas, a small flat-screen TV in the corner, tasseled wall sconces, and a domed oculus in the low ceiling, painted with clouds. Fisher's office is full of bulky antique furniture in dark wood with turned legs, armoires, walnut book-cases. Behind his desk are many photographs of his wife, Brooke Burke, a model and television personality. Were I differently placed on the Kinsey scale, I might even pronounce her "hot," dropping my voice an octave and adding an extra syllable to the word. She is a near-perfect beauty.

Fisher himself is also nice-looking, a handsome man in his early forties. Blue-eyed and chestnut-haired, he has a bit of the early-seventies Aqua Velva hunk about him. I ask him, looking directly at the enviable cleft in his chin, if he's had any work done himself. Very little. A tiny bit of botox between his brows and some veneers on his teeth. He also had his nose done, to correct some football injuries. To my dismay, he is similarly conservative in his approach to others. Of the eight potential patients he saw that day, he refused to take on seven of them. Some were not candidates while others had unreasonable expectations about what plastic surgery can realistically do, even now.

"This is the Dark Ages. This is like 1904," he says. Future generations will be amazed by the inevitable advances, he predicts. For now he is more than willing to allow other doctors to use their patient populations as the guinea pigs for new and experimental treatments. He has not done a penile augmentation, for example ("scary business"), neither does he offer those silicone pectoral or calf implants.

"I want a simple life. All I've got to do is do a good job and tell the truth."

The only reason he agrees to give me unsolicited advice is that he knows I am a writer (indeed, the only way I could get an appointment with two top Beverly Hills plastic surgeons is that they know I am a writer). He remains notably uncomfortable with the charade. "If someone comes in here like this," he pulls his ears out from his head like Dumbo, "and all they want fixed is the mole on their chin, then that's all I'm going to mention." Assured of my thick skin, he eventually allows as how he might "clean some things up" that steal focus from my eyes.

We go into an examining room where he keeps his computer simulator. The process begins with taking two photographs—the "befores." I look the way I always do, but it's embarrassing to see myself up on the monitor with another person sitting there. My profile looks careworn, simultaneously bald and hairy. My eyes are sunk into craters of liver-colored flesh, and my ear is a greasy nautilus, as if I'd just come from listening to a deep-fat fryer.

Fisher demonstrates his morphing tool by drawing a circle around my chin with the mouse. Pulling the cursor, he extends my jaw out like a croissant. It is a fabulous toy. I want to wrest the mouse from his control and really go to town, giving myself fleshy horns, pointy corkscrew ears. If he would only let me, I would pull out the flanges of my nostrils until they looked like the wings of Eero Saarinen's TWA terminal at JFK. "But your chin is perfect," he says, snapping it and me back to reality. "Three millimeters behind your bottom lip." Instead, he points out how the end of my nose droops down to the floor, while the arch of my nostrils is very high. (I write "too high" in my notebook before realizing that these are my words, not his.) He raises the tip, lowers my nostrils, and then straightens out the slope of the nose itself. It is subtle and aquiline. He then smoothes out the area under my eyes. In real life this would involve the removal of some fat and tightening up the skin. Finally, he points to the small vertical indentation between my brows, just like the one he had before botox. He recommends a small amount of the neurotoxin, just enough to smooth it out without robbing me of my capacity to emote. Of all the features that render me less than perfect, I've actually always sort of been attached to those that lend me an air of gravitas, covering up my shortcomings of character and intellect. I ask if it's all right to leave it as is. "Well," he shrugs, "it's okay if you're playing a lawyer or a judge." Instead, I get him to give me a slight Mick Jagger moue. "I don't like those lips, but I'll let you have them." He plumps up my mouth.

The photographs are printed out, the two images side by side against a dark background with no discernible seam between them. I am a set of twins. My original self seems a melancholic killjoy. His reengineered brother, on the other hand, looks clean and a little haughty. And how about that marvelous new nose! Pointy, sharp, a weapon. Despite that old stereotype about Jewish intellectual superiority, I think I appear cleverer as well ("perspicacious," as my ethnically cleansed self might say). Fisher's instinct about my new mouth was also right on the money. It gives me the beginnings of a snarl, like I've wedged a handful of Tic Tacs in front of my upper teeth.

15 But even my misbegotten new upper lip cannot dampen my spirits. I step out into the beautiful California dusk to catch a cab with a spring in my step. I'm feeling handsome, as though Fisher's changes were already manifest on my face and not just in the envelope of photographs I clutch. Reality soon sets in. The sidewalk of Santa Monica Boulevard simply ends without warning and I have to dart, terrified, across four lanes of traffic. I cannot find a taxi on the deserted leafy streets of Beverly Hills, and I have to walk all the way back to my hotel. "Good evening," the beautiful young doorman says to me when I arrive, an hour and a half later. He smiles in my direction, but his eyes are looking just above my left ear.

Studying the photographs the next morning, I am already experiencing some misgivings. It is not the regret of "What have I done?" that dogs me so much as a feeling that I want more. I briefly curse Garth Fisher's innate professionalism and hope that Richard Ellenbogen, my next surgeon, will not hang back and keep me from achieving my true physical glory.

If his office is any indication, I'm in luck. Where Fisher's was the McMansion version of the baths at Pompeii, Richard Ellenbogen's Sunset Boulevard practice (hard by the Hamburger Hamlet where Dean Martin are every day) defies easy aesthetic description. It is an astonishment of styles and motifs. The reception desk is framed by two arching female figureheads as might be found on the prow of a Spanish galleon. The walls of the waiting room are peach plaster set with Tudor timbers. There is an ornamental brick fireplace in the corner, sofas in floral chintz, and everywhere, absolutely everywhere—on the mantel, along the plate rail (hung with swags of floral chintz bunting)—are ormolu clocks, Bakelite and old wooden radios, commemorative plates, lamps and small sculptures of those young, barely pubescent deco-era girls, the kind who festoon old movie-palace plaster and frequently hold aloft globe lights. All of it in under 150 square feet.

There is a benevolence to this crowded exuberance; one's own physical flaws shrink to nothing in the midst of such riotous excess. The staff is friendly and funny. "Here to get your breasts done?" cracks one woman when she sees me. Another confides, "Sometimes he," meaning Ellenbogen, "will just say to a patient, 'You don't need this. Buy a new dress and save your money.' We love our patients."

Ellenbogen is known for fat grafting and facial reshaping. Instead of pulling and tightening a face, he replaces the fat in the areas that used to be fuller, before aging and gravity did their work. For a patient in their mid-fifties, for example, he will analyze a photograph of them at half that age and isolate the facial regions in need of filling. The patients I look at in his albums do seem *juicy*, for lack of a better word, although the result looks not so much younger as vegetal. They look like Arcimboldo paintings, those Renaissance portraits constructed entirely out of fruit. To give them their due, they don't look like drum-tight gorgons, either. In folder after folder, I do not come across even one of those monstrous surgerized analogues of Joan Rivers. Where are those faces, I wonder aloud to Ellenbogen?

20 "We call that the New York look," he says. Apparently, there is 20 less need for that kind of wholesale renovation in Los Angeles, where Hollywood hopefuls have been a self-selecting group for almost a century. "People are prettier here. It's now the children and grandchildren of Sandra Dee. In New York, you've still got all those great Jewish immigrant faces." Ellenbogen is allowed to say this, possessed of one as he is himself. (He's had some botox, his neck done, and lipo on his

love handles, although he still supports a somewhat cantilevered belly as befits a man of sixty.)

He doesn't do computer imaging. "It's hokey. It's used by people who aren't artists. It's not a true representation of what a surgeon can actually do. It's like a real estate agent saying, 'This would be such an incredible view if you just planted some trees here and put in a garden . . . '" Instead, he takes two Polaroids and, using a small brush, mixes together unbleached titanium and burnt umber and paints the changes on one of them. Like Fisher, even with carte blanche, Ellenbogen only envisions minor treatments. Again with the straightening of the nose and raising the tip (one hour), he would also build out my chin a little bit, using a narrow curving strip of milky white silicone—like something from the toe of a high-end running shoe—fed down through the mouth behind the lower lip (ten minutes), and a final procedure (fifteen minutes) in which he would inject fat into my extremely deep nasojugal folds, those tear troughs under my eyes. (Garth Fisher is not a fan of regrafting. "You'd love your doctor for six months," and no longer, he implies.) Total cost, around $12,000.

There is nothing so intimately known as our own face. Even the most deprived existence provides opportunities to gaze into a reflective surface now and then—puddles of standing water, soup spoons, the sides of toasters. We know what pleases us, and also have a fairly good sense of what we would change if we could. Sometimes, though, we just get it plain wrong. Ellenbogen shows me a photo of a young man in his twenties; a pale, strawberry blond with the kind of meek profile that gets shoved into lockers. "This kid came in and wanted me to fix his nose. 'It's too big!' he said. I told him, 'It's not your nose. I'll prove it to you. I'll build out your chin. If you don't like it, I'll take it out and do your nose for free.' " Ellenbogen was right. The merest moving forward of the jaw has made the nose recede. The change is remarkable.

The fellow may have been focusing on the wrong feature, but at least he wanted *something*. There is a reason that both Fisher and Ellenbogen were so reluctant to suggest procedures to me. An unspecified and overarching desire for change speaks to a dissatisfaction probably better served by a psychiatrist. One surgeon I spoke to will not treat people in their first year of widowhood for just that reason. To briefly rant about *The Swan*, the television show that takes depressed female contestants—all of whom seem to need little more than to change out of their sweat suits and get some therapy—and makes them all over to look like the same trannie hooker: what makes *The Swan* truly vile is that for the months that these women are being carved up like so much processed poultry, all of the mirrors in their lives are covered over. Such willing abrogation of any say or agency in how they will be transformed *by definition* means that in the real world, they would not be candidates for surgery. It is the very sleaziest of all the plastic-surgery makeover shows—quite a distinction, that; like being voted the Osbourne child with the fewest interests.

Garth Fisher, in what might be considered an unconscious act of penance for contributing to the culture in which something like *The Swan* can exist (he is the in-house surgeon for the comparatively classier *Extreme Makeover*), has created a five-hour DVD series called *The Naked Truth About Plastic Surgery*. Each hour-long disk is devoted to a different procedure and region of the body—breast augmentation, brow lifts, etc.

25 In spirit, *The Naked Truth* is more educational tool than sales 25 pitch. It is refreshingly up front about the complications that can arise, like bad scarring, hematoma, numbness, pigment irregularities, infection, skin loss, even embolism and death. In the liposuction section, there is a shot of Fisher in the operating room. The backs of the patient's legs are shiny brown from the pre-surgical iodine wash, and crisscrossed with felt-tip marker. Fisher is sawing away under the shuddering skin with the cannula, a tool resembling a sharp, narrow pennywhistle attached to a hose. There is a savagery to his movements, the way one might angrily go back and forth over a particularly tenacious piece of lint with a vacuum cleaner. He looks up at the camera, his arm going the whole time. Although wearing a mask, his eyes crinkle in an unmistakable "Well, hello there!" smile.

There are shots of clear plastic containers of extracted fat—frothy, orange-yellow foam floating atop a layer of dark blood—and pictures of postoperative faces looking like Marlon Brando after he's been worked over in *On the Waterfront*. Such footage might have once had a deterrent effect but is now familiar to any toddler who has ever been parked in front of The Learning Channel. That these images have to be followed up by the cautionary tone of a narrator who says, "just because something *can* be done does not mean it *should* be done" and "if you can reach your goal without surgery, then you are better off," speaks to how far down the rabbit hole we've tumbled. It's as if the whole country regularly watched newsreel footage of buses full of children going off of cliffs and was still blithely picking up the phone to make bookings with Greyhound.

I might be more apt to drink the Kool-Aid if I was more impressed by the results. The before and after photos of liposuction, for example, do show a reduction in volume. But if I were to endure the risks of general anesthetic, the pain, the constriction garment that must be worn like a sausage casing for weeks after the surgery, and the months-long wait for final results, I wouldn't just want a flatter stomach with no trace of love handles. I would insist upon the tortoiseshell reticulation of a six-pack, that abdominal Holy Grail. That's hard to achieve with liposuction. There is a procedure that replicates the look, called "etching," where the coveted tic-tac-toe pattern is suctioned out of the adipose tissue, giving the appearance of musculature with no muscles present; morphology absent of structure, like the false bones in McDonald's creepy McRib sandwich. Garth Fisher doesn't recommend or offer it. Gain weight, he points out, and the artificially differentiated lobes of your fat expand and rise from your stomach like a pan of buttermilk biscuits.

In the end, it is neither thrift nor fear of the knife that deters me. Far more than the physical transformation, it would be the very decision to go ahead with it that would render me unrecognizable to myself.

I once bleached my hair almost to platinum for a part in a short film. It lent me a certain Teutonic unapproachability, which I liked. But as it grew out, it faded to an acid, Marshmallow Peep yellow and my head started to look like a drugstore Easter-promotion window. Dark roots and straw-dry hair look fine on a college kid experimenting with peroxide, but I looked like a man of a certain age with a bad dye job clutching at his fleeting youth with bloody fingernails. I could see pity in the faces of strangers who passed me on the street. *Mutton dressed as lamb*, they were thinking. To all the world, I was the guy who broadcasts that heartbreaking and ambivalent directive: "Look at me, but for the reasons you used to!"

30   It must be murder to be an aging beauty, a former Tadzio, to see   30 your future as an ignored spectator rushing up to meet you like the hard pavement. What a small sip of gall to be able to time with each passing year the ever-shorter interval in which someone's eyes focus upon you. And then shift away.

Questions on Meaning

1. What does Rakoff tell us about his face and his basic appearance? Does he actually have any desire to have plastic surgery? Why does he visit the surgeons?

2. The first surgeon insists that he does only minimal work and then only if the patient requests the changes. Then he shows Rakoff how the imaging machine works. What new features does he give Rakoff?

3. The second surgeon insists that plastic surgery is an art and eschews machines for imaging. He then explains about intense changes such as liposuction and other surgeries that take months to recover from. What is Rakoff's response to such kinds of self-transformation?

4. The descriptions of the things that can happen if plastic surgery goes wrong are gory. What does Rakoff suggest might be the reason that some folks will give into such risks and torture?

5. What are the differences between the plastic surgeon who works with ordinary people and the one who works with movie stars? Why do movie stars want the changes they request?

Questions on Rhetorical Strategy and Style

1. This essay is gently humorous as Rakoff joins the ranks of the Jewish comedians who have fun laughing at themselves. How does Rakoff characterize his own looks? Why is this description funny?

2. Rakoff spends quite a few sentences on the difference between the two surgeons' office furnishings and staffs. How does he use these descriptions to differentiate between these two men and their practices?

3. Rakoff makes clear that he has no intention of having any kind of surgery, but these M.D.s see him anyway because he is a writer. Why is this point funny but also convincing? Why does everyone like to be the subject of an interview, as long, at least, as the interview promises to be friendly and even complimentary?

Writing Assignments

1. Have you ever considered or dreamed of plastic surgery? What would you like to have changed? Write about why we all would like to perfect something about ourselves.

2. What experiences have you had with the medical profession? Write about one or more of these experiences. Don't hesitate to be funny if that is the appropriate approach to take.

3. Try to describe two physical spaces in the way that Rakoff describes the offices of the two surgeons. Use the descriptions to characterize the people who occupy the spaces. For example, how do the offices of the chemistry department and the English department differ, or the residence hall rooms of a female friend and a male friend?

The Tipping Point

Malcolm Gladwell

Malcolm Gladwell (1963–   ) was born in England but grew up in Canada. He majored in history at the University of Toronto, graduating in 1984. In 1987 he began as a reporter for the Washington Post *where he worked first as a science writer and then as New York bureau chief. In 1996 he moved to the* New Yorker *where he works as a staff writer.* The Tipping Point *(2001), his best-selling book, is the source of this essay. The book theorizes the impact of building trends on events and ideas, showing that change takes place in sudden events rather than by gradual shifting.*

1   For Hush Puppies—the classic American brushed-suede shoes with the lightweight crepe sole—the Tipping Point came somewhere between late 1994 and early 1995. The brand had been all but dead until that point. Sales were down to 30,000 pairs a year, mostly to backwoods outlets and small-town family stores. Wolverine, the company that makes Hush Puppies, was thinking of phasing out the shoes that made them famous. But then something strange happened. At a fashion shoot, two Hush Puppies executives—Owen Baxter and Geoffrey Lewis—ran into a stylist from New York who told them that the classic Hush Puppies had suddenly become hip in the clubs and bars of downtown Manhattan. "We were being told," Baxter recalls, "that there were resale shops in the Village, in Soho, where the shoes were being sold. People were going to the Ma and Pa stores, the little stores that still carried them, and buying them up." Baxter and Lewis were baffled at first. It made no sense to them that shoes that were so obviously out of fashion could make a comeback. "We were told that Isaac Mizrahi was wearing the shoes himself,"

Lewis says. "I think it's fair to say that at the time we had no idea who Isaac Mizrahi was."

By the fall of 1995, things began to happen in a rush. First the designer John Bartlett called. He wanted to use Hush Puppies in his spring collection. Then another Manhattan designer, Anna Sui, called, wanting shoes for her show as well. In Los Angeles, the designer Joe Fitzgerald put a twenty-five-foot inflatable basset hound—the symbol of the Hush Puppies brand—on the roof of his Hollywood store and gutted an adjoining art gallery to turn it into a Hush Puppies boutique. While he was still painting and putting up shelves, the actor Pee-wee Herman walked in and asked for a couple of pairs. "It was total word of mouth," Fitzgerald remembers.

In 1995, the company sold 430,000 pairs of the classic Hush Puppies, and the next year it sold four times that, and the year after that still more, until Hush Puppies were once again a staple of the wardrobe of the young American male. In 1996, Hush Puppies won the prize for best accessory at the Council of Fashion Designers awards dinner at Lincoln Center, and the president of the firm stood up on the stage with Calvin Klein and Donna Karan and accepted an award for an achievement that—as he would be the first to admit—his company had almost nothing to do with. Hush Puppies had suddenly exploded, and it all started with a handful of kids in the East Village and Soho.

How did that happen? Those first few kids, whoever they were, weren't deliberately trying to promote Hush Puppies. They were wearing them precisely because no one else would wear them. Then the fad spread to two fashion designers who used the shoes to peddle something else—haute couture. The shoes were an incidental touch. No one was trying to make Hush Puppies a trend. Yet, somehow, that's exactly what happened. The shoes passed a certain point in popularity and they tipped. How does a thirty-dollar pair of shoes go from a handful of downtown Manhattan hipsters and designers to every mall in America in the space of two years?

I

5 There was a time, not very long ago, in the desperately poor New York City neighborhoods of Brownsville and East New York, when the streets would turn into ghost towns at dusk. Ordinary working

people wouldn't walk on the sidewalks. Children wouldn't ride their bicycles on the streets. Old folks wouldn't sit on stoops and park benches. The drug trade ran so rampant and gang warfare was so ubiquitous in that part of Brooklyn that most people would take to the safety of their apartment at nightfall. Police officers who served in Brownsville in the 1980s and early 1990s say that, in those years, as soon as the sun went down their radios exploded with chatter between beat officers and their dispatchers over every conceivable kind of violent and dangerous crime. In 1992, there were 2,154 murders in New York City and 626,182 serious crimes, with the weight of those crimes falling hardest in places like Brownsville and East New York. But then something strange happened. At some mysterious and critical point, the crime rate began to turn. It tipped. Within five years, murders had dropped 64.3 percent to 770 and total crimes had fallen by almost half to 355,893. In Brownsville and East New York, the sidewalks filled up again, the bicycles came back, and old folks reappeared on the stoops. "There was a time when it wasn't uncommon to hear rapid fire, like you would hear somewhere in the jungle in Vietnam," says Inspector Edward Messadri, who commands the police precinct in Brownsville. "I don't hear the gunfire anymore."[1]

The New York City police will tell you that what happened in New York was that the city's policing strategies dramatically improved. Criminologists point to the decline of the crack trade and the aging of the population. Economists, meanwhile, say that the gradual improvement in the city's economy over the course of the 1990s had the effect of employing those who might otherwise have become criminals. These are the conventional explanations for the rise and fall of social problems, but in the end none is any more satisfying than the statement that kids in the East Village caused the Hush Puppies revival. The changes in the drug trade, the population, and the economy are all long-term trends, happening all over the country. They don't explain why crime plunged in New York City so much more than in other cities around the country, and they don't explain why it all happened in such an extraordinarily short time. As for the improvements made by the police, they are important too. But there is a puzzling gap between the scale of the changes in policing and the size of the effect on places like Brownsville and East New York. After all, crime didn't just slowly ebb in New York as conditions gradually improved.

It plummeted. How can a change in a handful of economic and social indices cause murder rates to fall by two-thirds in five years?

II

The idea of the Tipping Point is very simple. It is that the best way to understand the emergence of fashion trends, the ebb and flow of crime waves, or, for that matter, the transformation of unknown books into bestsellers, or the rise of teenage smoking, or the phenomena of word of mouth, or any number of other mysterious changes that mark everyday life is to think of them as epidemics. Ideas and products and messages and behaviors spread just like viruses do.

The rise of Hush Puppies and the fall of New York's crime rate are textbook examples of epidemics in action. Although they may sound as if they don't have very much in common, they share a basic, underlying pattern. First of all, they are clear examples of contagious behavior. No one took out an advertisement and told people that the traditional Hush Puppies were cool and they should start wearing them. Those kids simply wore the shoes when they went to clubs or cafes or walked the streets of downtown New York, and in so doing exposed other people to their fashion sense. They infected them with the Hush Puppies "virus."

The crime decline in New York surely happened the same way. It wasn't that some huge percentage of would-be murderers suddenly sat up in 1993 and decided not to commit any more crimes. Nor was it that the police managed magically to intervene in a huge percentage of situations that would otherwise have turned deadly. What happened is that the small number of people in the small number of situations in which the police or the new social forces had some impact started behaving very differently, and that behavior somehow spread to other would-be criminals in similar situations. Somehow a large number of people in New York got "infected" with an anti-crime virus in a short time.

10 The second distinguishing characteristic of these two examples is 10 that in both cases little changes had big effects. All of the possible reasons for why New York's crime rate dropped are changes that happened at the margin; they were incremental changes. The crack trade leveled off. The population got a little older. The police force got a little better. Yet the effect was dramatic. So too with Hush Puppies.

How many kids are we talking about who began wearing the shoes in downtown Manhattan? Twenty? Fifty? One hundred—at the most? Yet their actions seem to have single-handedly started an international fashion trend.

Finally, both changes happened in a hurry. They didn't build steadily and slowly. It is instructive to look at a chart of the crime rate in New York City from, say, the mid-1960s to the late 1990s. It looks like a giant arch. In 1965, there were 200,000 crimes in the city and from that point on the number begins a sharp rise, doubling in two years and continuing almost unbroken until it hits 650,000 crimes a year in the mid-1970s. It stays steady at that level for the next two decades, before plunging downward in 1992 as sharply as it rose thirty years earlier. Crime did not taper off. It didn't gently decelerate. It hit a certain point and jammed on the brakes.

These three characteristics—one, contagiousness; two, the fact that little causes can have big effects; and three, that change happens not gradually but at one dramatic moment—are the same three principles that define how measles moves through a grade-school classroom or the flu attacks every winter. Of the three, the third trait—the idea that epidemics can rise or fall in one dramatic moment—is the most important, because it is the principle that makes sense of the first two and that permits the greatest insight into why modern change happens the way it does. The name given to that one dramatic moment in an epidemic when everything can change all at once is the Tipping Point.

III

A world that follows the rules of epidemics is a very different place from the world we think we live in now. Think, for a moment, about the concept of contagiousness. If I say that word to you, you think of colds and the flu or perhaps something very dangerous like HIV or Ebola. We have, in our minds, a very specific, biological notion of what contagiousness means. But if there can be epidemics of crime or epidemics of fashion, there must be all kinds of things just as contagious as viruses. Have you ever thought about yawning, for instance? Yawning is a surprisingly powerful act. Just because you read the word "yawning" in the previous two sentences—and the two additional "yawns" in this sentence—a good number of you will probably yawn within the next few minutes. Even as I'm writing this, I've yawned twice. If you're reading this in a public place, and you've just yawned, chances are that a good proportion of everyone who saw you yawn is now yawning too, and a good proportion of the people watching the people who watched you yawn are now yawning as well, and on and on, in an ever-widening, yawning circle.[2]

Yawning is incredibly contagious. I made some of you reading this yawn simply by writing the word "yawn." The people who yawned when they saw you yawn, meanwhile, were infected by the sight of you yawning—which is a second kind of contagion. They might even have yawned if they only heard you yawn, because yawning is also aurally contagious: if you play an audiotape of a yawn to blind people, they'll yawn too. And finally, if you yawned as you read this, did the thought cross your mind—however unconsciously and fleetingly—that you might be tired? I suspect that for some of you it did, which means that yawns can also be emotionally contagious. Simply by writing the word, I can plant a feeling in your mind. Can the flu virus do that? Contagiousness, in other words, is an unexpected property of all kinds of things, and we have to remember that, if we are to recognize and diagnose epidemic change.

15   The second of the principles of epidemics—that little changes can somehow have big effects—is also a fairly radical notion. We are, as humans, heavily socialized to make a kind of rough approximation between cause and effect. If we want to communicate a strong emotion, if we want to convince someone that, say, we love them, we realize that we need to speak passionately and forthrightly. If we want to break bad news to someone, we lower our voices and choose our words carefully. We are trained to think that what goes into any transaction or relationship or system must be directly related, in intensity and dimension, to what comes out. Consider, for example, the following puzzle. I give you a large piece of paper, and I ask you to fold it over once, and then take that folded paper and fold it over again, and then again, and again, until you have refolded the original paper 50 times. How tall do you think the final stack is going to be? In answer to that question, most people will fold the sheet in their mind's eye, and guess that the pile would be as thick as a phone book, or, if they're really courageous, they'll say that it would be as tall as a refrigerator. But the real answer is that the height of the stack would approximate the distance to the sun. And if you folded it over one

more time, the stack would be as high as the distance to the sun and back. This is an example of what in mathematics is called a geometric progression. Epidemics are another example of geometric progression: when a virus spreads through a population, it doubles and doubles again, until it has (figuratively) grown from a single sheet of paper all the way to the sun in fifty steps. As human beings we have a hard time with this kind of progression, because the end result—the effect—seems far out of proportion to the cause. To appreciate the power of epidemics, we have to abandon this expectation about proportionality. We need to prepare ourselves for the possibility that sometimes big changes follow from small events, and that sometimes these changes can happen very quickly.

This possibility of sudden change is at the center of the idea of the Tipping Point and might well be the hardest of all to accept. The expression first came into popular use in the 1970s to describe the flight to the suburbs of white living in the older cities of the American Northeast. When the number of incoming African Americans in a particular neighborhood reached a certain point—20 percent, say—sociologists observed that the community would "tip": most of the remaining whites would leave almost immediately. The Tipping Point is the moment of critical mass, the threshold, the boiling point. There was a Tipping Point for violent crime in New York in the early 1990s, and a Tipping Point for the reemergence of Hush Puppies, just as there is a Tipping Point for the introduction of any new technology. Sharp introduced the first low-priced fax machine in 1984, and sold about 80,000 of those machines in the United States in that first year. For the next three years, businesses slowly and steadily bought more and more faxes, until, in 1987, enough people had faxes that it made sense for everyone to get a fax. Nineteen eighty-seven was the fax machine Tipping Point. A million machines were sold that year, and by 1989 two million new machines had gone into operation. Cellular phones have followed the same trajectory. Through the 1990s, they got smaller and cheaper, and service got better until 1998, when the technology hit a Tipping Point and suddenly everyone had a cell phone[3]. . . .

All epidemics have Tipping Points. Jonathan Crane, a sociologist at the University of Illinois, has looked at the effect the number of role models in a community—the professionals, managers, teachers whom the Census Bureau has defined as "high status"—has on the lives of teenagers in the same neighborhood. He found little difference in pregnancy rates or school drop-out rates in neighborhoods of between 40 and 5 percent of high-status workers. But when the number of professionals dropped below 5 percent, the problems exploded. For black schoolchildren, for example, as the percentage of high-status workers falls just 2.2 percentage points—from 5.6 percent to 3.4 percent—drop-out rates more than double. At the same Tipping Point, the rates of childbearing for teenaged girls—which barely move at all up to that point—nearly double. We assume, intuitively, that neighborhoods and social problems decline in some kind of steady progression. But sometimes they may not decline steadily at all; at the Tipping Point, schools can lose control of their students, and family life can disintegrate all at once.

I remember once as a child seeing our family's puppy encounter snow for the first time. He was shocked and delighted and overwhelmed, wagging his tail nervously, sniffing about in this strange, fluffy substance, whimpering with the mystery of it all. It wasn't much colder on the morning of his first snowfall than it had been the evening before. It might have been 34 degrees the previous evening, and now it was 31 degrees. Almost nothing had changed, in other words, yet— and this was the amazing thing—everything had changed. Rain had become something entirely different. Snow! We are all, at heart, gradualists, our expectations set by the steady passage of time. But the world of the Tipping Point is a place where the unexpected becomes expected, where radical change is more than possibility. It is—contrary to all our expectations—a certainty. . . .

Notes

1. For a good summary of New York City crime statistics, see: Michael Massing, "The Blue Revolution," in the *New York Review of Books,* November 19, 1998, pp. 32–34. There is another good discussion of the anomalous nature of the New York crime drop in William Bratton and William Andrews, "What We've Learned About Policing," in *City Journal,* Spring 1999, p. 25.
2. The leader in research on yawning is Robert Provine, a psychologist at the University of Maryland. Among his papers on the subject are: Robert Provine, "Yawning as a Stereotyped Action Pattern and Releasing Stimulus," *Ethology* (1983), vol. 72, pp. 109–122.

Robert Provine, "Contagious Yawning and Infant Imitation," *Bulletin of the Psychonomic Society* (1989), vol. 27, no. 2, pp. 125–126.

3. The best way to understand the Tipping Point is to imagine a hypothetical outbreak of the flu. Suppose, for example, that one summer 1,000 tourists come to Manhattan from Canada carrying an untreatable strain of twenty-four-hour virus. This strain of flu has a 2 percent infection rate, which is to say that one out of every 50 people who come into close contact with someone carrying it catches the bug himself. Let's say that 50 is also exactly the number of people the average Manhattanite—in the course of riding the subways and mingling with colleagues at work—comes in contact with every day. What we have, then, is a disease in equilibrium. Those 1,000 Canadian tourists pass on the virus to 1,000 new people on the day they arrive. And the next day those 1,000 newly infected people pass on the virus to another 1,000 people, just as the original 1,000 tourists who started the epidemic are returning to health. With those getting sick and those getting well so perfectly in balance, the flu chugs along at a steady but unspectacular clip through the rest of the summer and the fall.

But then comes the Christmas season. The subways and buses get more crowded with tourists and shoppers, and instead of running into an even 50 people a day, the average Manhattanite now has close contact with, say, 55 people a day. All of a sudden, the equilibrium is disrupted. The 1,000 flu carriers now run into 55,000 people a day, and at a 2 percent infection rate, that translates into 1,100 cases the following day. Those 1,100, in turn, are now passing on their virus to 55,000 people as well, so that by day three there are 1,210 Manhattanites with the flu and by day four 1,331 and by the end of the week there are nearly 2,000, and so on up, in an exponential spiral, until Manhattan has a full-blown flu epidemic on its hands by Christmas Day. That moment when the average flu carrier went from running into 50 people a day to running into 55 people was the Tipping Point. It was the point at which an ordinary and stable phenomenon—a low-level flu outbreak—turned into a public health crisis. If you were to draw a graph of the progress of the Canadian flu epidemic, the Tipping Point would be the point on the graph where the line suddenly turned upward.

Tipping Points are moments of great sensitivity. Changes made right at the Tipping Point can have enormous consequences. Our Canadian flu became an epidemic when the number of New Yorkers running into a flu carrier jumped from 50 to 55 a day. But had that same small change happened in the opposite direction, if the number had dropped from 50 to 45, that change would have pushed the number of flu victims down to 478 within a week, and with a few weeks more at that rate, the Canadian flu would have vanished from Manhattan entirely. Cutting the number exposed from 70 to 65, or 65 to 60 or 60 to 55 would not have been sufficient to end the epidemic. But a change right at the Tipping Point, from 50 to 45, would.

The Tipping Point model has been described in several classic works of sociology. I suggest:

Mark Granovetter, "Threshold Models of Collective Behavior," *American Journal of Sociology* (1978), vol. 83, pp. 1420–1443.

Mark Granovetter and R. Soong, "Threshold Models of Diffusion and Collective Behavior," *Journal of Mathematical Sociology* (1983), vol. 9, pp. 165–179.

Thomas Schelling, "Dynamic Models of Segregation," *Journal of Mathematical Sociology* (1971), vol. I, pp. 143–186.

Thomas Schelling, *Micromotives and Macrobehavior* (New York: W. W. Norton, 1978).

Jonathan Crane, "The Epidemic Theory of Ghettos and Neighborhood Effects on Dropping Out and Teenage Childbearing," *American Journal of Sociology* (1989), vol. 95, no. 5, pp. 1226–1259.

Questions on Meaning

1. Two examples carry the basic message of the essay: the shoes called Hush Puppies, and crime in two New York City neighborhoods. Why does the rapid increase in Hush Puppies and the rapid decline in crime give the essay its title?
2. Gladwell notes the pattern of all epidemics: They are all contagious behavior; they have big effects; and they happen fast. Why does Gladwell propose that epidemics happen in many more areas than disease?
3. Does the example of the yawn work for you? Did you yawn? What other examples prove that the Tipping Point does exist?

Questions on Rhetorical Strategy and Style

1. The essay has a brief introduction and then three parts marked I, II, and III. What information is in each of the three parts? Why is the essay divided in this way?
2. The author has a reputation for making complex ideas understandable and readable. The style of the essay is conversational and detailed. Why does this style contribute to readability?
3. Many of the points in the essay are backed up with statistics. How does the use of data help to make the arguments both more clear and more understandable?

Writing Assignments

1. Trace a fashion trend that you have noticed and participated in during the past three or four years. Where did it begin (or where did you first notice it)? Why did you follow the trend?
2. Read about a current epidemic, such as AIDS. Where did it begin? When did it start to decline? What scientific explanations have been given? Would the Tipping Point argument work as well?
3. The real point of the essay is that, for the most part, people respond to all kinds of contagions. Try the experiment Gladwell uses in the essay. Sit in a public place and yawn. Count the responses. Then write about the phenomenon you observed.

"I'm Not Racist But ..."

Neil Bissoondath

Born in Trinidad, Neil Bissoondath (1955–) moved to Canada at age 18 to attend York University. Upon receiving a degree in French, Bissoondath taught both French and English before beginning his writing career. In choosing to be a full-time writer, he followed in the footsteps of his internationally known uncles, Shiva and V.S. Naipaul. Bissoondath's first book, the short story collection Digging Up the Mountains *(1985), received significant critical praise, and his nonfiction critique of multiculturalism,* Selling Illusions: The Cult of Multiculturalism in Canada *(1994), stirred a good deal of controversy. His book* The Innocence of Age *(1992) won the Canadian Authors Association Prize for fiction. Most of Bissoondath's work, both fiction and nonfiction, deals with the dislocation, alienation, and racial tension of non-white immigrants in Canadian society. In the following essay, the author questions the legitimacy of labeling all insensitive ethnic language as racism.*

1   Someone recently said that racism is as Canadian as maple syrup. I have no argument with that. History provides us with ample proof. But, for proper perspective, let us remember that it is also as American as apple pie, as French as croissants, as Jamaican as ackee, as Indian as aloo, as Chinese as chow mein, as. . . . Well, there's an entire menu to be written. This is not by way of excusing it. Murder and rape, too, are international, multicultural, as innate to the darker side of the human experience. But we must be careful that the inevitable rage evoked does not blind us to the larger context.

   The word "racism" is a discomforting one: It is so vulnerable to manipulation. We can, if we so wish, apply it to any incident involving people of different colour. And therein lies the danger. During the heat of altercation, we seize, as terms of abuse, on whatever is most obvious about the person. It is, often, a question of unfortunate convenience. A woman, because of her sex, easily becomes a female dog or an intimate part of her anatomy. A large person might be dubbed "a stupid ox," a small person "a little" whatever. And so a black might become "a nigger," a white "a honky," an Asian "a paki," a Chinese "a chink," an Italian "a wop," a French-Canadian "a frog."

There is nothing pleasant about these terms; they assault every decent sensibility. Even so, I once met someone who, in a stunning surge of naiveté, used them as simple descriptives and not as terms of racial abuse. She was horrified to learn the truth. While this may have been an extreme case, the point is that the use of such patently abusive words may not always indicate racial or cultural distaste. They may indicate ignorance or stupidity or insensitivity, but pure racial hatred—such as the Nazis held for Jews, or the Ku Klux Klan for blacks—is a thankfully rare commodity.

Ignorance, not the willful kind but that which comes from lack of experience, is often indicated by that wonderful phrase, "I'm not racist but. . . ." I think of the mover, a friendly man, who said, "I'm not racist, but the Chinese are the worst drivers on the road." He was convinced this was so because the shape of their eyes, as far as he could surmise, denied them peripheral vision.

Or the oil company executive, an equally warm and friendly man, who, looking for an apartment in Toronto, rejected buildings with East Indian tenants not because of their race—he was telling me this, after all—but because he was given to understand that cockroaches were symbols of good luck in their culture and that, when they moved into a new home, friends came by with gift-wrapped cockroaches.

Neither of these men thought of himself as racist, and I believe they were not, deep down. (The oil company executive made it clear he would not hesitate to have me as a neighbour; my East Indian descent was of no consequence to him, my horror of cockroaches was.) Yet their comments, so innocently delivered, would open them to the accusation, justifiably so if this were all one knew about them. But it is a charge which would undoubtedly be wounding to them. It is difficult to recognize one's own misconceptions.

True racism is based, more often than not, on willful ignorance, and an acceptance of—and comfort with—stereotype. We like to think, in this country, that our multicultural mosaic will help nudge us into a greater openness. But multiculturalism as we know it indulges in stereotype, depends on it for a dash of colour and the flash of dance. It fails to address the most basic questions people have about each other. Do those men doing the Dragon Dance really all belong to secret criminal societies? Do those women dressed in saris really coddle cockroaches for luck? Do those people in dreadlocks all smoke marijuana and live on welfare? Such questions do not seem to be the concern of the government's multicultural programs, superficial and exhibitionistic as they have become.

So the struggle against stereotype, the basis of all racism, becomes a purely personal one. We must beware of the impressions we create. A friend of mine once commented that, from talking to West Indians, she has the impression that their one great cultural contribution to the world is in the oft-repeated boast that "We (unlike everyone else) know how to party."

There are dangers, too, in community response. We must be wary of the self-appointed activists who seem to pop up in the media at every given opportunity spouting the rhetoric of retribution, mining distress for personal, political and professional gain. We must be skeptical about those who depend on conflict for their sense of self, the non-whites who need to feel themselves victims of racism, the whites who need to feel themselves purveyors of it. And we must be sure that, in addressing the problem, we do not end up creating it. Does the *Miss Black Canada Beauty Contest* still exist? I hope not. Not only do I find beauty contests offensive, but a racially segregated one even more so. What would the public reaction be, I wonder, if every year CTV broadcast the *Miss White Canada Beauty Pageant?* We give community-service awards only to blacks: Would we be comfortable with such awards only for whites? In Quebec, there are The Association of Black Nurses, The Association of Black Artists, The Congress of Black Jurists. Play tit for tat: The Association of White Nurses, White Artists, White Jurists: visions of apartheid. Let us be frank, racism for one is racism for others.

10   Finally, and perhaps most important, let us beware of abusing the   10
word itself.

Questions on Meaning

1. How does Bissoondath distinguish between what he considers simply unpleasant terms for women or ethnic minorities and true racism? To what extent do you agree or disagree with him?
2. How does Bissoondath characterize the Canadian government's attempts to foster multiculturalism? Why, according to the author, do these attempts fail to address true racism?
3. What does Bissoondath mean when he says that "we must be sure that, in addressing the problem [of racism], we do not end up creating it"? Do you agree with his reasoning? Why or why not?

Questions on Strategy and Style

1. Persuasion appeals sometimes to reason, sometimes to emotion, and sometimes to both. How would you characterize Bissoondath's primary appeal? Is this strategy successful, in your opinion? Explain your response.
2. What is Bissoondath's definition of racism? To what extent does this definition strengthen his argument about misusing the term?
3. Cite two examples used in this essay and explain how they support the author's argument.

Writing Assignments

1. Write a letter to Bissoondath, responding to his essay. Address the distinction he makes between real and imagined racism, and provide support for your position regarding this distinction.
2. Review your institution's policies on diversity, sexist/racist behavior, and offensive speech. Based on Bissoondath's essay, evaluate the effectiveness of those policies in curbing true racism.
3. Research the history of one of the racial/ethnic terms found in paragraph 2, and write an essay describing the evolution of that term from its origins to the present.

Don't You Think It's Time to Start Thinking?

Northrop Frye

Northrop Frye (1912–1991), one of Canada's most distinguished scholars, was reared in New Brunswick, and after attending school in Canada, received his MA from Oxford University, in England (1940). In 1939 Frye became a professor at the University of Toronto, where he wrote and taught until his death. His interests were literary criticism and school curriculum; his books include On Education *and* Myth and Metaphor. *The following essay insists that thinking happens only when a person writes down ideas "in the right words."*

1   A student often leaves high school today without any sense of language as a structure.

He may also have the idea that reading and writing are elementary skills that he mastered in childhood, never having grasped the fact that there are differences in levels of reading and writing as there are in mathematics between short division and integral calculus.

Yet, in spite of his limited verbal skills, he firmly believes that he can think, that he has ideas, and that if he is just given the opportunity to express them he will be all right. Of course, when you look at what he's written you find it doesn't make any sense. When you tell him this he is devastated.

Part of his confusion here stems from the fact that we use the word "think" in so many bad, punning ways. Remember James Thurber's Walter Mitty who was always dreaming great dreams of glory. When his wife asked him what he was doing he would say, "Has it ever occurred to you that I might be thinking?"

5   But, of course, he wasn't thinking at all. Because we use it for everything our minds do, worrying, remembering, daydreaming, we imagine that thinking is something that can be achieved without any training. But again it's a matter of practice. How well we can think depends on how much of it we have already done. Most students need to be taught, very carefully and patiently, that there is no such thing as an inarticulate idea waiting to have the right words wrapped around it.

They have to learn that ideas do not exist until they have been incorporated into words. Until that point you don't know whether you are pregnant or just have gas on the stomach.

The operation of thinking is the practice of articulating ideas until they are in the right words. And we can't think at random either. We can only add one more idea to the body of something we have already thought about. Most of us spend very little time doing this, and that is why there are so few people whom we regard as having any power to articulate at all. When such a person appears in public life, like Mr. Trudeau, we tend to regard him as possessing a gigantic intellect.

A society like ours doesn't have very much interest in literacy. It is compulsory to read and write because society must have docile and obedient citizens. We are taught to read so that we can obey the traffic signs and to cipher so that we can make out our income tax, but development of verbal competency is very much left to the individual.

And when we look at our day-to-day existence we can see that there are strong currents at work against the development of powers of articulateness. Young adolescents today often betray a curious sense of shame about speaking articulately, of framing a sentence with a period at the end of it.

10   Part of the reason for this is the powerful anti-intellectual drive which is constantly present in our society. Articulate speech marks you out as an individual, and in some settings this can be rather dangerous because people are often suspicious and frightened of articulateness. So if you say as little as possible and use only stereotyped, ready-made phrases you can hide yourself in the mass.

Then there are various epidemics sweeping over society which use unintelligibility as a weapon to preserve the present power structure. By making things as unintelligible as possible, to as many people as possible, you can hold the present power structure together.

Understanding and articulateness lead to its destruction. This is the kind of thing that George Orwell was talking about, not just in *Nineteen Eighty-Four,* but in all his work on language. The kernel of everything reactionary and tyrannical in society is the impoverishment of the means of verbal communication.

The vast majority of things that we hear today are prejudices and clichés, simply verbal formulas that have no thought behind them but are put up as pretence of thinking. It is not until we realize these things conceal meaning, rather than reveal it, that we can begin to develop our own powers of articulateness.

The teaching of humanities is, therefore, a militant job. Teachers are faced not simply with a mass of misconceptions and unexamined assumptions. They must engage in a fight to help the student confront and reject the verbal formulas and stock responses, to convert passive acceptance into active, constructive power. It is a fight against illiteracy and for the maturation of the mental process, for the development of skills which once acquired will never become obsolete.

Questions on Meaning

1. Frye says that our minds can do many things besides thinking—worrying, remembering, and daydreaming, for example. Why does he say that these are not thinking?

2. What is the difference between reading to understand a traffic sign and reading to understand a play such as *Romeo and Juliet*? Why does Frye think that the distinction is so important?

3. Are the vast majority of things people say prejudices and cliches? Frye says that they are and that people in power want it that way. Why does he think that this is true? Why does he refer to the novel *1984*?

Questions on Style and Structure

1. The style of this essay is sometimes quite forceful, such as "you don't know whether you are pregnant or just have gas." Why does this kind of style make Frye's point? What do we know about his feelings on the subject?

2. In this essay, Frye argues that humanities teachers are important, but he gets to his point at the end of the essay. What effect does this structure have on the reader?

3. Frye uses a forceful style in this essay because he feels strongly about his subject and he wants teachers to see how important their job really is. Find words and phrases that show the power of his emotions, and explain those emotions.

Writing Assignments

1. Find out about George Orwell. What political and social conditions caused Orwell to write his pessimistic novel *1984*? Write about the dangers of controlling people's thoughts.

2. Interview one of your humanities (history, literature, political science, philosophy) teachers. Ask the teacher about the responsibilities of the humanities to human freedom. Write about the interview, using your own responses as well as the teacher's perspectives.

3. Frye wrote in the second half of the twentieth century. Write about examples of complacency or laziness in political or social thought in the twenty-first century. How much have things changed? How much have they remained the same?

Food Product Design

Eric Schlosser

Eric Schlosser (1960–) was born in Manhattan. He studied American history at Princeton and British imperial history at Oxford University. He began his journalism career at The Atlantic Monthly *and is today a correspondent for that magazine. His work has also appeared in many magazines, including* The New Yorker, The Nation, Vanity Fair, *and* Rolling Stone. *Schlosser has lectured at colleges and universities around the country and has addressed the U.S. Senate on the risk to the U.S. food supply from bioterrorism. He has won awards for his journalism, including a National Magazine Award, the Loeb Award for business journalism, and a Sidney Hillman Foundation Award for Reporting. Other works include* Reefer Madness: Sex, Drugs, and Cheap Labor in the American Black Market *(2003); and* Chew on This: Everything You Don't Want to Know about Fast Food *(2006). The following selection is taken from Schlosser's best-known book,* Fast Food Nation: The Dark Side of the All-American Meal *(2001). It began as a two-part investigative piece published in* Rolling Stone. *As a best-selling book it has changed the image many have of the fast-food and meat-packing industries, and also exposed shoddy working conditions for employees. A Hollywood movie based on* Fast Food Nation *was released in 2006. The fast-food industry has, in response, prepared a public relations attack on Schlosser and his work in the hope of reversing the effects of his journalism on public perception. In this excerpt from* Fast Food Nation, *the author explains the "chemical wizardry" of the companies that keeps people coming back for more.*

1

The taste of McDonald's french fries has long been praised by customers, competitors, and even food critics.[1] James Beard loved McDonald's fries.[2] Their distinctive taste does not stem from the type of potatoes that McDonald's buys, the technology that processes them, or the restaurant equipment that fries them. Other chains buy their french fries from the same large processing companies, use Russet Burbanks, and have similar fryers in their restaurant kitchens. The taste of a fast food fry is largely determined by the cooking oil.[3] For decades, McDonald's cooked its french fries in a mixture of about 7 percent cottonseed oil and 93 percent beef tallow. The mix gave the fries their unique flavor—and more saturated beef fat per ounce than a McDonald's hamburger.[4]

Amid a barrage of criticism over the amount of cholesterol in their fries, McDonald's switched to pure vegetable oil in 1990. The switch presented the company with an enormous challenge: how to make fries that subtly taste like beef without cooking them in tallow. A look at the ingredients now used in the preparation of McDonald's french fries suggests how the problem was solved.[5] Toward the end of the list is a seemingly innocuous, yet oddly mysterious phrase: "natural flavor." That ingredient helps to explain not only why the fries taste so good, but also why most fast food—indeed, most of the food Americans eat today—tastes the way it does.

Open your refrigerator, your freezer, your kitchen cupboards, and look at the labels on your food. You'll find "natural flavor" or "artificial flavor" in just about every list of ingredients. The similarities between these two broad categories of flavor are far more significant than their differences. Both are man-made additives that give most processed food most of its taste. The initial purchase of a food item may be driven by its packaging or appearance, but subsequent purchases are determined mainly by its taste. About 90 percent of the money that Americans spend on food is used to buy processed food.[6] But the canning, freezing, and dehydrating techniques used to process food destroy most of its flavor. Since the end of World War II, a vast industry has arisen in the United States to make processed food palatable. Without this flavor industry, today's fast food industry could not exist. The names of the leading American fast food chains and their best-selling menu items have become famous worldwide, embedded in our popular culture. Few people, however, can name the companies that manufacture fast food's taste.

The flavor industry is highly secretive. Its leading companies will not divulge the precise formulas of flavor compounds or the identities of clients. The secrecy is deemed essential for protecting the reputation of beloved brands. The fast food chains, understandably, would like the public to believe that the flavors of their food somehow originate in their restaurant kitchens, not in distant factories run by other firms.

The New Jersey Turnpike runs through the heart of the flavor industry, an industrial corridor dotted with refineries and chemical plants. International Flavors & Fragrances (IFF), the world's largest flavor company, has a manufacturing facility off Exit 8A in Dayton, New Jersey; Givaudan, the world's second-largest flavor company, has a plant in East Hanover. Haarmann & Reimer, the largest German flavor company, has a plant in Teterboro, as does Takasago, the largest Japanese flavor company. Flavor Dynamics has a plant in South Plainfield; Frutarom is in North Bergen; Elan Chemical is in Newark. Dozens of companies manufacture flavors in the corridor between Teaneck and South Brunswick. Indeed, the area produces about two-thirds of the flavor additives sold in the United States.[7]

The IFF plant in Dayton is a huge pale blue building with a modern office complex attached to the front. It sits in an industrial park, not far from a BASF plastics factory, a Jolly French Toast factory, and a plant that manufactures Liz Claiborne cosmetics. Dozens of tractor-trailers were parked at the IFF loading dock the afternoon I visited, and a thin cloud of steam floated from the chimney. Before entering the plant, I signed a nondisclosure form, promising not to reveal the brand names of products that contain IFF flavors. The place reminded me of Willy Wonka's chocolate factory. Wonderful smells drifted through the hallways, men and women in neat white lab coats cheerfully went about their work, and hundreds of little glass bottles sat on laboratory tables and shelves. The bottles contained powerful but fragile flavor chemicals, shielded from light by the brown glass and the round plastic caps shut tight. The long chemical names on the little white labels were as mystifying to me as medieval Latin. They were the odd-sounding names of things that would be mixed and poured and turned into new substances, like magic potions.

I was not invited to see the manufacturing areas of the IFF plant, where it was thought I might discover trade secrets. Instead, I toured various laboratories and pilot kitchens, where the flavors of well-established brands are tested or adjusted, and where whole new flavors are created.

IFF's snack and savory lab is responsible for the flavor of potato chips, corn chips, breads, crackers, breakfast cereals, and pet food. The confectionery lab devises the flavor for ice cream, cookies, candies, toothpastes, mouthwashes, and antacids. Everywhere I looked, I saw famous, widely advertised products sitting on laboratory desks and tables. The beverage lab is full of brightly colored liquids in clear bottles. It comes up with the flavor for popular soft drinks, sport drinks, bottled teas, and wine coolers, for all-natural juice drinks, organic soy drinks, beers, and malt liquors. In one pilot kitchen I saw a dapper food technologist, a middle-aged man with an elegant tie beneath his lab coat, carefully preparing a batch of cookies with white frosting and pink-and-white sprinkles. In another pilot kitchen I saw a pizza oven, a grill, a milk-shake machine, and a french fryer identical to those I'd seen behind the counter at countless fast food restaurants.

In addition to being the world's largest flavor company, IFF manufactures the smell of six of the ten best-selling fine perfumes in the United States, including Estée Lauder's Beautiful, Clinique's Happy, Lancôme's Trésor, and Calvin Klein's Eternity.[8] It also makes the smell of household products such as deodorant, dishwashing detergent, bath soap, shampoo, furniture polish, and floor wax. All of these aromas are made through the same basic process: the manipulation of volatile chemicals to create a particular smell. The basic science behind the scent of your shaving cream is the same as that governing the flavor of your TV dinner.

The aroma of a food can be responsible for as much as 90 percent of its flavor.[9] Scientists now believe that human beings acquired the sense of taste as a way to avoid being poisoned. Edible plants generally taste sweet; deadly ones, bitter. Taste is supposed to help us differentiate food that's good for us from food that's not. The taste buds on our tongues can detect the presence of half a dozen or so basic tastes, including: sweet, sour, bitter, salty, astringent, and umami (a taste discovered by Japanese researchers, a rich and full sense of deliciousness triggered by amino acids in foods such as shellfish, mushrooms, potatoes, and seaweed).[10] Taste buds offer a relatively limited means of detection, however, compared to the human olfactory system, which can perceive thousands of different chemical aromas. Indeed "flavor" is primarily the smell of gases being released by the chemicals you've just put in your mouth.

10   The act of drinking, sucking, or chewing a substance releases its   10
volatile gases. They flow out of the mouth and up the nostrils, or up the passageway in the back of the mouth, to a thin layer of nerve cells called

the olfactory epithelium, located at the base of the nose, right between the eyes. The brain combines the complex smell signals from the epithelium with the simple taste signals from the tongue, assigns a flavor to what's in your mouth, and decides if it's something you want to eat.

Babies like sweet tastes and reject bitter ones; we know this because scientists have rubbed various flavors inside the mouths of infants and then recorded their facial reactions. A person's food preferences, like his or her personality, are formed during the first few years of life, through a process of socialization. Toddlers can learn to enjoy hot and spicy food, bland health food, or fast food, depending upon what the people around them eat. The human sense of smell is still not fully understood and can be greatly affected by psychological factors and expectations. The color of a food can determine the perception of its taste. The mind filters out the overwhelming majority of chemical aromas that surround us, focusing intently on some, ignoring others. People can grow accustomed to bad smells or good smells; they stop noticing what once seemed overpowering. Aroma and memory are somehow inextricably linked. A smell can suddenly evoke a long-forgotten moment. The flavors of childhood foods seem to leave an indelible mark, and adults often return to them, without always knowing why. These "comfort foods" become a source of pleasure and reassurance, a fact that fast food chains work hard to promote. Childhood memories of Happy Meals can translate into frequent adult visits to McDonald's, like those of the chain's "heavy users," the customers who eat there four or five times a week.[11]

The human craving for flavor has been a largely unacknowledged and unexamined force in history. Royal empires have been built, unexplored lands have been traversed, great religions and philosophies have been forever changed by the spice trade. In 1492 Christopher Columbus set sail to find seasoning. Today the influence of flavor in the world marketplace is no less decisive. The rise and fall of corporate empires—of soft drink companies, snack food companies, and fast food chains—is frequently determined by how their products taste.

The flavor industry emerged in the mid-nineteenth century, as processed foods began to be manufactured on a large scale. Recognizing the need for flavor additives, the early food processors turned to perfume companies that had years of experience working with essential oils and volatile aromas. The great perfume houses of England, France, and the Netherlands produced many of the first flavor compounds. In the early part of the twentieth century, Germany's powerful chemical industry assumed the technological lead in flavor production. Legend has it that a German scientist discovered methyl anthranilate, one of the first artificial flavors, by accident while mixing chemicals in his laboratory. Suddenly the lab was filled with the sweet smell of grapes. Methyl anthranilate later became the chief flavoring compound of grape Kool-Aid. After World War II, much of the perfume industry shifted from Europe to the United States, settling in New York City near the garment district and the fashion houses. The flavor industry came with it, subsequently moving to New Jersey to gain more plant capacity. Man-made flavor additives were used mainly in baked goods, candies, and sodas until the 1950s, when sales of processed food began to soar. The invention of gas chromatographs and mass spectrometers—machines capable of detecting volatile gases at low levels—vastly increased the number of flavors that could be synthesized. By the mid-1960s the American flavor industry was churning out compounds to supply the taste of Pop Tarts, Bac-Os, Tab, Tang, Filet-O-Fish sandwiches, and literally thousands of other new foods.

The American flavor industry now has annual revenues of about $1.4 billion.[12] Approximately ten thousand new processed food products are introduced every year in the United States. Almost all of them require flavor additives. And about nine out of every ten of these new food products fail.[13] The latest flavor innovations and corporate realignments are heralded in publications such as *Food Chemical News, Food Engineering, Chemical Market Reporter,* and *Food Product Design.* The growth of IFF has mirrored that of the flavor industry as a whole. IFF was formed in 1958, through the merger of two small companies. Its annual revenues have grown almost fifteenfold since the early 1970s, and it now has manufacturing facilities in twenty countries.[14]

15 The quality that people seek most of all in a food, its flavor, is usually present in a quantity too infinitesimal to be measured by any traditional culinary terms such as ounces or teaspoons. Today's sophisticated spectrometers, gas chromatographs, and headspace vapor analyzers provide a detailed map of a food's flavor components, detecting chemical aromas in amounts as low as one part per billion. The human nose, however, is still more sensitive than any machine yet invented. A nose can detect aromas present in quantities of a few parts per trillion—an amount equivalent to 0.000000000003 percent. Complex aromas, like those of coffee or roasted meat, may be composed of volatile gases from

nearly a thousand different chemicals. The smell of a strawberry arises from the interaction of at least 350 different chemicals that are present in minute amounts. The chemical that provides the dominant flavor of bell pepper can be tasted in amounts as low as .02 parts per billion; one drop is sufficient to add flavor to five average size swimming pools.[15] The flavor additive usually comes last, or second to last, in a processed food's list of ingredients. As a result, the flavor of a processed food often costs less than its packaging. Soft drinks contain a larger proportion of flavor additives than most products. The flavor in a twelve-ounce can of Coke costs about half a cent.[16]

The color additives in processed foods are usually present in even smaller amounts than the flavor compounds. Many of New Jersey's flavor companies also manufacture these color additives, which are used to make processed foods look appealing. Food coloring serves many of the same purposes as lipstick, eye shadow, mascara—and is often made from the same pigments. Titanium dioxide, for example, has proved to be an especially versatile mineral. It gives many processed candies, frosting, and icing their bright white color; it is a common ingredient in women's cosmetics; and it is the pigment used in many white oil paints and house paints. At Burger King, Wendy's, and McDonald's, coloring agents have been added to many of the soft drinks, salad dressings, cookies, condiments, chicken dishes, and sandwich buns.

Studies have found that the color of a food can greatly affect how its taste is perceived. Brightly colored foods frequently seem to taste better than bland-looking foods, even when the flavor compounds are identical. Foods that somehow look off-color often seem to have off tastes. For thousands of years, human beings have relied on visual cues to help determine what is edible. The color of fruit suggests whether it is ripe, the color of meat whether it is rancid. Flavor researchers sometimes use colored lights to modify the influence of visual cues during taste tests. During one experiment in the early 1970s, people were served an oddly tinted meal of steak and French fries that appeared normal beneath colored lights. Everyone thought the meal tasted fine until the lighting was changed. Once it became apparent that the steak was actually blue and the fries were green, some people became ill.

The Food and Drug Administration does not require flavor companies to disclose the ingredients of their additives, so long as all the chemicals are considered by the agency to be GRAS (Generally Regarded As Safe). This lack of public disclosure enables the companies to maintain the secrecy of their formulas. It also hides the fact that flavor compounds sometimes contain more ingredients than the foods being given their taste. The ubiquitous phrase "artificial strawberry flavor" gives little hint of the chemical wizardry and manufacturing skill that can make a highly processed food taste like a strawberry.

A typical artificial strawberry flavor, like the kind found in a Burger King strawberry milk shake, contains the following ingredients: amyl acetate, amyl butyrate, amyl valerate, anethol, anisyl formate, benzyl acetate, benzyl isobutyrate, butyric acid, cinnamyl isobutyrate, cinnamyl valerate, cognac essential oil, diacetyl, dipropyl ketone, ethyl acetate, ethyl amylketone, ethyl butyrate, ethyl cinnamate, ethyl heptanoate, ethyl heptylate, ethyl lactate, ethyl methylphenylglycidate, ethyl nitrate, ethyl propionate, ethyl valerate, heliotropin, hydroxyphenyl-2-butanone (10 percent solution in alcohol), α-ionone, isobutyl anthranilate, isobutyl butyrate, lemon essential oil, maltol, 4-methylacetophenone, methyl anthranilate, methyl benzoate, methyl cinnamate, methyl heptine carbonate, methyl naphthyl ketone, methyl salicylate, mint essential oil, neroli essential oil, nerolin, neryl isobutyrate, orris butter, phenethyl alcohol, rose, rum ether, γ-undecalactone, vanillin, and solvent.[17]

20 Although flavors usually arise from a mixture of many different 20 volatile chemicals, a single compound often supplies the dominant aroma. Smelled alone, that chemical provides an unmistakable sense of the food. Ethyl-2-methyl butyrate, for example, smells just like an apple. Today's highly processed foods offer a blank palette: whatever chemicals you add to them will give them specific tastes. Adding methyl-2-peridylketone makes something taste like popcorn. Adding ethyl-3-hydroxybutanoate makes it taste like marshmallow. The possibilities are now almost limitless. Without affecting the appearance or nutritional value, processed foods could even be made with aroma chemicals such as hexanal (the smell of freshly cut grass) or 3-methyl butanoic acid (the smell of body odor).

The 1960s were the heyday of artificial flavors. The synthetic versions of flavor compounds were not subtle, but they did not need to be, given the nature of most processed food. For the past twenty years food processors have tried hard to use only "natural flavors" in their products. According to the FDA, these must be derived entirely from natural sources—from herbs, spices, fruits, vegetables, beef, chicken, yeast, bark, roots, etc. Consumers prefer to see natural flavors on a label, out of a belief that they are healthier. The distinction between artificial and natural flavors can be somewhat arbitrary and absurd, based more on how the flavor has been made than on what it actually contains. "A natural flavor," says Terry Acree, a professor of food science at Cornell University, "is a flavor that's been derived with an out-of-date technology."[18] Natural flavors and artificial flavors sometimes contain exactly the same chemicals, produced through different methods. Amyl acetate, for example, provides the dominant note of banana flavor. When you distill it from bananas with a solvent, amyl acetate is a natural flavor. When you produce it by mixing vinegar with amyl alcohol, adding sulfuric acid as a catalyst, amyl acetate is an artificial flavor. Either way it smells and tastes the same. The phrase "natural flavor" is now listed among the ingredients of everything from Stonyfield Farm Organic Strawberry Yogurt to Taco Bell Hot Taco Sauce.

A natural flavor is not necessarily healthier or purer than an artificial one. When almond flavor (benzaldehyde) is derived from natural sources, such as peach and apricot pits, it contains traces of hydrogen cyanide, a deadly poison. Benzaldehyde derived through a different process—by mixing oil of clove and the banana flavor, amyl acetate—does not contain any cyanide. Nevertheless, it is legally considered an artificial flavor and sells at a much lower price. Natural and artificial flavors are now manufactured at the same chemical plants, places that few people would associate with Mother Nature. Calling any of these flavors "natural" requires a flexible attitude toward the English language and a fair amount of irony.

The small and elite group of scientists who create most of the flavor in most of the food now consumed in the United States are called "flavorists." They draw upon a number of disciplines in their work: biology, psychology, physiology, and organic chemistry. A flavorist is a chemist with a trained nose and a poetic sensibility. Flavors are created by blending scores of different chemicals in tiny amounts, a process governed by scientific principles but demanding a fair amount of art. In an age when delicate aromas, subtle flavors, and microwave ovens do not easily coexist, the job of the flavorist is to conjure illusions about processed food and, in the words of one flavor company's literature, to ensure "consumer likeability."[19] The flavorists with whom I spoke were charming, cosmopolitan, and ironic. They were also discreet, in keeping with the dictates of their trade. They were the sort of scientist who not only enjoyed fine wine, but could also tell you the chemicals that gave each vintage its unique aroma. One flavorist compared his work to composing music. A well-made flavor compound will have a "top note," followed by a "dry-down," and a "leveling-off," with different chemicals responsible for each stage. The taste of a food can be radically altered by minute changes in the flavoring mix. "A little odor goes a long way," one flavorist said.

In order to give a processed food the proper taste, a flavorist must always consider the food's "mouthfeel"—the unique combination of textures and chemical interactions that affects how the flavor is perceived. The mouthfeel can be adjusted through the use of various fats, gums, starches, emulsifiers, and stabilizers. The aroma chemicals of a food can be precisely analyzed, but mouthfeel is much harder to measure. How does one quantify a french fry's crispness? Food technologists are now conducting basic research in rheology, a branch of physics that examines the flow and deformation of materials. A number of companies sell sophisticated devices that attempt to measure mouthfeel. The TA.XT2i Texture Analyzer, produced by the Texture Technologies Corporation, performs calculations based on data derived from as many as 250 separate probes.[20] It is essentially a mechanical mouth. It gauges the most important rheological properties of a food—the bounce, creep, breaking point, density, crunchiness, chewiness, gumminess, lumpiness, rubberiness, springiness, slipperiness, smoothness, softness, wetness, juiciness, spreadability, springback, and tackiness.

25   Some of the most important advances in flavor manufacturing are now occurring in the field of biotechnology. Complex flavors are being made through fermentation, enzyme reactions, fungal cultures, and tissue cultures. All of the flavors being created through these methods—including the ones being synthesized by funguses—are considered natural flavors by the FDA.[21] The new enzyme-based processes are responsible for extremely lifelike dairy flavors. One company now offers not just butter flavor, but also fresh creamy butter, cheesy butter, milky butter, savory melted butter, and super-concentrated butter flavor, in liquid or powder form. The development of new fermentation techniques, as well as new techniques for heating mixtures of sugar and amino acids, have led to the creation of much more realistic meat flavors. The McDonald's Corporation will not reveal the exact origin of the natural flavor added to its french fries. In response to inquiries from *Vegetarian Journal,* however, McDonald's did acknowledge that its fries derive some of their characteristic flavor from "animal products."[22]

Other popular fast foods derive their flavor from unexpected sources. Wendy's Grilled Chicken Sandwich, for example, contains beef extracts.[23] Burger King's BK Broiler Chicken Breast Patty contains "natural smoke flavor."[24] A firm called Red Arrow Products Company specializes in smoke flavor, which is added to barbecue sauces and processed meats. Red Arrow manufactures natural smoke flavor by charring sawdust and capturing the aroma chemicals released into the air. The smoke is captured in water and then bottled, so that other companies can sell food which seems to have been cooked over a fire.

The Vegetarian Legal Action Network recently petitioned the FDA to issue new food labeling requirements for foods that contain natural flavors. The group wants food processors to list the basic origins of their flavors on their labels. At the moment, vegetarians often have no way of knowing whether a flavor additive contains beef, pork, poultry, or shellfish. One of the most widely used color additives—whose presence is often hidden by the phrase "color added"—violates a number of religious dietary restrictions, may cause allergic reactions in susceptible people, and comes from an unusual source. Cochineal extract (also known as carmine or carminic acid) is made from the desiccated bodies of female Dactlyopius coccus Costa, a small insect harvested mainly in Peru and the Canary Islands. The bug feeds on red cactus berries and color from the berries accumulated in the females and their unhatched larvae. The insects are collected, dried, and ground into pigment. It takes about 70,000 of them to produce one pound of carmine, which is used to make processed foods look pink, red, or purple. Dannon strawberry yogurt gets its color from carmine, as do many frozen fruit bars, candies, fruit fillings, and Ocean Spray pink-grapefruit juice drink.

In a meeting room at IFF, Brian Grainger let me sample some of the company's flavors. It was an unusual taste test; there wasn't any food to taste. Grainger is a senior flavorist at IFF, a soft-spoken chemist with graying hair, an English accent, and a fondness for understatement. He could easily be mistaken for a British diplomat or the owner of a West End brasserie with two Michelin stars. Like many in the flavor industry, he has an Old World, old-fashioned sensibility which seems out of step with our brand-conscious, egocentric age. When I suggested that IFF should put its own logo on the products that contain its flavors—instead of allowing other brands to enjoy the consumer loyalty and affection inspired by those flavors—Grainger politely disagreed, assuring me such a thing would never be done. In the absence of public credit or acclaim, the small and secretive fraternity of flavor chemists praises one another's work. Grainger can often tell, by analyzing the flavor formula of a product, which of his counterparts at a rival firm devised it. And he enjoys walking down supermarket aisles, looking at the many products that contain his flavors, even if no one else knows it.

Grainger had brought a dozen small glass bottles from the lab. After he opened each bottle, I dipped a fragrance testing filter into it. The filters were long white strips of paper designed to absorb aroma chemicals without producing off-notes. Before placing the strips of paper before my nose, I closed my eyes. Then I inhaled deeply, and one food after another was conjured from the glass bottles. I smelled fresh cherries, black olives, sautéed onions, and shrimp. Grainger's most remarkable creation took me by surprise. After closing my eyes, I suddenly smelled a grilled hamburger. The aroma was uncanny, almost miraculous. It smelled like someone in the room was flipping burgers on a hot grill. But when I opened my eyes, there was just a narrow strip of white paper and a smiling flavorist.

Why the Fries Taste Good

30 *Food: A Culinary History* (New York: Columbia University Press, 30
1999), edited by Jean-Louis Flandrin and Massimo Montanari, traces the cultural and technological changes in food preparation from prehistoric campfires to the kitchens at McDonald's. A good account of the history of American food processing can be found in John M. Connor and William A. Schiek, *Food Processing: An Industrial Powerhouse in Transition* (New York: John Wiley & Sons, 1997). Harvey Levenstein's *Paradox of Plenty: A Social History of Eating in Modern America* (New York: Oxford University Press, 1993) has a fine chapter on the implications of postwar advances in food processing. For consolidation in the food processing industry and its effects on American farmers, I learned a great deal from the following sources: Charles R. Handy and Alden C. Manchester, "Structure and Performance of the Food System Beyond the Farm Gate," Commodities Economics Division White Paper, USDA Economic Research Service, April 1990; Alden C. Manchester, "The Transformation of U.S. Food Marketing," in *Food and Agricultural Markets: The Quiet Revolution,* edited by Lyle

P. Schertz and Lynn M. Daff (Washington, D.C.: National Planning Association, 1994); *Concentration in Agriculture, A Report of the USDA Advisory Committee on Agricultural Concentration* (Washington, D.C.: USDA Agricultural Marketing Service, June 1996); *A Time to Act: Report of the USDA National Commission on Small Farms* (Washington, D.C.: United States Department of Agriculture, 1998); and William Heffernan, "Consolidation in the Food and Agriculture System," Report to the National Farmers Union, February 5, 1999. A telephone interview, extending for hours, with J. R. Simplot provided much information on the details of his life and the origins of the potato industry in Idaho. Simplot was blunt, charismatic, entertaining, and seemingly tireless. Fred Zerza, the vice president for public and government relations at the J. R. Simplot Company, helped confirm the accuracy of Simplot's remarks. I also relied on "Origins of the J. R. Simplot Company," J. R. Simplot Company, 1997; and James W. Davis, *Aristocrat in Burlap: A History of the Potato in Idaho* (Boise: Idaho Potato Commission, 1992). Paul Patterson, an extension professor of agricultural economics at the University of Idaho, graciously explained to me how potatoes are grown, processed, and sold today. Bert Moulton, at the Potato Growers of Idaho, gave me a sense of the challenges that farmers in his state must now confront. I am grateful to Ben Strand, at the Simplot Food Group, and Bud Mandeville, at Lamb Weston, for giving me tours of their french fry facilities.

The reference books on flavor technology were a pleasure to read; they reminded me of medieval texts on the black arts. Among the works I consulted were *Fenaroli's Handbook of Flavor Ingredients,* vol. 2 (Ann Arbor, Mich.: CRC Press, 1995); Henry B. Heath, *Source Book of Flavors* (Westport, Conn.: Avi Publishing, 1981); Martin S. Peterson and Arnold H. Johnson, *Encyclopedia of Food Science* (Westport, Conn.: Avi Publishing, 1978); Y. H. Hui, *Encyclopedia of Food Science and Technology,* vol. 2 (New York: John Wiley & Sons, 1992); Carl W. Hall, A. W. Farrall, and A. L. Rippen, *Encyclopedia of Food Engineering* (Westport, Conn.: Avi Publishing, 1986); *Flavor Science: Sensible Principles and Techniques,* edited by Terry E. Acree and Roy Teranishi (Washington, D.C.: American Chemical Society, 1993); *Biotechnology for Improved Foods and Flavors,* edited by Gary R. Takeoka, Roy Teranishi, Patrick J. Williams, and Akio Kobayashi (Washington, D.C.: American Chemical Society, 1995); *Flavor Analyses Developments in Isolation and Characterization,* edited by Cynthia J. Mussinan and

Michael J. Novello (Washington, D.C.: American Chemical Society, 1998). I found many useful articles on the flavor industry in journals such as *Food Product Design, Food Engineering, Food Processing, Food Manufacture, Chemistry and Industry, Chemical Market Reporter,* and *Soap-Cosmetics-Chemical Specialties* (now published as *Soap & Cosmetics*). A good overview of the flavor business can be found in *Industry and Trade Summary: Flavor and Fragrance Materials* (Washington, D.C.: U.S. International Trade Commission, USITC Publication 3162, March 1999). Ellen Ruppel Shell wrote a fine article on the work of flavorists more than a decade ago: "Chemists Whip Up a Tasty Mess of Artificial Flavors," *Smithsonian,* May 1986. Terry Acree, a professor of food science technology at Cornell University, was a wonderful resource on the subjects of smell, taste, flavor, and the flavor industry. Bob Bauer, executive director of the National Association of Fruits, Flavors, and Syrups, outlined when and where the flavor industry settled in New Jersey. At International Flavors & Fragrances, I am grateful to Nancy Ciancaglini, Diane Mora, and Brian Grainger, who patiently answered many questions. The flavorists at other firms whom I interviewed shall remain anonymous.

End Notes

1. Since the publication of *Fast Food Nation,* the McDonald's Corporation has been more forthcoming about the ingredients in their fries. For the origins of the new policy, see pages 278–80 of the Afterword.
2. See Elizabeth Mehren, "From Whisks to Molds, James Beard's Personal Possessions to Be Auctioned," *Los Angeles Times,* September 12, 1985.
3. See Olivia Wu, "Fats and Oils in a New Light," *Restaurants and Institutions,* January 15, 1997; and Candy Sagon, "Fry, Fry Again: The Secret of Great French Fries? Frying and more Frying," *Washington Post,* July 9, 1997.
4. A small McDonald's hamburger weighed 102 grams and had 3.6 grams of saturated fat; a small order of fries weighed 68 grams and had 5.05 grams of saturated fat. See "Where's the Fat," *USA Today,* April 5, 1990; Marian Burros, "The Slimming of Fat Fast Food," *New York Times,* July 25, 1990; and Michael F. Jacobson and Sarah Fritscher, *The Completely Revised and Updated Fast-Food Guide* (New York: Workman Publishing, 1991).
5. See "McDonald's Nutrition Facts," McDonald's Corporation, July 1997.
6. See "Personal Consumption Expenditures Table, 1999," Bureau of Economic Analysis, U.S. Department of Commerce.
7. Cited in Joyce Jones, "Labs Conjure Up Fragrances and Flavors to Add Allure," *New York Times,* December 26, 1993.
8. Interview with Nancy Ciancaglini, International Flavors & Fragrances.

9. Cited in Ruth Sambrook, "Do You Smell What I Smell? The Science of Smell and Taste," Institute of Food Research March 1999.

10. See Marilynn Larkin, "Truncated Glutamate Receptor Holds Key to the Fifth Primary Taste," *Lancet,* January 29, 2000; and Andy Coghlan, "In Good Taste," *New Scientist,* January 29, 2000.
Babies like sweet tastes: See Julie A. Mennella and Gary K. Beauchamp, "Early Flavor Experiences: When Do They Start?" *Nutrition Today,* September 1994.

11. See Jennifer Ordonez, "Hamburger Joints Call Them 'Heavy Users,'" *Wall Street Journal,* January 12, 2000.

12. Interview with Nancy Ciancaglini. *Approximately ten thousand new processed food products:* Cited in Susan Carroll, "Flavors Market Is Poised for Recovery This Year," *Chemical Market Report,* July 19, 1999.

13. Cited in Andrew Bary, "Take a Whiff: Why International Flavors & Fragrances Looks Tempting Right Now," *Barron's,* July 20, 1998.

14. *Its annual revenues have grown almost fifteenfold:* IFF's sales were about $103 million in 1970 and about $1.4 billion in 1999. The first figure comes from "Company History," IFF Advertising and Public Relations. The second is cited in Catherine Curan, "Perfume Company Banks on CEO's Nose for Business," *Crain's NY Business,* June 26, 2000.

15. The chemical is isobutylmethoxy pyrazine. Its minute taste recognition threshold is noted in "Flavor Chemistry Seminar," International Flavors & Fragrances.

16. An industry source provided me with the cost of the flavor in a six-pack of Coke, and I did the rest of the math.

17. This recipe comes from *Fenaroli's Handbook of Flavor Ingredients,* vol. 2, p. 831.

18. Interview with Terry Acree.

19. Quoted in "What Is Flavor? An IFF Consumer Insights Perspective."

20. For a description of such contraptions, see Ray Marsili, "Texture and Mouthfeel: Making Rheology Real," *Food Product Design,* August 1993.

21. See Leticia Mancini, "Expanding Flavor Horizons," *Food Engineering,* November 1991; and Kitty Kevin, "A Brave New World: Capturing the Flavor Bug: Flavors from Microorganisms," *Food Processing,* March 1995.

22. See Jeanne-Marie Bartas, "Vegan Menu Items at Fast Food and Family-Style Restaurants—Part 2," *Vegetarian Journal,* January/February 1998.

23. See "Wendy's Nutrition/Ingredient Guide," Wendy's International, Inc., 1997.

24. See "Nutritional Information," Burger King, 1999.

Questions on Meaning

1. Where does the title of this selection come from? Why do you think the author chose it?
2. According to the author, what percentage of our nation's food is considered processed? Why is this fact a cause for concern?
3. What is the difference between natural and artificial flavors? How did you react to the author's description of how these flavors are created?
4. What is the Universal TA-XT2 Texture Analyzer? What is the field called "rheology"?

Questions on Rhetorical Strategy and Style

1. Why does the author include heavy doses and long lists of technical and scientific diction and data in this selection? What effect might this have on the reader? How is this strategy both objective and emotional?
2. How does the author characterize the companies that form the "flavor industry"? Why does the IFF company remind him of Willy Wonka's chocolate factory? What impression is that analogy intended to create?
3. What is the purpose of the author's brief profile of the senior flavorist Brian Grainger? Why does this selection end with it?

Writing Assignments

1. Write a two-page response to this selection. Where are you inclined to agree with the author's concerns about the fast food industry? On the other hand, where did you question his use of evidence?
2. Write a paper describing the role of the FDA in our society. In your opinion, is the FDA doing enough to protect consumers? Does it have enough leverage or authority? In what ways is it, in your opinion, bogged down by bureaucracy and politics?

If You Are What You Eat,
Then What Am I?

Geeta Kothari

Geeta Kothari came with her parents from India as a child. She lived with them in the United States with her sister but far from her extended family in northern India. She married an American and became a writing instructor at the University of Pittsburgh. Her edited collection Did My Mama Like to Dance and Other Stories about Mothers and Daughters *(1994), as well as many stories and articles in magazines and newspapers, have earned her recognition as an important present-day writer. In this essay, she asks about the identity of people like her who have grown up between cultures. She uses her experiences with both American and Indian food to define the predicament of her life. As a child, she wanted to be like other children and eat sandwiches, but her mother had no idea how to make American sandwiches. At the same time, when she visited India with her parents, she could not tolerate the types of bacteria that populated Indian drink and food. She became ill by merely drinking from a bottle of Fanta soda. After marrying her husband, she found herself repelled by the smell of meat on his skin, never being able herself to face a rare steak or even a pork chop. This essay investigates the links in her life between food and identity. It is part of a longer work from the* Kenyon Review.

> *To belong is to understand the tacit codes of the people you live with.*
> —Michael Ignatieff, *Blood and Belonging*

Reprinted from *Kenyon Review* 21, no. 1 (winter 1999), by permission of the author and the Kenyon Review.

1 The first time my mother and I open a can of tuna, I am nine years old. We stand in the doorway of the kitchen, in semi-darkness, the can tilted toward daylight. I want to eat what the kids at school eat: bologna, hot dogs, salami—foods my parents find repugnant because they contain pork and meat byproducts, crushed bone and hair glued together by chemicals and fat. Although she has never been able to tolerate the smell of fish, my mother buys the tuna, hoping to satisfy my longing for American food.

Indians, of course, do not eat such things.

The tuna smells fishy, which surprises me because I can't remember anyone's tuna sandwich actually smelling like fish. And the tuna in those sandwiches doesn't look like this, pink and shiny, like an internal organ. In fact, this looks similar to the bad foods my mother doesn't want me to eat. She is silent, holding her face away from the can while peering into it like a half-blind bird.

"What's wrong with it?" I ask.

5 She has no idea. My mother does not know that the tuna everyone else's mothers made for them was tuna *salad*.

"Do you think it's botulism?"

I have never seen botulism, but I have read about it, just as I have read about but never eaten steak and kidney pie.

There is so much my parents don't know. They are not like other parents, and they disappoint me and my sister. They are supposed to help us negotiate the world outside, teach us the signs, the clues to proper behavior: what to eat and how to eat it.

We have expectations, and my parents fail to meet them, especially my mother, who works full-time. I don't understand what it means, to have a mother who works outside and inside the home; I notice only the ways in which she disappoints me. She doesn't show up for school plays. She doesn't make chocolate-frosted cupcakes for my class. At night, if I want her attention, I have to sit in the kitchen and talk to her while she cooks the evening meal, attentive to every third or fourth word I say.

10 We throw the tuna away. This time my mother is disappointed. I go to school with tuna eaters. I see their sandwiches, yet cannot explain the discrepancy between them and the stinking, oily fish in my mother's hand. We do not understand so many things, my mother and I.

When we visit our relatives in India, food prepared outside the house is carefully monitored. In the hot, sticky monsoon months in New

Delhi and Bombay, we cannot eat ice cream, salad, cold food, or any fruit that can't be peeled. Definitely no meat. People die from amoebic dysentery, unexplained fevers, strange boils on their bodies. We drink boiled water only, no ice. No sweets except for jalebi, thin fried twists of dough in dripping hot sugar syrup. If we're caught outside with nothing to drink, Fanta, Limca, Thums Up (after Coca-Cola is thrown out by Mrs. Gandhi[1]) will do. Hot tea sweetened with sugar, served with thick creamy buffalo milk, is preferable. It should be boiled, to kill the germs on the cup.

My mother talks about "back home" as a safe place, a silk cocoon frozen in time where we are sheltered by family and friends. Back home, my sister and I do not argue about food with my parents. Home is where they know all the rules. We trust them to guide us safely through the maze of city streets for which they have no map, and we trust them to feed and take care of us, the way parents should.

Finally, though, one of us will get sick, hungry for the food we see our cousins and friends eating, too thirsty to ask for a straw, too polite to insist on properly boiled water.

At my uncle's diner in New Delhi, someone hands me a plate of aloo tikki, fried potato patties filled with mashed channa dal and served with a sweet and a sour chutney. The channa, mixed with hot chilies and spices, burns my tongue and throat. I reach for my Fanta, discard the paper straw, and gulp the sweet orange soda down, huge drafts that sting rather than soothe.

15   When I throw up later that day (or is it the next morning, when a   15 stomachache wakes me from deep sleep?), I cry over the frustration of being singled out, not from the pain my mother assumes I'm feeling as she holds my hair back from my face. The taste of orange lingers in my mouth, and I remember my lips touching the cold glass of the Fanta bottle.

At that moment, more than anything, I want to be like my cousins.

In New York, at the first Indian restaurant in our neighborhood, my father orders with confidence, and my sister and I play with the silverware until the steaming plates of lamb biryani arrive.

What is Indian food? my friends ask, their noses crinkling up.

Later, this restaurant is run out of business by the new Indo-Pak-Bangladeshi combinations up and down the street, which serve similar food. They use plastic cutlery and Styrofoam cups. They do not distinguish between North and South Indian cooking, or between Indian, Pakistani, and Bangladeshi cooking, and their customers do not care. The food is fast, cheap, and tasty. Dosa, a rice flour crepe stuffed with masala potato, appears on the same trays as chicken makhani.

20   Now my friends want to know, Do you eat curry at home?   20

One time my mother makes lamb vindaloo for guests. Like dosa, this is a South Indian dish, one that my Punjabi[2] mother has to learn from a cookbook. For us, she cooks everyday food—yellow dal, rice, chapati, bhaji. Lentils, rice, bread, and vegetables. She has never referred to anything on our table as "curry" or "curried," but I know she has made chicken curry for guests. Vindaloo, she explains, is a curry too. I understand then that curry is a dish created for guests, outsiders, a food for people who eat in restaurants.

I look around my boyfriend's freezer one day and find meat: pork chops, ground beef, chicken pieces, Italian sausage. Ham in the refrigerator, next to the homemade bolognese sauce. Tupperware filled with chili made from ground beef and pork.

He smells different from me. Foreign. Strange.

I marry him anyway.

25   He has inherited blue eyes that turn gray in bad weather, light   25
brown hair, a sharp pointy nose, and excellent teeth. He learns to make chili with ground turkey and tofu, tomato sauce with red wine and portobello mushrooms, roast chicken with rosemary and slivers of garlic under the skin.

He eats steak when we are in separate cities, roast beef at his mother's house, hamburgers at work. Sometimes I smell them on his skin. I hope he doesn't notice me turning my face, a cheek instead of my lips, my nose wrinkled at the unfamiliar, musky smell.

I have inherited brown eyes, black hair, a long nose with a crooked bridge, and soft teeth with thin enamel. I am in my twenties, moving to a city far from my parents, before it occurs to me that jeera, the spice my sister avoids, must have an English name. I have to learn that haldi = turmeric, methi = fenugreek. What to make with fenugreek, I do not know. My grandmother used to make methi roti for our breakfast, cornbread with fresh fenugreek leaves served with a lump of homemade butter. No one makes it now that she's gone, though once in a while my mother will get a craving for it and produce a facsimile ("The cornmeal here is wrong") that only highlights what she's really missing: the smells and tastes of her mother's house.

I will never make my grandmother's methi roti or even my mother's unsatisfactory imitation of it. I attempt chapati; it takes six hours, three phone calls home, and leaves me with an aching back. I have to write translations down: jeera = cumin. My memory is unreliable. But I have always known garam = hot.

If I really want to make myself sick, I worry that my husband will one day leave me for a meat-eater, for someone familiar who doesn't sniff him suspiciously for signs of alimentary infidelity.

30 Indians eat lentils. I understand this as absolute, a decree from an unidentifiable authority that watches and judges me.

So what does it mean that I cannot replicate my mother's dal? She and my father show me repeatedly, in their kitchen, in my kitchen. They coach me over the phone, buy me the best cookbooks, and finally write down their secrets. Things I'm supposed to know but don't. Recipes that should be, by now, engraved on my heart.

Living far from the comfort of people who require no explanation for what I do and who I am, I crave the foods we have shared. My mother convinces me that moong is the easiest dal to prepare, and yet it fails me every time: bland, watery, a sickly greenish yellow mush. These imperfact imitations remind me only of what I'm missing.

But I have never been fond of moong dal. At my mother's table it is the last thing I reach for. Now I worry that this antipathy toward dal signals something deeper, that somehow I am not my parents' daughter, not Indian, and because I cannot bear the touch and smell of raw meat, though I can eat it cooked (charred, dry, and overdone), I am not American either.

I worry about a lifetime purgatory in Indian restaurants where I will complain that all the food looks and tastes the same because they've used the same masala.

End Notes

1. Coca-Cola was banned in India for twenty years beginning in the mid-1970s, when Indira Gandhi was prime minister, because the company would not reveal its formula to the government. Fanta, Limca, and Thums Up are other soft drinks popular in India.
2. Native of the state of Punjab, in northern India.

Questions on Meaning

1. Indians often have a difficult time with American food. What does Kothari's family prefer to eat, and how does that food differ from American fare?
2. What dangers lurk in Indian food culture for one accustomed to American sanitation? Why can Kothari's cousins eat and drink from cutlery and glassware and not her? Why do Americans get sick when they go to Asian countries?
3. Kothari finds herself unable to cook Indian food. Why has she never learned to cook the food from her parents' culture? How many kinds of food are there in India? What is the importance of spices and types of lentils?

Questions on Rhetorical Strategy and Style

1. Finding an identity challenges each child, but why is that task particularly difficult for a child whose parents are first-generation Americans? Why does Kothari as a child become angry with her parents for not understanding American food? Does she herself ever really become a part of the American food culture?
2. Kothari stresses her relationship with her mother. Why does she find her mother inadequate as a guide through American culture? Why is it more difficult for an immigrant mother to help her children? What kinds of school activities does her mother miss? What can she not provide for her children?
3. How does the food difference interfere with Kothari's relationship with her husband? Why does the smell of the meat that he has eaten on his breath and skin so offend her? What is she saying about the deep-seated problems of marrying outside of one's culture?

Writing Assignments

1. Describe a food that your family considered to be "home cooking." What did it take to prepare the food? Who did the cooking? What did the food represent to your family? Would you still cook it today?
2. Think of a perfume or aftershave that you do not like. Imagine dating someone who uses this product. Would you ask this per-

son to change products? If the scent came from eating a food, would you ask this person to give up the food? What impact does food preference have on relationships?

3. Describe a time that you have felt isolated and alienated. What aspects of this experience are most powerful in your memory? Help your reader to understand your experience by using vivid sensory descriptions to explain how you felt. Keep in mind the description of the tuna fish in this essay. Have you experienced any food or scent so foreign?

Take My Privacy, Please

David Pogue

David Pogue, former columnist for Macworld, *writes a technology column for the* New York Times. *After Pogue earned a music degree from Yale University in 1985, he began writing music software, working with music on Broadway, and teaching computer skills. He has also created a line of printed manuals for computer products that don't have manuals. In this article, Pogue examines a common fear in the computer age: that the vast storage capacity of the computers that compose the Internet will make the most intimate details of our personal and financial lives available to anyone.*

Could Somebody Remind Me Why We're Panicking?

1 Hey, want to have an instant best-seller? Write a book about the loss of privacy in the Information Age. Want to sell newspapers? Run a headline about how the evil Software Conspiracy tracks our every move. Movie? Novel? Party conversation? With high-tech surveillance, you've got yourself a winning theme.

I don't dispute that some tracking is going on. Our phone calls, credit card transactions, and plane reservations have been recorded on some computer somewhere, for years. No, what I'd like to know is, what—in practical, nonhysterical terms—is wrong with this kind of data collection? Reporters, moviemakers, and publishers have glommed on to the invasion-of-privacy thing because it sells, but the thinking never seems to go much further than "They're watching you."

So, aside from our visceral negative reactions, what's the downside? The few possibilities I've come across revolve around these arguments:

"Take My Privacy, Please" by David Pogue, published in *Macworld*, December 2000.

- We'll be targeted by marketers. If you visit Amazon.com, you're greeted by ads for books in categories you've bought from recently. When you do a search for car information on Yahoo, the results page may offer a car ad at the top of the screen. The writing is on the wall: Pretty soon, they'll send us ads targeting our interests!

5   And the problem is . . . ? I say, bring it on! If I have to look at advertising, why not see ads for products that interest me, for heaven's sake? My interests are Macs, gadgets, Broadway musicals, magic, tennis, books, kids—let the targeting begin!

No, our problem is that not enough ads are aimed at specific audiences. When companies spend millions to show me ads for SUVs and adult diapers, they're wasting their dollars and my time.

- We'll be caught. Nobody wants to get caught being naughty. People hate the thought that their criminal, extramarital, or pornographic interests might one day come to light.

In my book, that's a pretty flimsy reason for championing privacy. If you want only to cover up violations of the law—moral, marital, or other—your problem isn't the threat of losing privacy; it's living in a society that has laws and a conscience.

- Our information will be made public someday. No doubt about it: life as a political candidate or celebrity is no picnic. Thanks to massive databases that shadow our every life event, public officials are open to scrutiny by every reporter and opponent.

10   On the other hand, aren't we better off knowing about Richard Nixon's deception, Gary Hart's affair, Bill Clinton's draft dodge? Whether you're a supporter or an opponent, knowing is better than not knowing.

- It's just creepy. It is creepy to think that someone is watching us. It makes us nervous, fuels dramatic opinion columns, and keeps the producers of Big Brother from using the TV camera over the toilet.

But scary-sounding high-tech paranoia schemes have been foisted upon us before, and they almost never pan out. Remember the Y2K bug? There were people digging bomb shelters in Montana, for heaven's sake, and a lot of publishers got rich on what turned out to be a marketing scam, for all practical purposes. So far, the theft-of-privacy threat remains mostly in the realm of the theoretical and the someday.

Spam and Privacy Tragedies

I'm not claiming that there are no downsides to living in a database nation. Junk e-mail, for example, is a true annoyance.

Nor do I need reminders of the real, if isolated, tragedies caused by the abuse of personal information: the credit-report error that haunts someone for years, the wife beater who tracks down his ex-spouse's new address, or the AIDS patient who's denied a job because of medical records. These stories are genuinely upsetting.

15 But there are costs to fearmongering, too. I know people who 15 have turned off their browsers' cookies (preference files for Web sites) out of paranoia—and who therefore have to type out convoluted user IDs and access codes with every visit to a restricted site. Thousands of people refuse to buy anything online—never mind that their credit card numbers are at infinitely greater risk of being stolen at a gas station or restaurant. I know a guy who pays for everything at stores, in cash, for fear of giving any private information to anyone. But take it from someone whose credit card company refunds 2 percent of his annual purchases: that kind of paranoia can cost you.

Look, I don't want Big Business to invade every corner of our lives. I'll back any law against sending spam, sharing medical records, or collecting our personal data without telling us. My issue is with the marketing of privacy hysteria. There are different ways to lose your privacy—and not all are scary.

Questions on Meaning

1. How many times have you given someone personal information, such as your driver's-license number, your Social Security number, your phone number, and your address, in the last week? Which people or organizations (parents, schools, insurance companies, and others) have regular access to information about you?
2. Pogue argues that people are too paranoid about snooping and privacy. What are his main reasons for believing this?

Questions on Rhetorical Strategy and Style

1. Pogue uses a kidding tone to undermine fears of snooping. Find and analyze a few sentences that illustrate his "don't take this too seriously" attitude.
2. Does Pogue's irony persuade you to relax about surveillance? Why or Why not? Were you already relaxed about it, or were you worried?

Writing Assignments

1. Investigate the student record system in your school. Find out who has access to personal information about you. Write an informative article about the topic that might be printed in your school newspaper.
2. The Fourth Amendment to the U.S. Constitution reads as follows: "The right of the people to be secure in their persons, houses, papers, and effects, against unreasonable searches and seizures, shall not be violated, and no Warrants shall issue, but upon probable cause, supported by Oath or affirmation, and particularly describing the place to be searched, and the persons or things to be seized." Write an essay in which you oppose Pogue's thesis. Use the Constitution as your authority.

Girl

Jamaica Kincaid

*Born Elaine Potter Richardson in St. John's, Antigua, in
the West Indies, Jamaica Kincaid (1949-) left Antigua for
New York when she was seventeen, took classes at a com-
munity college, studied photography at the New School for
Social Research, and attended Franconia College. She has
been a staff writer for* The New Yorker *and has published
her work in* Rolling Stone, The Village Voice, *and* The
Paris Review. *Her first book,* At the Bottom of the River
*(1983) won an award from the American Academy and
Institute of Arts and Letters. Her more recent works include*
The Autobiography of My Mother *(1996) and* My
Brother *(1997). The following selection originally appeared in* The New Yorker *and was included in* At the
Bottom of the River. *It vividly narrates a relationship between a powerful mother and her young daughter and con-
fronts us with the advice the daughter must listen to.*

1   Wash the white clothes on Monday and put them on the
stone heap; wash the color clothes on Tuesday and put
them on the clothesline to dry; don't walk barehead in the
hot sun; cook pumpkin fritters in very hot sweet oil; soak your little
clothes right after you take them off; when buying cotton to make
yourself a nice blouse, be sure that it doesn't have gum on it, because
that way it won't hold up well after a wash; soak salt fish overnight before you cook it; is it true that you sing benna in Sunday school?; always eat your food in such a way that it won't turn someone else's
stomach; on Sundays try to walk like a lady and not like the slut you
are so bent on becoming; don't sing benna in Sunday school; you

mustn't speak to wharf-rat boys, not even to give directions; don't eat fruits on the street—flies will follow you; *but I don't sing benna on Sundays at all and never in Sunday school*; this is how to sew on a button; this is how to make a buttonhole for the button you have just sewed on; this is how to hem a dress when you see the hem coming down and so to prevent yourself from looking like the slut I know you are so bent on becoming; this is how you iron your father's khaki shirt so that it doesn't have a crease; this is how you iron your father's khaki pants so that they don't have a crease; this is how you grow okra—far from the house, because okra tree harbors red ants; when you are growing dasheen, make sure it gets plenty of water or else it makes your throat itch when you are eating it; this is how you sweep a corner; this is how you sweep a whole house; this is how you sweep a yard; this is how you smile to someone you don't like too much; this how you smile to someone you don't like at all; this is how you smile to someone you like completely; this is how you set a table for tea; this is how you set a table for dinner; this is how you set a table for dinner with an important guest; this is how you set a table for lunch; this is how you set a table for breakfast; this is how to behave in the presence of men who don't know you very well, and this way they won't recognize immediately the slut I have warned you against becoming; be sure to wash every day, even if it is with your own spit; don't squat down to play marbles—you are not a boy, you know; don't pick people's flowers—you might catch something; don't throw stones at blackbirds, because it might not be a blackbird at all; this is how to make a bread pudding; this is how to make doukona; this is how to make pepper pot; this is how to make a good medicine for a cold; this is how to make a good medicine to throw away a child before it even becomes a child; this is how to catch a fish; this is how to throw back a fish you don't like, and that way something bad won't fall on you; this is how to bully a man; this is how a man bullies you; this is how to love a man, and if this doesn't work there are other ways, and if they don't work don't feel too bad about giving up; this is how to spit up in the air if you feel like it and this is how to move quick so that it doesn't fall on you; this is how to make ends meet; always squeeze bread to make sure it's fresh; *but what if the baker won't let me feel the bread?*; you mean to say that after all you are really going to be the kind of woman who the baker won't let near the bread?

Questions on Meaning

1. In this short piece, Kincaid gives us a glimpse into the relationship between a mother and daughter. How would you describe that relationship?
2. How would you characterize the advice offered by the mother in this story? What information about her community and its assumptions regarding gender roles can you infer from it?

Questions on Rhetorical Strategy and Style

1. What is this story's texture? How does it make you feel? Why do you think Kincaid chose to present it as a brief monologue?
2. Kincaid doesn't describe the physical setting of "Girl" directly, but provides clues in the content of the mother's advice. Go through the story and find as many details about place as you can, then write a description of the characters' home and neighborhood.
3. "Girl" makes an interesting use of example: Kincaid strings together a barrage of examples to tell her reader something about the characters, but doesn't explain precisely what they're meant to illustrate. What point do you think she is trying to make with them?

Writing Assignments

1. Write a short narrative piece about a time when someone with authority over you gave you advice. What kind of advice was it? How did you feel about receiving it? What was your response? In your narrative, try to convey a sense of the mood surrounding the exchange by the way you describe the things around you.
2. Write an essay about your relationship with one of your parents. Recount in detail significant moments you spent together. Your purpose is to convey something about the understandings you share.

Pornography

Margaret Atwood

Margaret Atwood (1939–), born in Ottawa, Canada, attended the University of Toronto, Radcliffe, and Harvard. At a young age she decided to become a writer, and she has published a remarkable list of novels, poetry, and essays, along with forays into other genres such as children's stories and television scripts. She is best known, however, for her novels: The Edible Women *(1969),* Surfacing *(1972),* Lady Oracle *(1976),* Life Before Man *(1979),* Bodily Harm *(1982),* The Handmaid's Tale *(1985),* Cat's Eye *(1989),* The Robber Bride *(1994),* Alias Grace *(1996),* The Blind Assassin *(2000),* Oryx and Crake *(2003), which was shortlisted for the Giller Prize, and the Man Booker Prize,* The Penelopiad *(2005), and* The Tent *(2006). In the following selection, first published in 1988, she explores a topic she first became involved in when doing research for a novel. As a gifted stylist, Atwood is well aware of the power of language—which she uses in this essay to describe vividly the violence of pornography.*

1   When I was in Finland a few years ago for an international writers' conference, I had occasion to say a few paragraphs in public on the subject of pornography. The context was a discussion of political repression, and I was suggesting the possibility of a link between the two. The immediate result was that a male journalist took several large bites out of me. Prudery and pornography are two halves of the same coin, said he, and I was clearly a prude. What could you expect from an Anglo-Canadian? Afterward,

a couple of pleasant Scandinavian men asked me what I had been so worked up about. All "pornography" means, they said, is graphic depictions of whores, and what was the harm in that?

Not until then did it strike me that the male journalist and I had two entirely different things in mind. By "pornography," he meant naked bodies and sex. I, on the other hand, had recently been doing the research for my novel *Bodily Harm,* and was still in a state of shock from some of the material I had seen, including the Ontario Board of Film Censors' "outtakes." By "pornography," I meant women getting their nipples snipped off with garden shears, having meat hooks stuck into their vaginas, being disemboweled; little girls being raped; men (yes, there are some men) being smashed to a pulp and forcibly sodomized. The cutting edge of pornography, as far as I could see, was no longer simple old copulation, hanging from the chandelier or otherwise: it was death, messy, explicit and highly sadistic. I explained this to the nice Scandinavian men. "Oh, but that's just the United States," they said. "Everyone knows they're sick." In their country, they said, violent "pornography" of that kind was not permitted on television or in movies; indeed, excessive violence of any kind was not permitted. They had drawn a clear line between erotica, which earlier studies had shown did not incite men to more aggressive and brutal behavior toward women, and violence, which later studies indicated did.

Some time after that I was in Saskatchewan, where, because of the scenes in *Bodily Harm,* I found myself on an open-line radio show answering questions about "pornography." Almost no one who phoned in was in favor of it, but again they weren't talking about the same stuff I was, because they hadn't seen it. Some of them were all set to stamp out bathing suits and negligees, and, if possible, any depictions of the female body whatsoever. God, it was implied, did not approve of female bodies, and sex of any kind, including that practised by bumblebees, should be shoved back into the dark, where it belonged. I had more than a suspicion that *Lady Chatterley's Lover,* Margaret Laurence's *The Diviners,* and indeed most books by most serious modern authors would have ended up as confetti if left in the hands of these callers.

For me, these two experiences illustrate the two poles of the emotionally heated debate that is now thundering around this issue. They also underline the desirability and even the necessity of defining the terms. "Pornography" is now one of those catchalls, like "Marxism" and "feminism," that have become so broad they can mean almost anything, ranging from certain verses in the Bible, ads for skin lotion and sex texts for children to the contents of Penthouse, Naughty '90s postcards and films with titles containing the word *Nazi* that show vicious scenes of torture and killing. It's easy to say that sensible people can tell the difference. Unfortunately, opinions on what constitutes a sensible person vary.

5   But even sensible people tend to lose their cool when they start talking about this subject. They soon stop talking and start yelling, and the name-calling begins. Those in favor of censorship (which may include groups not noticeably in agreement on other issues, such as some feminists and religious fundamentalists) accuse the others of exploiting women through the use of degrading images, contributing to the corruption of children, and adding to the general climate of violence and threat in which both women and children live in this society; or, though they may not give much of a hoot about actual women and children, they invoke moral standards and God's supposed aversion to "filth," "smut" and deviated *perversion,* which may mean ankles.

The camp in favor of total "freedom of expression" often comes out howling as loud as the Romans would have if told they could no longer have innocent fun watching the lions eat up Christians. It too may include segments of the population who are not natural bedfellows: those who proclaim their God-given right to freedom, including the freedom to tote guns, drive when drunk, drool over chicken porn and get off on videotapes of women being raped and beaten, may be waving the same anticensorship banner as responsible liberals who fear the return of Mrs. Grundy, or gay groups for whom sexual emancipation involves the concept of "sexual theatre." *Whatever turns you on* is a handy motto, as is *A man's home is his castle* (and if it includes a dungeon with beautiful maidens strung up in chains and bleeding from every pore, that's his business).

Meanwhile, theoreticians theorize and speculators speculate. Is today's pornography yet another indication of the hatred of the body, the deep mind-body split, which is supposed to pervade Western Christian society? Is it a backlash against the women's movement by men who are threatened by uppity female behavior in real life, so like to fantasize about women done up like outsize parcels, being turned into hamburger, kneeling at their feet in slavelike adoration or sucking off guns? Is it a sign of collective impotence, of a generation of men who can't relate to real women at all but have to make do with bits of celluloid and paper? Is the current flood just a result of smart marketing and aggressive promotion by the money men in what has now become a multibillion-dollar industry? If they were selling movies about men getting their testicles stuck full of knitting needles by women with swastikas on their sleeves, would they do as well, or is this penchant somehow peculiarly male? If so, why? Is pornography a power trip rather than a sex one? Some say that those ropes, chains, muzzles and other restraining devices are an argument for the immense power female sexuality still wields in the male imagination: you don't put these things on dogs unless you're afraid of them. Others, more literary, wonder about the shift from the 19th-century Magic Women or Femme Fatale image to the lollipop-licker, airhead or turkey-carcass treatment of women in porn today. The proporners don't care much about theory: they merely demand product. The antiporners don't care about it in the final analysis either: there's dirt on the street, and they want it cleaned up, now.

It seems to me that this conversation, with its *You're-a-prude/You're-a-pervert* dialectic, will never get anywhere as long as we continue to think of this material as just "entertainment." Possibly we're deluded by the packaging, the format: magazine, book, movie, theatrical presentation. We're used to thinking of these things as part of the "entertainment industry," and we're used to thinking of ourselves as free adult people who ought to be able to see any kind of "entertainment" we want to. That was what the First Choice pay-TV debate was all about. After all, it's only entertainment, right? Entertainment means fun, and only a killjoy would be antifun. What's the harm?

This is obviously the central question: *What's the harm?* If there isn't any real harm to any real people, then the antiporners can tsk-tsk and/or throw up as much as they like, but they can't rightfully expect more legal controls or sanctions. However, the no-harm position is far from being proven.

10 (For instance, there's a clear-cut case for banning—as the federal government has proposed—movies, photos and videos that depict children engaging in sex with adults: real children are used to make the movies, and hardly anybody thinks this is ethical. The possibilities for coercion are too great.) 10

To shift the viewpoint, I'd like to suggest three other models for looking at "pornography"—and here I mean the violent kind.

Those who find the idea of regulating pornographic materials repugnant because they think it's Fascist or Communist or otherwise not in accordance with the principles of an open democratic society should consider that Canada has made it illegal to disseminate material that may lead to hatred toward any group because of race or religion. I suggest that if pornography of the violent kind depicted these acts being done predominantly to Chinese, to blacks, to Catholics, it would be off the market immediately, under the present laws. Why is hate literature illegal? Because whoever made the law thought that such material might incite real people to do real awful things to other real people. The human brain is to a certain extent a computer: garbage in, garbage out. We only hear about the extreme cases (like that of American multimurderer Ted Bundy) in which pornography has contributed to the death and/or mutilation of women and/or men. Although pornography is not the only factor involved in the creation of such deviance, it certainly has upped the ante by suggesting both a variety of techniques and the social acceptability of such actions. Nobody knows yet what effect this stuff is having on the less psychotic.

Studies have shown that a large part of the market for all kinds of porn, soft and hard, is drawn from the 16-to-21-year-old population of young men. Boys used to learn about sex on the street, or (in Italy, according to Fellini movies) from friendly whores, or, in more genteel surroundings, from girls, their parents, or, once upon a time, in school, more or less. Now porn has been added, and sex education in the schools is rapidly being phased out. The buck has been passed, and boys are being taught that all women secretly like to be raped and that real men get high on scooping out women's digestive tracts.

Boys learn their concept of masculinity from other men: is this what most men want them to be learning? If word gets around that rapists are "normal" and even admirable men, will boys feel that in order to be normal, admirable and masculine they will have to be rapists? Human beings are enormously flexible, and how they turn out depends a lot on how they're educated, by the society in which they're immersed as well as by their teachers. In a society that advertises and glorifies rape or even implicitly condones it, more women get raped. It becomes socially acceptable. And at a time when men and the traditional male role have taken a lot of flak and men are confused and casting around for an acceptable way of being male (and, in some cases, not getting much comfort from women on that score), this must be at times a pleasing thought.

15   It would be naïve to think of violent pornography as just harmless entertainment. It's also an educational tool and a powerful propaganda device. What happens when boy educated on porn meets girl brought up on Harlequin romances? The clash of expectations can be heard around the block. She wants him to get down on his knees with a ring, he wants her to get down on all fours with a ring in her nose. Can this marriage be saved?

Pornography has certain things in common with such addictive substances as alcohol and drugs: for some, though by no means for all, it induces chemical changes in the body, which the user finds exciting and pleasurable. It also appears to attract a "hard core" of habitual users and a penumbra of those who use it occasionally but aren't dependent on it in any way. There are also significant numbers of men who aren't much interested in it, not because they're undersexed but because real life is satisfying their needs, which may not require as many appliances as those of users.

For the "hard core," pornography may function as alcohol does for the alcoholic: tolerance develops, and a little is no longer enough. This may account for the short viewing time and fast turnover in porn theatres. Mary Brown, chairwoman of the Ontario Board of Film Censors, estimates that for every one mainstream movie requesting entrance to Ontario, there is one porno flick. Not only the quantity consumed but the quality of explicitness must escalate, which may account for the growing violence: once the big deal was breasts, then it was genitals, then copulation, then that was no longer enough and the hard users had to have more. The ultimate kick is death, and after that, as the Marquis de Sade so boringly demonstrated, multiple death.

The existence of alcoholism has not led us to ban social drinking. On the other hand, we do have laws about drinking and driving, excessive drunkenness and other abuses of alcohol that may result in injury or death to others.

This leads us back to the key question: what's the harm? Nobody knows, but this society should find out fast, before the saturation point is reached. The Scandinavian studies that showed a connection between depictions of sexual violence and increased impulse toward it on the part of male viewers would be a starting point, but many more questions remain to be raised as well as answered. What, for instance, is the crucial difference between men who are users and men who are not? Does using affect a man's relationship with actual women, and, if so, adversely? Is there a clear line between erotica and violent pornography, or are they on an escalating continuum? Is this a "men versus women" issue, with all men secretly siding with the proporners and all women secretly siding against? (I think not; there *are* lots of men who don't think that running their true love through the Cuisinart is the best way they can think of to spend a Saturday night, and they're just as nauseated by films of someone else doing it as women are.) Is pornography merely an expression of the sexual confusion of this age or an active contributor to it?

20   Nobody wants to go back to the age of official repression, when even piano legs were referred to as "limbs" and had to wear pantaloons to be decent. Neither do we want to end up in George Orwell's *1984,* in which pornography is turned out by the State to keep the proles in a state of torpor, sex itself is considered dirty and the approved practise is only for reproduction. But Rome under the emperors isn't such a good model either.

If all men and women respected each other, if sex were considered joyful and life-enhancing instead of a wallow in germ-filled glop, if everyone were in love all the time, if, in other words, many people's lives were more satisfactory for them than they appear to be now, pornography might just go away on its own. But since this is obviously not happening, we as a society are going to have to make some informed and responsible decisions about how to deal with it.

Questions on Meaning

1. What does Atwood mean when she says violent pornography is "an educational tool and a powerful propaganda device"?
2. Atwood speculates about the possible causes for what she sees as an explosion of pornography in modern times. List some of these causes. Does she argue for one cause rather than another? Explain why or why not.
3. The essay asks far more questions about pornography than it attempts to answer, but Atwood still has a clear point to make. State her primary theme in your own words.

Questions on Rhetorical Strategy and Style

1. Atwood's style is quite graphic in some places in this essay, such as in the second paragraph where she describes violent details of the pornographic film out-takes she saw from the Ontario Board of Film Censors. What effect did such descriptions have on you as you read the essay? Explain how this style is appropriate for what she has to say about her subject.
2. One goal of this essay is simply to define pornography. After establishing that different people mean very different things by the word, Atwood does attempt to define it. What writing techniques does she use to define what she means by pornography?
3. To explain the argument that pornography should be regulated by laws, Atwood compares it to hate literature. Examine how she uses this strategy of comparison and contrast explicitly in that part of the essay but also implicitly throughout by associating the concepts of hatred and pornography.

Writing Assignments

1. The term "date rape" has arisen in the last decade to describe a specific kind of sexual coercion. Date rape has become so common on most college campuses that colleges and universities have developed programs for purposes of education and prevention. Research what is being done on your own campus to help overcome this problem.
2. Atwood comments that when discussing pornography, people "soon stop talking and start yelling." Think of other social issues about which people become highly emotional. Without getting

into a debate on the issue itself, write an essay exploring why you think it is so difficult for people on both sides of such issues to calmly and rationally debate the question.

3. Atwood mentions how much better it would be "if sex were considered joyful and life-enhancing." Consider all the different ways you have seen sex portrayed in reality and in the media. Write an essay in which you compare and contrast different representations of sex.

There Will Come Soft Rains

Ray Bradbury

Ray Douglas Bradbury (1920–) was born in Waukegan, Illinois. A storywriter and novelist, a playwright, a screenwriter, and a poet, Bradbury is one of the most distinguished and beloved science fiction writers. In 1934, Bradbury moved to Los Angeles, California where he met such famous people as the great comedian, George Burns, who paid Bradbury for his very first work—a joke for Burns's comedy show. In 1947 Bradbury published his first collection of short stories, Dark Carnival. The Martian Chronicles *(1950), in which he imagined humans colonizing Mars, made him famous. In 1953* Fahrenheit 451 *struck a darker note as it imagined a world where books were burned and ideas suppressed. Bradbury has won the O. Henry Memorial Award; the Benjamin Franklin Award (1954); the Aviation-Space Writer's Association Award for Best Space Article in an American Magazine (1967); and the World Fantasy Award for Lifetime Achievement. His work was included in the* Best American Short Stories *collections for 1946, 1948, and 1952. Bradbury's most unusual honor came when an Apollo astronaut named Dandelion Crater on the moon after Bradbury's novel,* Dandelion Wine.

"There Will Come Soft Rains" was first published in Colliers *magazine on May 6, 1950. The story revolves around a house that was built to withstand nuclear blasts and to run itself for human convenience. In the story the*

house stands, but the family is burned into the outer wall by a blast. The tale ends with the house reading Sara Teasedale's poem about the world without humans.

1   In the living room the voice-clock sang, *Tick-tock, seven o'clock, time to get up, time to get up, seven o'clock!* as if it were afraid that nobody would. The morning house lay empty. The clock ticked on, repeating and repeating its sounds into the emptiness. *Seven-nine, breakfast time, seven-nine!*

In the kitchen the breakfast stove gave a hissing sigh and ejected from its warm interior eight pieces of perfectly browned toast, eight eggs sunnyside up, sixteen slices of bacon, two coffees, and two cool glasses of milk.

"Today is August 4, 2026," said a second voice from the kitchen ceiling, "in the city of Allendale, California." It repeated the date three times for memory's sake. "Today is Mr. Featherstone's birthday. Today is the anniversary of Tilita's marriage. Insurance is payable, as are the water, gas, and light bills."

Somewhere in the walls, relays clicked, memory tapes glided under electric eyes.

5   *Eight-one, tick-tock, eight-one o'clock, off to school, off to work, run, run, eight-one!* But no doors slammed, no carpets took the soft tread of rubber heels. It was raining outside. The weather box on the front door sang quietly: "Rain, rain, go away; rubbers, raincoats for today . . ." And the rain tapped on the empty house, echoing.

Outside, the garage chimed and lifted its door to reveal the waiting car. After a long wait the door swung down again.

At eight-thirty the eggs were shriveled and the toast was like stone. An aluminum wedge scraped them into the sink, where hot water whirled them down a metal throat which digested and flushed them away to the distant sea. The dirty dishes were dropped into a hot washer and emerged twinkling dry.

Nine-fifteen, sang the clock, *time to clean.*

Out of warrens in the wall, tiny robot mice darted. The rooms were acrawl with the small cleaning animals, all rubber and metal. They thudded against chairs, whirling their mustached runners, kneading the rug nap, sucking gently at hidden dust. Then, like mysterious invaders, they popped into their burrows. Their pink electric eyes faded. The house was clean.

10   *Ten o'clock.* The sun came out from behind the rain. The house stood alone in a city of rubble and ashes. This was the one house left standing. At night the ruined city gave off a radioactive glow which could be seen for miles.

   Ten-fifteen. The garden sprinklers whirled up in golden founts, filling the soft morning air with scatterings of brightness. The water pelted windowpanes, running down the charred west side where the house had been burned evenly free of its white paint. The entire west face of the house was black, save for five places. Here the silhouette in paint of a man mowing a lawn. Here, as in a photograph, a woman bent to pick flowers. Still farther over, their images burned on wood in one titanic instant, a small boy, hands flung into the air; higher up, the image of a thrown ball, and opposite him a girl, hands raised to catch a ball which never came down.

   The five spots of paint—the man, the woman, the children, the ball—remained. The rest was a thin charcoaled layer.

   The gentle sprinkler rain filled the garden with falling light.

   Until this day, how well the house had kept its peace. How carefully it had inquired, "Who goes there? What's the password?" and, getting no answer from lonely foxes and whining cats, it had shut up its windows and drawn shades in an old- maidenly preoccupation with self-protection which bordered on a mechanical paranoia.

15   It quivered at each sound, the house did. If a sparrow brushed a window, the shade shapped up. The bird, startled, flew off! No, not even a bird must touch the house!

   The house was an altar with ten thousand attendants, big, small, servicing, attending, in choirs. But the gods had gone away, and the ritual of the religion continued senselessly, uselessly.

   Twelve noon.

   A dog whined, shivering, on the front porch.

   The front door recognized the dog voice and opened. The dog, once huge and fleshy, but now gone to bone and covered with sores, moved in and through the house, tracking mud. Behind it whirred angry mice, angry at having to pick up mud, angry at inconvenience.

20   For not a leaf fragment blew under the door but what the wall panels flipped open and the copper scrap rats flashed swiftly out. The

offending dust, hair, or paper, seized in miniature steel jaws, was raced back to the burrows. There, down tubes which fed into the cellar, it was dropped into the sighing vent of an incinerator which sat like evil Baal in a dark corner.

The dog ran upstairs, hysterically yelping to each door, at last realizing, as the house realized, that only silence was here.

It sniffed the air and scratched the kitchen door. Behind the door, the stove was making pancakes which filled the house with a rich baked odor and the scent of maple syrup.

The dog frothed at the mouth, lying at the door, sniffing, its eyes turned to fire. It ran wildly in circles, biting at its tail, spun in a frenzy, and died. It lay in the parlor for an hour.

Two o'clock, sang a voice.

25 Delicately sensing decay at last, the regiments of mice hummed out as softly as blown gray leaves in an electrical wind.

Two-fifteen.

The dog was gone.

In the cellar, the incinerator glowed suddenly and a whirl of sparks leaped up the chimney.

Two thirty-five.

30 Bridge tables sprouted from patio walls. Playing cards fluttered onto pads in a shower of pips. Martinis manifested on an oaken bench with egg-salad sandwiches. Music played.

But the tables were silent and the cards untouched.

At four o'clock the tables folded like great butterflies back through the paneled walls.

Four-thirty.

The nursery walls glowed.

35 Animals took shape: yellow giraffes, blue lions, pink antelopes, lilac panthers cavorting in crystal substance. The walls were glass. They looked out upon color and fantasy. Hidden films clocked through well-oiled sprockets, and the walls lived. The nursery floor was woven to resemble a crisp, cereal meadow. Over this ran aluminum roaches and iron crickets, and in the hot still air butterflies of delicate red tissue wavered among the sharp aroma of animal spoors! There was the sound like a great matted yellow hive of bees within a dark bellows, the lazy bumble of a purring lion. And there was the patter of okapi feet and the murmur of a fresh jungle rain, like other

hoofs, falling upon the summer-starched grass. Now the walls dissolved into distances of parched weed, mile on mile, and warm endless sky. The animals drew away into thorn brakes and water holes.

It was the children's hour.

Five o'clock. The bath filled with clear hot water.

Six, seven, eight o'clock. The dinner dishes manipulated like magic tricks, and in the study a *click.* In the metal stand opposite the hearth where a fire now blazed up warmly, a cigar popped out, half an inch of soft gray ash on it, smoking, waiting.

Nine o'clock. The beds warmed their hidden circuits, for nights were cool here.

40   *Nine-five.* A voice spoke from the study ceiling: 40

"Mrs. McClellan, which poem would you like this evening?"

The house was silent.

The voice said at last, "Since you express no preference, I shall select a poem at random." Quiet music rose to back the voice. "Sara Teasdale. As I recall, your favorite. . . .

"There will come soft rains and the smell of the ground,
And swallows circling with their shimmering sound;

And frogs in the pools singing at night,
And wild plum trees in tremulous white;

Robins will wear their feathery fire,
Whistling their whims on a low fence-wire;

And not one will know of the war, not one
Will care at last when it is done.

Not one would mind, neither bird nor tree,
If mankind perished utterly;

And Spring herself, when she woke at dawn
Would scarcely know that we were gone."

The fire burned on the stone hearth and the cigar fell away into a mound of quiet ash on its tray. The empty chairs faced each other between the silent walls, and the music played.

45   At ten o'clock the house began to die.   45

    The wind blew. A falling tree bough crashed through the kitchen window. Cleaning solvent, bottled, shattered over the stove. The room was ablaze in an instant!

    "Fire!" screamed a voice. The house lights flashed, water pumps shot water from the ceilings. But the solvent spread on the linoleum, licking, eating, under the kitchen door, while the voices took it up in chorus: "Fire, fire, fire!"

    The house tried to save itself. Doors sprang tightly shut, but the windows were broken by the heat and the wind blew and sucked upon the fire.

    The house gave ground as the fire in ten billion angry sparks moved with flaming ease from room to room and then up the stairs. While scurrying water rats squeaked from the walls, pistoled their water, and ran for more. And the wall sprays let down showers of mechanical rain.

50   But too late. Somewhere, sighing, a pump shrugged to a stop.   50
The quenching rain ceased. The reserve water supply which had filled baths and washed dishes for many quiet days was gone.

    The fire crackled up the stairs. It fed upon Picassos and Matisses in the upper halls, like delicacies, baking off the oily flesh, tenderly crisping the canvases into black shavings.

    Now the fire lay in beds, stood in windows, changed the colors of drapes!

    And then, reinforcements.

    From attic trapdoors, blind robot faces peered down with faucet mouths gushing green chemical.

55   The fire backed off, as even an elephant must at the sight of a   55
dead snake. Now there were twenty snakes whipping over the floor, killing the fire with a clear cold venom of green froth.

    But the fire was clever. It had sent flames outside the house, up through the attic to the pumps there. An explosion! The attic brain which directed the pumps was shattered into bronze shrapnel on the beams.

    The fire rushed back into every closet and felt of the clothes hung there.

    The house shuddered, oak bone on bone, its bared skeleton cringing from the heat, its wire, its nerves revealed as if a surgeon had torn the skin off to let the red veins and capillaries quiver in the scalded air. Help, help! Fire! Run, run! Heat snapped mirrors like the brittle winter ice. And the voices wailed Fire, fire, run, run, like a tragic nursery rhyme, a dozen voices, high, low, like children dying in a forest, alone, alone. And the voices fading as the wires popped their sheathings like hot chestnuts. One, two, three, four, five voices died.

In the nursery the jungle burned. Blue lions roared, purple giraffes bounded off. The panthers ran in circles, changing color, and ten million animals, running before the fire, vanished off toward a distant steaming river. . . .

60   Ten more voices died. In the last instant under the fire avalanche, other choruses, oblivious, could be heard announcing the time, playing music, cutting the lawn by remote-control mower, or setting an umbrella frantically out and in the slamming and opening front door, a thousand things happening, like a clock shop when each clock strikes the hour insanely before or after the other, a scene of maniac confusion, yet unity; singing, screaming, a few last cleaning mice darting bravely out to carry the horrid ashes away! And one voice, with sublime disregard for the situation, read poetry aloud in the fiery study, until all the film spools burned, until all the wires withered and the circuits cracked.

The fire burst the house and let it slam flat down, puffing out skirts of spark and smoke.

In the kitchen, an instant before the rain of fire and timber, the stove could be seen making breakfasts at a psychopathic rate, ten dozen eggs, six loaves of toast, twenty dozen bacon strips, which, eaten by fire, started the stove working again, hysterically hissing!

The crash. The attic smashing into kitchen and parlor. The parlor into cellar, cellar into sub-cellar. Deep freeze, armchair, film tapes, circuits, beds, and all like skeletons thrown in a cluttered mound deep under.

Smoke and silence. A great quantity of smoke.

65   Dawn showed faintly in the east. Among the ruins, one wall stood alone. Within the wall, a last voice said, over and over again and again, even as the sun rose to shine upon the heaped rubble and steam:

"Today is August 5, 2026, today is August 5, 2026, today is . . ."

Questions on Meaning

1. What is the significance of a house that can withstand destruction and humans who cannot? Why does the house survive? What does the death of the dog mean?
2. What kind of people lived in a house that did all the housework and even planned the days? What is the story saying about our tendency to rely on technology? Are we able to take care of ourselves without that technology?
3. Why is the poem so poignant? What does it say about the ability of nature to come back even if all the brilliant humans have disappeared? Is the poem hopeful or negative or both? Why?

Questions on Rhetorical Strategy and Style

1. The story plays on human fears by introducing the worst of those fears being fulfilled at the beginning of the tale. Why does the image of the dying dog seem to end all human hope?
2. The house reads the poem as the center of the story. Why does the poem work as the centerpiece of the tale? How does it work as the turning point for both humanity and for the house?
3. At the end of the story the house begins to self-destruct, just as the human race has done. What are the stages of the destruction? How do these stages show the breakdown of society?

Writing Assignments

1. Bradbury wrote this story just after the first atomic bombs were dropped on Japan. Find images of the destruction of the Japanese cities, and write about the images of them.
2. Many people think that terrorism is the worst that the human race has faced. Read about the Cuban missile crisis. How close did the world come to atomic destruction? Write about the Cold War and its fear factors, and compare those factors to the world today.
3. Consider the images in the poem that centers the story. Write about the world of nature and the human effects on nature. Would nature be better off without the destructive species that humans have proved to be? What could we do better?

Shooting an Elephant

George Orwell

George Orwell is the pen name used by the British author Eric Blair (1903–1950). Orwell was born in the Indian village of Motihari, near Nepal, where his father was stationed in the Civil Service. India was then part of the British Empire; Orwell's grandfather too had served the Empire in the Indian Army. From 1907 to 1922 Orwell lived in England, returning to India and Burma and a position in the Imperial Police, which he held until 1927. This is the period about which he writes in "Shooting an Elephant." Thereafter he lived in England, Paris, Spain, and elsewhere, writing on a wide range of topics. He fought in the Spanish Civil War and was actively engaged in several political movements, always against totalitarianism of any kind. He is best known today for two novels of political satire: Animal Farm *(1945) and* 1984 *(1949). He was also a prolific journalist and essayist, with his essays collected in five volumes. "Shooting an Elephant" was first published in 1936 and later collected in a book of the same name in 1950. Note that Orwell is writing as an older, wiser man about events that took place when he was in his early twenties some two decades previously. This combined perspective of the young man experiencing the incident and the older man looking back on it is part of the rich reading experience.*

1   In Moulmein, in Lower Burma, I was hated by large numbers of people—the only time in my life that I have been important enough for this to happen to me. I was sub-divisional police officer of the town, and in an aimless, petty, kind of way anti-European feel-

From *Shooting an Elephant and Other Essays* by George Orwell. Published by Harcourt Brace and Company. Harcourt Brace and Company and Heath & Co., Ltd. Reprinted from *Shooting an Elephant and Other Essays* (1950), by permission of Penguin Group Ltd., A.M. Heath, and Harcourt Brace and Company.

ing was very bitter. No one had the guts to raise a riot, but if a European woman went through the bazaars alone somebody would probably spit betel juice over her dress. As a police officer I was an obvious target and was baited whenever it seemed safe to do so. When a nimble Burman tripped me up on the football field and the referee (another Burman) looked the other way, the crowd yelled with hideous laughter. This happened more than once. In the end the sneering yellow faces of young men that met me everywhere, the insults hooted after me when I was at a safe distance, got badly on my nerves. The young Buddhist priests were the worst of all. There were several thousand of them in the town and none of them seemed to have anything to do except stand on street corners and jeer at Europeans.

All this was perplexing and upsetting. For at that time I had already made up my mind that imperialism was an evil thing and the sooner I chucked up my job and got out of it the better. Theoretically—and secretly, of course—I was all for the Burmese and all against their oppressors, the British. As for the job I was doing, I hated it more bitterly than I can perhaps make clear. In a job like that you see the dirty work of Empire at close quarters. The wretched prisoners huddling in the stinking cages of the lock-ups, the grey, cowed faces of the long-term convicts, the scarred buttocks of the men who had been flogged with bamboos—all these oppressed me with an intolerable sense of guilt. But I could get nothing into perspective. I was young and ill-educated and I had had to think out my problems in the utter silence that is imposed on every Englishman in the East. I did not even know that the British Empire is dying, still less did I know that it is a great deal better than the younger empires that are going to supplant it. All I knew was that I was stuck between my hatred of the empire I served and my rage against the evil-spirited little beasts who tried to make my job impossible. With one part of my mind I thought of the British Raj as an unbreakable tyranny, as something clamped down, in *saecula saeculorum,* upon the will of prostrate peoples; with another part I thought that the greatest joy in the world would be to drive a bayonet into a Buddhist priest's guts. Feelings like these are the normal by-products of imperialism; ask any Anglo-Indian official, if you can catch him off duty.

One day something happened which in a roundabout way was enlightening. It was a tiny incident in itself, but it gave me a better glimpse than I had had before of the real nature of imperialism—the real motives for which despotic governments act. Early one morning the sub-inspector at a police station the other end of the town rang me up on the 'phone and said that an elephant was ravaging the bazaar. Would I please come and do something about it? I did not know what I could do, but I wanted to see what was happening and I got on to a pony and started out. I took my rifle, an old .44 Winchester and much too small to kill an elephant, but I thought the noise might be useful *in terrorem*. Various Burmans stopped me on the way and told me about the elephant's doings. It was not, of course, a wild elephant, but a tame one which had gone "must." It had been chained up, as tame elephants always are when their attack of "must" is due, but on the previous night it had broken its chain and escaped. Its mahout, the only person who could manage it when it was in that state, had set out in pursuit, but had taken the wrong direction and was now twelve hours' journey away, and in the morning the elephant had suddenly reappeared in the town. The Burmese population had no weapons and were quite helpless against it. It had already destroyed somebody's bamboo hut, killed a cow and raided some fruit-stalls and devoured the stock; also it had met the municipal rubbish van and, when the driver jumped out and took to his heels, had turned the van over and inflicted violence upon it.

The Burmese sub-inspector and some Indian constables were waiting for me in the quarter where the elephant had been seen. It was a very poor quarter, a labyrinth of squalid bamboo huts, thatched with palm-leaf, winding all over a steep hillside. I remember that it was a cloudy, stuffy, morning at the beginning of the rains. We began questioning the people as to where the elephant had gone and, as usual, failed to get any definite information. That is invariably the case in the East; a story always sounds clear enough at a distance, but the nearer you get to the scene of events the vaguer it becomes. Some of the people said that the elephant had gone in one direction, some said that he had gone in another, some professed not even to have heard of any elephant. I had almost made up my mind that the whole story was a pack of lies, when we heard yells a little distance away. There was a loud, scandalized cry of "Go away, child! Go away this instant!" and an old woman with a switch in her hand came round the corner of a hut, violently shooing away a crowd of naked children. Some more women followed, clicking their tongues and exclaiming; evidently there was something that the children ought not to have seen. I rounded the hut and saw a man's dead body sprawling in the mud. He was an Indian, a black Dravidian coolie, almost naked, and he could not have been dead many minutes. The people said that the elephant had come suddenly upon him round the corner of the hut, caught him with its trunk, put its foot on his back and ground him into the earth. This was the rainy season and the ground was soft, and his face had scored a trench a foot deep and a couple of yards long. He was lying on his belly with arms crucified and head sharply twisted to one side. His face was coated with mud, the eyes wide open, the teeth bared and grinning with an expression of unendurable agony. (Never tell me, by the way, that the dead look peaceful. Most of the corpses I have seen looked devilish.) The friction of the great beast's foot had stripped the skin from his back as neatly as one skins a rabbit. As soon as I saw the dead man I sent an orderly to a friend's house nearby to borrow an elephant rifle. I had already sent back the pony, not wanting it to go mad with fright and throw me if it smelt the elephant.

5   The orderly came back in a few minutes with a rifle and five cartridges, and meanwhile some Burmans had arrived and told us that the elephant was in the paddy fields below, only a few hundred yards away. As I started forward practically the whole population of the quarter flocked out of the houses and followed me. They had seen the rifle and were all shouting excitedly that I was going to shoot the elephant. They had not shown much interest in the elephant when he was merely ravaging their homes, but it was different now that he was going to be shot. It was a bit of fun to them, as it would be to an English crowd; besides they wanted the meat. It made me vaguely uneasy. I had no intention of shooting the elephant—I had merely sent for the rifle to defend myself if necessary—and it is always unnerving to have a crowd following you. I marched down the hill, looking and feeling a fool, with the rifle over my shoulder and an evergrowing army of people jostling at my heels. At the bottom, when you got away from the huts, there was a metalled road and beyond that a miry waste of paddy fields a thousand yards across, not yet ploughed but soggy from the first rains and dotted with coarse grass. The elephant was standing eight yards from the road, his left side towards us. He took not the slightest notice of the crowd's approach. He was tearing up bunches of grass, beating them against his knees to clean them and stuffing them into his mouth.

I had halted on the road. As soon as I saw the elephant I knew with perfect certainty that I ought not to shoot him. It is a serious matter to shoot a working elephant—it is comparable to destroying a huge and costly piece of machinery—and obviously one ought not to do it if it can possibly be avoided. And at that distance, peacefully eating, the elephant looked no more dangerous than a cow. I thought then and I think now that his attack of "must" was already passing off; in which case he would merely wander harmlessly about until the mahout came back and caught him. Moreover, I did not in the least want to shoot him. I decided that I would watch him for a little while to make sure that he did not turn savage again, and then go home.

But at that moment I glanced round at the crowd that had followed me. It was an immense crowd, two thousand at the least and growing every minute. It blocked the road for a long distance on either side. I looked at the sea of yellow faces above the garish clothes—faces all happy and excited over this bit of fun, all certain that the elephant was going to be shot. They were watching me as they would watch a conjurer about to perform a trick. They did not like me, but with the magical rifle in my hands I was momentarily worth watching. And suddenly I realized that I should have to shoot the elephant after all. The people expected it of me and I had got to do it; I could feel their two thousand wills pressing me forward, irresistibly. And it was at this moment, as I stood there with the rifle in my hands, that I first grasped the hollowness, the futility of the white man's dominion in the East. Here was I, the white man with his gun, standing in front of the unarmed native crowd—seemingly the leading actor of the piece; but in reality I was only an absurd puppet pushed to and fro by the will of those yellow faces behind. I perceived in this moment that when the white man turns tyrant it is his own freedom that he destroys. He becomes a sort of hollow, posing dummy, the conventionalized figure of a sahib. For it is the condition of his rule that he shall spend his life in trying to impress the "natives," and so in every crisis he has got to do what the "natives" expect of him. He wears a mask, and his face grows to fit it. I had got to shoot the elephant. I had committed myself to doing it when I sent for the rifle. A sahib has got to act like a sahib; he has got to appear resolute, to know his own mind and do definite things. To come all that way, rifle in hand, with a thousand people marching at my heels, and then to trail feebly away, having done nothing—no, that was impossible. The crowd would laugh at me. And my whole life, every white man's life in the East, was one long struggle not to be laughed at.

But I did not want to shoot the elephant. I watched him beating his bunch of grass against his knees, with that preoccupied grandmotherly air that elephants have. It seemed to me that it would be murder to shoot him. At that age I was not squeamish about killing animals, but I had never shot an elephant and never wanted to. (Somehow it always seems worse to kill a *large* animal.) Besides, there was the beast's owner to be considered. Alive, the elephant was worth at least a hundred pounds; dead, he would only be worth the value of his tusks, five pounds, possibly. But I had got to act quickly. I turned to some experienced-looking Burmans who had been there when we arrived, and asked them how the elephant had been behaving. They all said the same thing: he took no notice of you if you left him alone, but he might charge if you went too close to him.

It was perfectly clear to me what I ought to do. I ought to walk up to within, say, twenty-five yards of the elephant and test his behavior. If he charged, I could shoot; if he took no notice of me, it would be safe to leave him until the mahout came back. But also I knew that I was going to do no such thing. I was a poor shot with a rifle and the ground was soft mud into which one would sink at every step. If the elephant charged and I missed him, I should have about as much chance as a toad under a steam-roller. But even then I was not thinking particularly of my own skin, only of the watchful yellow faces behind. For at that moment, with the crowd watching me, I was not afraid in the ordinary sense, as I would have been if I had been alone. A white man mustn't be frightened in front of "natives"; and so, in general, he isn't frightened. The sole thought in my mind was that if anything went wrong those two thousand Burmans would see me pursued, caught, trampled on and reduced to a grinning corpse like that Indian up the hill. And if that happened it was quite probable that some of them would laugh. That would never do. There was only one alternative. I shoved the cartridges into the magazine and lay down on the road to get a better aim.

10 The crowd grew very still, and a deep, low, happy sigh, as of people who see the theatre curtain go up at last, breathed from innumerable throats. They were going to have their bit of fun after all. The rifle was a beautiful German thing with cross-hair sights. I did not then know that in shooting an elephant one would shoot to cut an imaginary bar running from ear-hole to ear-hole. I ought, therefore, as the elephant was sideways on, to have aimed straight at his ear-hole; actually 10

I aimed several inches in front of this, thinking the brain would be further forward.

When I pulled the trigger I did not hear the bang or feel the kick—one never does when a shot goes home—but I heard the devilish roar of glee that went up from the crowd. In that instant, in too short a time, one would have thought, even for the bullet to get there, a mysterious, terrible change had come over the elephant. He neither stirred nor fell, but every line of his body had altered. He looked suddenly stricken, shrunken, immensely old, as though the frightful impact of the bullet had paralysed him without knocking him down. At last, after what seemed a long time—it might have been five seconds, I dare say—he sagged flabbily to his knees. His mouth slobbered. An enormous senility seemed to have settled upon him. One could have imagined him thousands of years old. I fired again into the same spot. At the second shot he did not collapse but climbed with desperate slowness to his feet and stood weakly upright, with legs sagging and head drooping. I fired a third time. That was the shot that did for him. You could see the agony of it jolt his whole body and knock the last remnant of strength from his legs. But in falling he seemed for a moment to rise, for as his hind legs collapsed beneath him he seemed to tower upward like a huge rock toppling, his trunk reaching skywards like a tree. He trumpeted, for the first and only time. And then down he came, his belly towards me, with a crash that seemed to shake the ground even where I lay.

I got up. The Burmans were already racing past me across the mud. It was obvious that the elephant would never rise again, but he was not dead. He was breathing very rhythmically with long rattling gasps, his great mound of a side painfully rising and falling. His mouth was wide open—I could see far down into caverns of pale pink throat. I waited a long time for him to die, but his breathing did not weaken. Finally I fired my two remaining shots into the spot where I thought his heart must be. The thick blood welled out of him like red velvet, but still he did not die. His body did not even jerk when the shots hit him, the tortured breathing continued without a pause. He was dying, very slowly and in great agony, but in some world remote from me where not even a bullet could damage him further. I felt that I had got to put an end to that dreadful noise. It seemed dreadful to see the great beast lying there, powerless to move and yet powerless to die, and not even to be able to finish him. I sent back for my small rifle and poured shot after shot into his heart and down his throat. They seemed to make no impression. The tortured gasps continued as steadily as the ticking of a clock.

In the end I could not stand it any longer and went away. I heard later that it took him half an hour to die. Burmans were bringing dahs and baskets even before I left, and I was told they had stripped his body almost to the bones by the afternoon.

Afterwards, of course, there were endless discussions about the shooting of the elephant. The owner was furious, but he was only an Indian and could do nothing. Besides, legally I had done the right thing, for a mad elephant has to be killed, like a mad dog, if its owner fails to control it. Among the Europeans opinion was divided. The older men said I was right, the younger men said it was a damn shame to shoot an elephant for killing a coolie, because an elephant was worth more than any damn Coringhee coolie. And afterwards I was very glad that the coolie had been killed; it put me legally in the right and it gave me a sufficient pretext for shooting the elephant. I often wondered whether any of the others grasped that I had done it solely to avoid looking a fool.

Questions on Meaning

1. Orwell confesses to many strong emotions about the Burmese people, such as his comment "I thought that the greatest joy in the world would be to drive a bayonet into a Buddhist priest's guts." Does he actually hate these people? Explain your answer with examples from the essay.
2. At the beginning of the third paragraph Orwell introduces the "tiny incident" that will for him reveal the "real motives for which despotic governments act." What are those motives, as revealed by the incident and Orwell's later comments?
3. Even before the incident with the elephant, Orwell tells us he had discovered that "imperialism was an evil thing." How many different kinds of "evil" are shown through the course of the essay?

Questions on Rhetorical Strategy and Style

1. The primary rhetorical strategy used in this essay is narration—telling the story of shooting the elephant. In addition to the story itself, Orwell keeps up a sort of running commentary on the meaning of the story, helping us understand it as he analyzes the events of the story. Reread the essay and chart how Orwell moves back and forth between narration and analysis.
2. Orwell is particularly vivid in his descriptive language, often achieving a larger meaning through descriptive details and figurative language. Reread the section of the essay that describes the elephant's slow death as he seems "thousands of years old" (paragraph 11) What meanings are suggested by the language Orwell uses in this descriptive passage?

Writing Assignments

1. Fear of embarrassment before others can be a powerful motivating force, as the young Orwell discovers in this incident. Search your memory for a time when you yourself took some action simply to avoid embarrassment. How did it feel at the time? Did you feel foolish afterwards? Would you do the same again now in the same circumstances? Try to be as honest in your self-evaluation as Orwell was in his.
2. Have you ever been among a large group of people very different from yourself, either in another country or in a different cultural

group in the United States? Did your concerns lead to fears or negative feelings about these others? Some social scientists have said that people naturally fear things or other people that are very different from themselves, that negative reactions are "normal" even if not healthy or fair to the others. Do you think there is such a natural impulse in people? What are the good and bad effects of this impulse? Present your thoughts in an essay exploring the topic.

3. We all have a "public self" and a "private self." Your public self may be the self you show to others in the academic world or on the job. It may be similar to your private self, what you really are like inside, or it may be very different. The two selves may be harmonious or in conflict, as they were for Orwell. Write an essay defining the difference between these two selves and exploring both the constructive and problematic aspects of this duality.

Freedom Denied

Samantha Nutt

Among the many degrees Samantha Nutt (1970–) has earned a BA and an MD from McMaster University, and an MS in Public Health and Developing Countries from the University of London School of Hygiene and Tropical Medicine. She specializes in women's health in developing countries, and has worked in war zones for more than a decade. After serving in Burundi, Somalia, and Liberia with UNICEF, Nutt co-founded War Child Canada in 1999, an organization whose projects have included HIV education in Ethiopia. She is an associate of the Center for International Health at McMaster University and was the Inaugural Fellow in International Women's Health at Women's College Hospital, University of Toronto. Nutt was named to the 2000 Honour Roll for Maclean's *magazine and the Top Forty Under 40 for* Report on Business *magazine. She has written many papers and reports on the impact of war on the health of women and children in Africa and the Middle East, published by UNICEF, the U.N. Department of Humanitarian Affairs, the* Toronto Star; *and* Maclean's. *In this article from* Maclean's, *Nutt reports that despite the fall of the Taliban in Afghanistan, women in that country still live in fear and under oppression.*

1   Peshawar is a dusty, rundown border town in Pakistan comprised mainly of low-rise buildings and decrepit Afghan refugee camps. The sweltering heat and traffic congestion combine to produce a haze of pollution so thick that by mid-morning it's impossible to see the mountains and the famous Khyber Pass in the distance. During 23 years of war and brutal oppression at the hands of foreign invaders,   1

warlords and the extremist Taliban regime, millions of Afghan refugees fled across the pass to Peshawar. More than two million have returned to their homeland since the U.S. overthrew the Taliban in 2001, but more than two million, fearing even greater poverty and political persecution at home, remain stranded in desolation.

The refugees are resisting moves to coerce them back to Afghanistan. In recent months, such efforts have included the alleged demolition of at least one camp, public harassment and the threatened closure of refugee schools. Even though almost 17,000 American and European troops are attempting to bring order to Afghanistan, most of the women I meet in Peshawar are afraid to return. They are too scarred by past atrocities to believe suggestions that they would be safe in their war-shattered country. At a meeting of refugee widows held by the Afghan Women's Council, a local non-governmental group, they tell excruciating stories of tragedy and loss: families killed in war, how they've suffered from hunger and unremitting fear. They are so desperate to remain in Pakistan that Mheer, a woman who lost her husband and a son during the war against the Russians in the 1980s, sold her 15-year-old daughter for 10,000 rupees (US$170) to a person she describes as an "ugly old man with many wives."

As Mheer explains that she only sold her daughter to buy food for her remaining six children, other women in the group console her, but with a certain disdain—selling a daughter to a man of questionable character is regarded as a heinous act. When Mheer is finished, I ask the women when they will go back to Afghanistan, particularly with the promise of freedom they would ostensibly now enjoy under President Hamid Karzai's government. "We will not go back," one woman insists while the others nod in agreement. "It is not safe."

Later I visit the Esmat School for Girls. It's the last day of classes before summer, and the graduates giggle and daringly allow their chadors to slip off their heads and onto their shoulders. One young woman, Masooda, 19, is less confident than her peers; she is the only student in the class who was in Afghanistan during the Taliban years, fleeing with her family to Pakistan so she could receive an education. Masooda wants to be a human rights lawyer so she can help women in her country, but is concerned about the situation in Kabul. "It is too dangerous," she laments, "and the conditions are not good." As I leave the school, a young girl stops and pleads with one of my Canadian colleagues. "Please take me with you," she begs. "There is no future for me here."

We leave the women of Peshawar behind, and travel through the Khyber Pass into Afghanistan. In Kabul, we meet Marzia Meena, a foreign-educated Afghan woman participating in the drafting of the country's new constitution, which is expected to be adopted by the Loya Jirga, an assembly of tribal leaders, this October after nationwide consultations. She has cropped, dyed hair and is the only woman I meet in Kabul who walks around government offices with her legs exposed to mid-calf. With the defeat of the Taliban, she says, "there was hope and promise for women." But, she adds, "in a practical sense, the only real advancement had been that women don't have to wear the burka. That doesn't translate into an actual advancement of their rights."

Even with the large number of foreign troops in Kabul, most women don't feel safe. And those outside the capital must contend with warlords and their militias, who are often as harsh as the Taliban were. In warlord-dominated areas such as Herat, 700 km west of Kabul, women are not even allowed to occupy the same office space as men or to go to public places unaccompanied—a policy that is enforced by flogging. "When women are not allowed to leave the house to go to the doctor even when they are in labour," says Meena, "how can they participate in public consultations surrounding the new constitution?"

Therein lies the paradox: efforts to liberate Afghan women are progressing at a speed too fast for religious conservatives, but far too slow for those who believed that the fall of the Taliban would end oppression. Tajwar Kakar is the deputy minister of women's affairs, and one of only a handful of women occupying top political positions in Karzai's government. She is an outspoken supporter of women's rights and has received numerous death threats. Kakar is also fiercely critical of the Western media's overly optimistic portrayal of her country since the war. "The views and judgments in the West about Afghan women after the fall of the Taliban were premature and propagandistic," she says. "In reality, women can never be free without first feeling secure."

And how can you feel secure, in a society where reports of kidnappings, rapes, forced marriages and beatings are widespread? Among young women, such stories take on a life of their own, and are offered up as a rationale for wearing the burka, missing school and never travelling unaccompanied by a male. "A young girl walking for ice cream in Kabul was raped by 20 men," a young Afghan woman whispers to me at a social gathering in her aunt's home. "It's better not to go out."

In reality, it's difficult to ascertain the truth behind some of the stories. But since July 2002, the Afghan Independent Human Rights Commission, chaired by Karzai's former deputy prime minister Sima Samar, has received 800 complaints, ranging from killings and burnings to live burials, kidnappings and rapes. It is believed the attacks are being carried out by religious extremists unhappy with the government's lax attitude toward women, former mujahedeen gunmen, and rogue members of the Northern Alliance, which was allied with the U.S. in the Afghan war.

10   The Karzai government had hoped to broaden its authority outside of Kabul and rebuild the country's shattered infrastructure. But those efforts have been hurt by sporadic attacks staged by remnants of the Taliban, al-Qaeda, and fighters loyal to disgruntled warlords. And although more than $2 billion in foreign aid has been received, it's well short of the $8.3 billion to $12.2 billion the World Bank says is needed to rebuild the country.

Nigel Fisher, a Canadian who was until recently the UN secretary general's special representative in Afghanistan, says progress to increase security across the country has been slow. "Most of the human rights abuses are committed by military commanders under the control of the warlords," Fisher says over lunch at the UN's walled enclave in Kabul. Fisher says the U.S. supplied weapons to some of the warlords in the fight against the Taliban, but, he adds, "now they have to help rein them in." It will be difficult. "There are still deep-rooted suspicions at all levels," explains Fisher. "At one time or another, every group has been responsible for the massacre of another group. To whom do they give their weapons?"

A drive to reduce the number of weapons is underway, and the UN plans to demobilize 100,000 Afghan fighters. In exchange for giving up their weapons, they will be enrolled in employment programs; 6,000 have been targeted for this year. But UN officials are moving slowly because there are not enough jobs for the soldiers, and if they are released from the military without work they could end up looting and pillaging among innocent civilians. To help the UN create a more secure environment, Fisher urges "any government that has made commitments to Afghanistan to fulfill them in a hurry."

But as Afghanistan waits for the promises of peace to be fulfilled, women continue to pay the price for decades of oppression. In Tundara, about a one-hour drive from Kabul, I meet with four Afghan women, all of whom in their own way reflect the attitudes of women across the country. Sheela is 12 years old and the eldest of eight children. She recently attended school for the first time and is feisty and confident. I ask her whether she wears the burka to school. "I do not!" she announces proudly. "And if I want to wear it or not, it is no one's business."

Sheela claims not to remember life under the Taliban, and when she tires of my questioning she demands to be excused. I turn to 14-year-old Farzanna, who was tested at the Grade 1 level but does not go to school because her father will not allow it. She is sullen, almost depressed. When I ask what she would like to do when she is older, she replies, "I cannot think of my future, because I cannot think of solving my problems in the near future." Najeeba, 22, is a health-care worker and attended school secretly throughout the Taliban's rule. Her father is a wealthy general, and she is an attractive, graceful young woman. Her husband died of cancer at 25, but unlike the Afghan widows I met in Peshawar, Najeeba has financial resources. "I hope one day my children will be able to leave my home and live and work independently," she says, "even in this strict environment."

15 Khanum is less hopeful. Unsure of her age, she believes she is in her 40s. She wears a burka, and describes a life that has left her grief-stricken and defeated. Russian soldiers shot her husband and son; she is poor, with thick, darkened hands and a deeply lined face. During our conversation she is tearful but open, offering up personal details of a troubled lifetime. "We have never seen a good day," she confides. "I hope there will be peace in the world as well as peace for us." 15

In the end, only democracy will bring security for women, says Ishaq Gailani, chairman of the National Solidarity Movement, representing more than 40 political parties in Afghanistan. A national election is expected in 2004. But unfortunately, he says, the reality of implementing elections in Afghanistan is proving difficult: there can be no election without voter registration, and there can be no effective means of voter registration and participation without sufficient security—especially for women. "It has been a year and a half, and still the people of Afghanistan are eating from the gun," he sighs. For Afghan women, it is a daily reality that is painfully difficult to swallow.

Questions on Meaning

1. Why do the women in the Peshawar refugee camp refuse to return to Afghanistan? What dangers do they believe they will face in their home country? How do they respond to Western assurances that oppression of women ended with the fall of the Taliban?
2. What reasons do Nutt's sources offer for the slow pace of women's liberation in Afghanistan? How do the occupying forces fail to address the issue of women's security?
3. According to Nutt, why is the Karzai government unable to extend its influence into the regions beyond Kabul? How does this situation affect the plight of women in rural areas?

Questions on Rhetorical Strategy and Style

1. An important feature of persuasion is an appeal to authority. List the authorities that Nutt uses to support her position. What are their credentials? How does their testimony lend validity to her interpretation of the situation in Afghanistan?
2. Nutt opens with a vivid description of Peshawar, Pakistan. How does this description set the tone for the rest of the article? How does it underscore the hopelessness of the women in both the refugee camps and in Afghanistan itself?
3. Why does Nutt use Sheela, Farzanna, Najeeba, and Khanum as examples of Afghan women? What does each of these women represent in terms of women's rights? How does Nutt's presentation of them affect her argument?

Writing Assignments

1. Tajwar Kakar claims that, "women can never be free without first feeling secure." In what ways might this statement apply to life in the United States or Canada? For example, to what extent does fear of assault impede women's freedom to walk unaccompanied through a city park or even a large campus at night? Think of other examples of the impact of security concerns on freedom. In an extended paragraph, discuss the relationship between freedom and security.

2. A preliminary constitution for Afghanistan was adopted in January 2004. Read accounts of this event in newspapers and news-magazines. Write an essay discussing the ways in which the new constitution addresses women's rights. Consider questions such as the following: How effective do experts believe it will be in securing freedom for women? What obstacles still interfere with the achievement of equality for women? To what extent will Afghanistan have to rely on help from the West to enforce these rights?

Microbes on the Move

Jeffrey Goldberg

Investigative journalist and award-winning independent television producer Jeff Goldberg has written about many subjects for a broad range of periodicals, including People, Omni, *and the* New York Times Magazine. *His most recent book,* Plague Wars: The Terrifying Reality of Biological Warfare *(co-authored with Tom Mangold) chronicles the stockpiling of biological weapons in third-world countries. An earlier book,* Anatomy of a Scientific Discovery, *recounts the breakthrough discovery of endorphins, the body's natural pain killers. In this selection, originally printed in the* New York Times Magazine, *Goldberg uses stories of easily transportable viruses to argue for a truly global approach to the study of disease and public health.*

1 In late November, 1995, while on a reporting trip to the island of Zanzibar, off the coast of East Africa, I was bit repeatedly by mosquitoes. This is not uncommon, and I paid it no mind—I was already suffering from what I believed to have been shigella, a nasty gastrointestinal parasite, and I was feeling miserable anyway.

It wasn't until early December, while hiking in the Bwindi Impenetrable Forest of Uganda, that I began to suffer from a prostrating fever and severe shakes. A short while later, atop a mountain, I fell unconscious. This was an unfortunate place to fall unconscious, for two reasons. One, while unconscious, I was attacked by fire ants. Two, the Ugandan parks service owns no medevac helicopters, so once I awoke—the paroxysm of fever having subsided for the moment—I

"Microbes on the Move," by Jeffrey Goldberg, reprinted from the *New York Times Magazine*, October 10, 1999, pp. 21, 23.

had to crawl down the mountain with the help of a very kind park official, who told me he would lose his job if I died on him.

I was driven later that day to the town of Kabale, where I stayed the night. At one point, a friend had to throw himself across my body to keep me from shaking myself off the bed. The town doctor came, and made an on-the-spot diagnosis: falciparum malaria. He gave me pills that began to kill the parasite. The pills cost $8 each, which at the time was twice what the Ugandan Government spent on public health per capita each year.

When I finally made it to Kampala, the capital, I decided to check in to the Sheraton, rather than the city's main hospital, because the Sheraton was more antiseptic. I stayed there for a week, able to walk only on he fifth day. I was lucky; I didn't die. Almost one million Africans, mostly children, are killed by malaria each year. One hundred million people in sub-Saharan Africa are made sick each year by malaria. Few, if any, can afford to recuperate at a Sheraton.

5   I tell this story for cautionary reasons: in the next decade—as the earth grows warmer, and as pathogens, aided by increased global trade, political chaos and the destruction of rain forests, find new hosts—Americans who have never set foot in Africa will be contracting malaria, just as last month Americans who never set foot in Africa contracted the West Nile virus, which was discovered in Uganda in 1937 and had never been seen in this hemisphere.

"There's no question we will have malaria in this country in the next decade," the acting deputy director of the Centers for Disease Control and Prevention, Stephen Ostroff, told me recently. New York City has, in fact, already seen two cases of indigenous malaria this decade—infection in people who have not traveled to malarial zones. "That was a kind of warning shot," Ostroff said.

The problem is, we keep getting warning shots, and we keep ignoring them. West Nile, which is believed to be responsible for the deaths of at least five people here so far, is a warning shot. H.I.V., of course, is a particularly vicious warning shot. What we are being warned about is that "pathogens have no borders," says the Surgeon General, David Satcher.

Americans tend to be sanguine about the outbreak of exotic diseases in faraway places—perhaps because entire oceans separate us from the rest of the world, perhaps because we overestimate the effectiveness of our public health system or perhaps because Hollywood has hijacked the issue: when we think of tropical disease, we tend to picture Dustin Hoffman chasing monkeys through the woods. But "Outbreak"—or at least the first half-hour of "Outbreak"—actually does present a plausible scenario for the spread of a newly emerged disease from Africa to America.

It is a scenario that greatly worries the nation's leading health official, including Satcher and Harold Varmus, the director of the National Institutes of Health. The argument they have embraced in response is this: The biological national security of the United States is threatened by the unchecked spread of infectious disease in Africa; therefore, Africa's health is very much our problem.

10   "The outbreak in New York teaches us that we can't protect the   10
American people by focusing just on what happens inside our borders," Satcher says. Africa "suffers form poverty, poor sanitation, and political instability, and this puts the whole world at risk," he adds. "It's not humanitarian when we intervene to help Africa or other poor countries. From a selfish perspective, we must have a global system of public health and disease surveillance in place. If we had been able to identify H.I.V. sooner, we might have been able to save lives."

This theory of biological containment—confirmed, it appears, by the identification of the West Nile virus in New York—is a controversial one. Reflexive defenders of Africa interpret it as an attack on Africans, a way to stigmatize and isolate a contingent full of people who are already stigmatized and isolated.

But this theory is not meant to attack Africans; it is meant to ignite an attack on the diseases that kill Africans in horrific numbers. Of course, it is not only Africa that has served as a petri dish for emerging pathogens—Europe has a long and storied history of exporting deadly disease, around the world, and West Nile and similar viruses are also found in Asia. But Africa is hotter, wetter, poorer and more chaotic than any other continent, and pathogens need precisely these conditions to flourish. Just this year, an outbreak of the fatal Marburg virus (a cousin of Ebola) struck gold miners in northeastern Congo, an isolated corner of a war-ravaged country, initially unobserved by the disease-surveillance experts of the West.

"It was going on for as long as six months before it came to anyone's attention," Ostroff says. "And it only came to our attention because the district health officer died from the disease." If one of the gold miners had visited his family in Kinshasa, and then one of his relatives had boarded a plane to another part of Africa, or to Europe, or to Kennedy International Airport, the Marburg virus might have spread far beyond the northeastern corner of Congo. It is not just Marburg that could escape the rain forests of central Africa. Scientists believe that pathogens still unknown to man lurk in the tropics, and as the forests continue to be knocked down at an alarming rate, these microbes will seek new hosts—the men who are invading the forests, presumably.

Unfortunately for Americans, Congress is not the easiest place to make the argument for increased foreign aid to Africa, even aid to fight infectious disease. The prevailing Congressional posture toward Africa was summed up last month by Senator Larry Craig, a Republican from Idaho, who complained about the $42 million it cost to send President Clinton to Africa last year, as well as additional outlays to send the President to Child and China. The effects of the Clinton trip were ephemeral and symbolic—the President apologized for slavery, for one thing—but, for at least two weeks, Africa was on the agenda. Not Senator Craig's agenda, however. "It seems to me that's an awful high price tag to pay for an apology," he said. Then he amplified his remarks in high Strangelovian fashion. "Remember in the closing days of our military engagement over Kosovo, we ran out of smart bombs?" he asked. "The amount of money on these three trips would have acquired 3,000 smart bombs."

15 Senator Craig—and, by extension, all too many American tax- 15 payers—may consider U.S. engagement in Africa unworthy of $42 million, but what Senator Craig doesn't understand is that Idaho is not as far from Africa as he thinks.

Questions on Meaning

1. According to Goldberg, why should we pay more attention to disease in Africa?
2. What are some of the "warning shots" that have been ignored in the United States? What does Goldberg say about the consequences of ignoring those warnings?
3. What conditions in Africa make the continent an ideal breeding ground for microbes?

Questions on Rhetorical Strategy and Style

1. Persuasion often relies on the use of authorities for support. Name several of the authorities cited by Goldberg in this essay and explain how they contribute to the effectiveness of his argument.
2. Goldberg offers several causes for the appearance of exotic diseases in the United States. Identify two of these causes and explain how they affect the health of Americans.
3. Goldberg's final anecdote about Senator Craig provides an example of what point in the essay? How effectively do you think the story illustrates that point? Explain your response.

Writing Assignments

1. Using Goldberg's evidence, write a letter to your congressional representative arguing for more aid to fight and study disease in Africa.
2. Research newspaper and news magazine accounts from the past several years of the African health crisis. Write an essay explaining in detail the effects of poverty, political unrest, and the natural environment on the health of the African population.

For Some, the Blogging Never Stops

Katie Hafner and Tim Gnatek

Katie Hafner has a degree in German literature from the University of California, San Diego and a degree in journalism from Columbia University. She is currently a technology reporter for The New York Times *and a contributing editor for* Newsweek. *She has also published articles in* Business Week, Esquire, The New Republic, The New York Times Magazine, Wired, *and* Working Woman. *She has written four books:* Cyberpunk: Outlaws and Hackers on the Computer Frontier *(co-author, 1991);* The House at the Bridge: A Story of Modern Germany *(1995);* Where Wizards Stay Up Late: The Origins of the Internet *(co-author, 1996); and* The Well: A Story of Love, Death & Real Life in the Seminal Online Community *(2001). She lives in Marin County, California. Tim Gnatek, who contributed reporting for the following selection, has a degree in journalism from Columbia University and in 2003 and 2004 won the Wired Magazine Award for New Media Journalism.*

1   To celebrate four years of marriage, Richard Wiggins and his wife, Judy Matthews, recently spent a week in Key West, Fla. Early on the morning of their anniversary, Ms. Matthews heard her husband get up and go into the bathroom. He stayed there for a long time.

"I didn't hear any water running, so I wondered what was going on," Ms. Matthews said. When she knocked on the door, she found him

---

seated with his laptop balanced on his knees, typing into his Web log, a collection of observations about the technical world, over a wireless link.

Blogging is a pastime for many, even a livelihood for a few. For some, it becomes an obsession. Such bloggers often feel compelled to write several times daily and feel anxious if they don't keep up. As they spend more time hunkered over their computers, they neglect family, friends and jobs. They blog at home, at work and on the road. They blog openly or sometimes, like Mr. Wiggins, quietly so as not to call attention to their habit.

"It seems as if his laptop is glued to his legs 24/7," Ms. Matthews said of her husband.

5   The number of bloggers has grown quickly, thanks to sites like blogger.com, which makes it easy to set up a blog. Technorati, a blog-tracking service, has counted some 2.5 million blogs.

Of course, most of those millions are abandoned or, at best, maintained infrequently. For many bloggers, the novelty soon wears off and their persistence fades.

Sometimes, too, the realization that no one is reading sets in. A few blogs have thousands of readers, but never have so many people written so much to be read by so few. By Jupiter Research's estimate, only 4 percent of online users read blogs.

Indeed, if a blog is likened to a conversation between a writer and readers, bloggers like Mr. Wiggins are having conversations largely with themselves.

Mr. Wiggins, 48, a senior information technologist at Michigan State University in East Lansing, does not know how many readers he has; he suspects it's not many. But that does not seem to bother him.

10   "I'm just getting something off my chest," he said.

Nor is he deterred by the fact that he toils for hours at a time on his blog for no money. He gets satisfaction in other ways. "Sometimes there's an 'I told you so' aspect to it," he said. Recent ruminations on wigblog.blogspot.com have focused on Gmail, Google's new e-mail service. Mr. Wiggins points with pride to Wigblog posts that voiced early privacy concerns about Gmail.

Perhaps a chronically small audience is a blessing. For it seems that the more popular a blog becomes, the more some bloggers feel the need to post.

Tony Pierce started his blog three years ago while in search of a distraction after breaking up with a girlfriend. "In three years, I don't think I've missed a day," he said. Now Mr. Pierce's blog (www.tonypierce.com/blog/bloggy.htm), a chatty diary of Hollywood, writing and women in which truth sometimes mingles with fiction, averages 1,000 visitors a day.

Where some frequent bloggers might label themselves merely ardent, Mr. Pierce is more realistic. "I wouldn't call it dedicated, I would call it a problem," he said. "If this were beer, I'd be an alcoholic."

15 Mr. Pierce, who lives in Hollywood and works as a scheduler in the entertainment industry, said blogging began to feel like an addiction when he noticed that he would rather be with his computer than with his girlfriend—for technical reasons.

"She's got an iMac, and I don't like her computer," Mr. Pierce said. When he is at his girlfriend's house, he feels "antsy." "We have little fights because I want to go home and write my thing," he said.

Mr. Pierce described the rush he gets from what he called "the fix" provided by his blog. "The pleasure response is twofold," he said. "You can have instant gratification; you're going to hear about something really good or bad instantly. And if I feel like I've written something good, it's enjoyable to go back and read it."

"And," he said, "like most addictions, those feelings go away quickly. So I have to do it again and again."

Joseph Lorenzo Hall, 26, a graduate student at the School of Information Management and Systems at the University of California at Berkeley who has studied bloggers, said that for some people blogging has supplanted e-mail as a way to procrastinate at work.

20 People like Mr. Pierce, who devote much of their free time to the care and feeding of their own blogs and posting to other blogs, do so largely because it makes them feel productive even if it is not a paying job.

The procrastination, said Scott Lederer, 31, a fellow graduate student with Mr. Hall, has a collective feel to it. "You feel like you're participating in something important, because we're all doing it together," he said.

Jeff Jarvis, president of Advance.net, a company that builds Web sites for newspapers and magazines, and a blogging enthusiast, defended what he called one's "obligation to the blog."

"The addictive part is not so much extreme narcissism," Mr. Jarvis said. "It's that you're involved in a conversation. You have a connection to people through the blog."

Some compulsive bloggers take their obligation to extremes, blogging at the expense of more financially rewarding tasks.

25   Mr. Wiggins has missed deadline after deadline at Searcher, an
online periodical for which he is a paid contributor.

Barbara Quint, the editor of the magazine, said she did all she
could to get him to deliver his columns on time. Then she discovered
that Mr. Wiggins was busily posting articles to his blog instead of sending her the ones he had promised, she said. "Here he is working all
night on something read by five second cousins and a dog, and I'm willing to pay him," she said.

Ms. Quint has grown more understanding of his reasons, if not
entirely sympathetic. "The Web's illusion of immortality is sometimes
more attractive than actual cash," she said.

Jocelyn Wang, a 27-year-old marketing manager in Los Angeles,
started her blog, a chronicle of whatever happens to pop into her
head (www.jozjozjoz.com), 18 months ago as an outlet for boredom.

Now she spends at least four hours a day posting to her blog and
reading other blogs. Ms. Wang's online journal is now her life. And the
people she has met through the blog are a large part of her core of friends.

30   "There is no real separation in my life," she said. Like Mr. Wiggins,
Ms. Wang blogs while on vacation. She stays on floors at the Hotel
Nikko in San Francisco with access to a free Internet connection. ("So I
can blog," she explains.)

Blogging for a cause can take on a special urgency. Richard Khoe, a
political consultant in Washington who in his spare time helps run a
pro-John Kerry group called Run Against Bush, posts constantly to the
blog embedded in the group's Web site (www.runagainstbush.org). He
blogs late into the night, although he knows that the site still attracts
relatively few visitors.

"Sometimes you get really particular with the kind of link you
want, so you search a little more, then a little more, then you want to
see what other people are saying about that link you chose," he said.
"And before you know it, some real time has passed."

Others find they are distracted to the point of neglectfulness.
Tom Lewis, 35, a project manager for a software firm in western
Massachusetts who has a photo blog (tomdog.buzznet.com/user), has
occasionally shown up "considerably late" for events and has put off
more than a few work-related calls to tend to his blog.

Mr. Jarvis characterizes the blogging way of life as a routine rather
than an obsession. "It's a habit," he said. "What you're really doing is
telling people about something that they might find interesting.

When that becomes part of your life, when you start thinking in blog, it becomes part of you."

35   The constant search for bloggable moments is what led Gregor J. Rothfuss, a programmer in Zurich, to blog to the point of near-despair. Bored by his job, Mr. Rothfuss, 27, started a blog that focused on technical topics.

    "I was trying to record all thoughts and speculations I deemed interesting," he said. "Sort of creating a digital alter ego. The obsession came from trying to capture as much as possible of the good stuff in my head in as high fidelity as possible."

    For months, Mr. Rothfuss said, he blogged at work, at home, late into the night, day in and day out until it all became a blur—all the while knowing, he added, "that no one was necessarily reading it, except for myself."

    When traffic to the blog, greg.abstract.ch started to rise, he began devoting half a day every day and much of the weekend to it. Mr. Rothfuss said he has few memories of that period in his life aside from the compulsive blogging.

    He was saved from the rut of his online chronicle when he traveled to Asia. The blog became more of a travelogue. Then Mr. Rothfuss switched jobs, finding one he enjoyed, and his blogging grew more moderate.

40   He still has the blog, but posts to it just twice a week, he said, "as opposed to twice an hour." He feels healthier now. "It's part of what I do now, it's not what I do," he said.

    Suffering from a similar form of "blog fatigue," Bill Barol, a freelance writer in Santa Monica, Calif., simply stopped altogether after four years of nearly constant blogging.

    "It was starting to feel like work, and it was never supposed to be a job," Mr. Barol said. "It was supposed to be an anti-job."

    Even with some 200 visitors to his blog each day, he has not posted to his blog since returning from a month of travel.

    Still, Mr. Barol said, he does not rule out a return to blogging someday.

45   "There is this seductive thing that happens, this kind of snowball-rolling-down-a-hill thing, where the sheer momentum of several years' posting becomes very keenly felt," he said. "And the absence of posting feels like—I don't know, laziness or something."

Questions on Meaning

1. What issues about blogging get raised in this article? Is it an obsession, an addiction, or something else?
2. People have always kept journals with little thought given to an actual reader. Yet blogs are sometimes represented as self-indulgent. Do you agree or disagree? Explain. How are blogs similar to and different from journals or day books?
3. Beyond the availability of technology, why have the number of blogs increased so dramatically? As with any form of communication, what does the prevalence of blogs suggest about our culture?

Questions on Rhetorical Strategy and Style

1. Why did the writer choose to begin the article with an anecdote about the couple celebrating their anniversary?
2. What is the writer's attitude toward bloggers? Where is this most apparent? How did she attempt to offer a balance of perspectives and how successful was she?
3. Why does Hafner close her piece with Bill Barol's perspectives on blogging? How does this frame the article and reinforce the tone in perhaps a different way?

Writing Assignments

1. If you have a blog of your own, write an essay explaining to a cynic why it is important to you. What role does your blog play in your life? If you don't have a blog, perhaps you've been thinking of creating one. Most likely you know people who have started their own blogs. You can write a profile of one such person.
2. Write an essay extending your response to question no. 3 under Questions on Meaning above. Think about blogs as a genre, a type of writing that shapes, and is shaped by, social circumstances and conditions. Speculate on what social conditions, in your opinion, have given rise to the blog.

The Ethnobiologist's Dilemma

Jared Diamond

Jared Mason Diamond (1937–) was born in Boston and attended Harvard and Cambridge universities. He teaches physiology at UCLA, where he specializes in evolutionary biology by studying the birds of New Guinea. He writes regularly for Natural History *and* Discover *magazines. His 1992 book,* The Third Chimpanzee, *collects his essays on human prehistory, the biology of human nature, unique human traits, and the human place in history. Diamond's book* Guns, Germs, and Steel *(1998), which argues that environment and biology explain the European conquest of the Americas, won a Pulitzer prize for nonfiction. Diamond's latest book,* Collapse: How Societies Choose to Fail or Succeed, *discusses the sets of factors that contribute to whether societies fail or succeed. "The Ethnobiologist's Dilemma," published in the scientific journal* Natural History *in June 1989, suggests that humans develop quite different systems of communication based on their cultures and environments.*

1 "Listen, I already told you. The reason I said your VW didn't start was its solenoid was no good. Like I said, what the solenoid does is. . . . OK, forget it, you don't need to understand it. All you have to know is I fixed it and you owe me $203.67 and you can drive it again."

My car mechanic must have seen my eyes glaze over, just as I had seen my physiology students' eyes glaze over when I tried to explain osmotic diuresis to them in my lecture that same morning last month. It's humiliating to feel like an ignoramus, as I do about cars. At least

"The Ethnobiologist's Dilemma" by Jared Diamond, published in *Natural History*, June 1989.

I feel OK in my own areas of scientific expertise. So do most other scientists in their specialty: scientists are generally the experts who know more about their subject matter than do any other people. But there's one science in which this usual directional flow of information is often stood on its head. That's the branch of cultural anthropology termed *ethnobiology*—the study of how people from different cultures perceive and classify animals and plants.

In my column in the April 1989 issue I described how many New Guinea tribesmen are walking encyclopedias of facts about locally occurring species. This month's piece is about the cruel dilemma that arises when these walking encyclopedias are quizzed by an ethnobiologist, or even by a professional ornithologist naïve about New Guinea birds, as I was when I began working in New Guinea twenty-five years ago. I'll mainly discuss birds, but similar issues arise with classifications of other species. I eventually realized that the ethnobiologist's dilemma illustrates the frustrations that all of us face in everyday life, whenever we have to a quiz experts like our doctor or car mechanic.

As you may recall from my last column, New Guineans have distinct names in their local languages for almost every bird species living in the vicinity. Their knowledge of the behavior and life history of many species far exceeds what Western scientists know. The same is true of some other "primitive" peoples living elsewhere in the world, such as Amazonian Indians. I and other biologists working in such areas want this expertise for its own sake. I would need several lifetimes of observation to discover for myself what New Guineans already know about the birds I study. By learning names for New Guinea birds in local languages, I can tap into this knowledge. Foré tribesmen wouldn't understand me if I asked about the "blue bird of paradise," but they talked for hours when I asked about the *kongonámu*, their Foré name for this species.

5 Ethnobiologists are also interested in this expertise, but for another reason. They want to know how different human cultures perceive and organize information. Nothing is as fascinating as understanding how another human being thinks. It's challenging enough to understand someone who shares your language, culture, and much of your life, like your spouse; it becomes infinitely more challenging when the person belongs to a different society. Ethnobiology offers a well-defined approach to this problem, because species possess an objective reality, and some of the same species occur in areas

occupied by different human cultures. Particular goals of ethnobiologists include discovering what units people choose to name (species or other groupings?), whether tribesmen group units hierarchically as we group species into genera and families, and whether the answers to these questions vary among peoples.

The first step in an ethnobiological study is a seemingly simple one: to gather from informants a list of names of birds (or of other animals or plants) in a local language and to determine which bird each name refers to. Yet the apparent simplicity of this task is deceptive, as I gradually came to realize while gathering such lists in New Guinea, talking with ethnobiologists, reading their papers, and reinterviewing tribespeople previously studied by ethnobiologists. Anthropologists focus on theoretically interesting questions posed by naming but often fail to appreciate the pitfalls in that mundane first step of obtaining a correct list of bird names. While the goal is to understand a people whose perceptions differ from ours, those very differences make it hard for us to discern their perceptions. To compound this problem, most anthropologists know much less about the local birds than do the tribesmen they're interviewing. Let's consider three stimuli that scientists have used to gather lists of bird names: pictures in bird books, dead specimens of birds, and live birds encountered in the jungle.

To Western scientists accustomed to book learning, the most obvious approach is to show a tribesman a book with pictures of bird species likely to occur in his area, and ask him to name the birds depicted. The virtues of this method are that a compact field guide may depict hundreds of species, you don't have to find and identify birds in the jungle, and every informant is shown the same birds. Among the many anthropologists and linguists who used this method were Leonard Glick and Kenneth McElhanon in their respective studies of New Guinea's Gimi and Selepet peoples.

During my early years in New Guinea, I too used this method until I realized that the results were too variable to trust. When shown pictures of bird species that I knew occurred in the vicinity, local people sometimes gave names in agreement with the names they gave when they and I together observed the same bird species alive in the jungle. But sometimes the names disagreed. In other cases people failed even to recognize pictures of common local birds or professed to recognize bird species that could not possibly occur in the area.

A glaring error of naming on Vella Lavella Island in the Solomon archipelago finally made me understand one of the flaws in the picture method. I had spent the day bird watching with some knowledgeable old men who named and described the habits of fifty-five bird species that we encountered. In the evening I showed them bird pictures in a field guide. When we came to the picture of a lesser frigatebird, I expected my guides to apply the name *belama*, which they had used for the frigatebirds we saw soaring that day. In fact, they pronounced it to be a *pitikole*, the name they had used for the willie wagtail.

10   A more ludicrous mistake would be impossible to imagine.   10
Frigatebirds are huge seabirds (eight-foot wingspread), have deeply forked tails, soar high in flocks, catch fish, and are usually silent. Willie wagtails are small flycatchers (eight inches long), have a fan-shaped tail that they wave incessantly, hop on the ground in villages, catch insects, and call noisily. The only feature shared by frigatebirds, and willie wagtails is that both are black and white.

Shocked by this gross failure of the experts, I reexamined the pictures from a fresh perspective, as if I were a Vella Lavella islander shown a bird book for the first time. On a printed page was a black-and-white pattern about four inches across. Having spent several decades reading books, I was accustomed to conjuring up a large, three-dimensional sketch. But the islanders weren't used to this leap of imagination. Instead, they saw what was really there: a flat, black-and-white, bird-shaped image, much closer in size to a real willie wagtail than to a real frigatebird.

I'm not arguing that pictures are of no value as an ethnobiological tool. It's just that, for informants from a barely literate society, identifications based on pictures are unreliable unless confirmed by a better technique. The picture method's failures illustrate the risk of using our own perceptions to devise tests for the perceptions of other peoples.

An ethnobiological technique that avoids some drawbacks of the picture method is to show people actual specimens of local birds that have been shot. Whenever I was making collections of New Guinea birds, I routinely asked local villagers to name each of my specimens, and so have many other ornithologists. Most anthropologists can't apply this method because they aren't collecting bird specimens. In Peru, however, anthropologists Brent Berlin and James Boster collaborated with ornithologist John O'Neill to test this approach rigorously. They showed locally collected specimens of 157 bird species to Aguaruna Jívaro Indians, asked each Indian to name each specimen, and did three such naming trials on twenty-eight, twenty-five, and twenty-seven Indians, respectively.

In my experience, names elicited by specimens agree better with names elicited by live birds than do names elicited by pictures. Nevertheless, problems of discrepancies and inabilities to name some locally common species still occur. A superb New Guinea informant named Mero, who lived at Kiunga on the Fly River, helped me see what was going wrong. Mero had described for me 125 local bird species, named many fruits that each frugivorous bird species ate, and guided me to one of New Guinea's rarest birds, the white-bellied pitohui. Far more abundant than the white-bellied pitohui, though, is the related rusty pitohui, one of the most conspicuous and distinctive birds of the New Guinea lowlands. It constantly gives loud calls audible hundreds of yards away, dives in and out of vine tangles, and scours the whole jungle from the understory to the canopy. In groups of up to ten, rusty pitohuis lead flocks of other bird species in their search for food (see "Strange Traveling Companions," December 1988). Thus, after Mero had named for me such rarities as the whitebellied pitohui, I was astonished when he could not decide what to name a specimen of the rusty pitohui that I handed him.

15 As I had done on Vella Lavella, I tried to see the situation from Mero's point of view. Here he stood holding a dead, silent, motionless, utterly undistinctive brown bird, stripped of all the characteristics that he associated with the rusty pitohui.

Gone were the bugling calls, the shaking of the vine tangles, the excitement as the jungle came alive and as dozens of other birds swept after the pitohuis. For Mero, the rusty pitohui was that noise and excitement, not this drab carcass. Perhaps the same conclusion lay behind a remark that a Kaluli tribesman named Jubi, living barely a hundred miles east of Mero's village, made to ethnobiologist Steven Feld. After Feld had been attempting for months to decipher Kaluli bird names, Jubi suddenly lost his patience and blurted out, "Listen—to you they are birds, to me they are voices in the forest."

Berlin's, Boster's, and O'Neill's accounts of their experiments suggest that bird specimens may pose similar problems for Peruvian Indians as for Mero and Jubi. In response to specimens of the 157 bird species, Indians came up with 275 bird names, less than half of which appeared to Berlin and his colleagues to be valid names (as judged by being applied consistently to a given specimen or to several very similar species). Indians volunteered eight names of birds said to be relatives of the most distinctive local woodpecker. Yet when Indians were shown specimens of eight local woodpecker species, only one species received the same name from all informants, and only two names were confined to a single woodpecker species (but each of those species more often received a different name).

Much of this variability among Indian informants was undoubtedly due to some of them knowing more about birds than others. However, another contributing factor is surely that Indians distinguish live woodpeckers by call, drumming pattern, habitat, and perch, as well as by appearance. Dead specimens were stripped of those recognition marks, just as was the dead rusty pitohui for Mero.

The basic problem with trying to elicit bird names by pictures or specimens is that these methods fail to present birds in the way that New Guinea hunters normally perceive them. To elicit names under natural circumstances, I routinely have one or two local hunters accompany me through the jungle whenever I am bird watching in New Guinea. I ask them to name each bird that we see or hear, and I check their identifications by asking them to tell me details of the bird's habits. This method has proved to be reliable because whenever I have worked in areas where biologists of the Whitney South Seas Expedition used the same method in the 1920s and 1930s, identifications of names obtained by me and by the Whitney biologists agree closely.

20 I also ask hunters to describe and name all the birds that they 20 know, in addition to the ones that we have seen or heard together. When they eventually run out of names, I prod them for any they might have forgotten by asking them to describe all nocturnal birds or all ground-dwelling birds or all birds similar to a parrot or some other type of bird that they have already described. At all costs, I avoid yes/no questions. I also avoid giving people a complete description of some bird and asking them to name it, for that would leave me no way of checking whether they really know the species in question.

It often still happens that I want to find out whether a hunter knows some particular bird species that he hasn't as yet spontaneously described to me. In that case I give a brief description of the bird. If the hunter claims to know it, I ask him to describe more about it so I can tell if he really knows that bird. But I still have to remind myself that New Guinea hunters don't experience birds as we see them—through binoculars or displayed in Peterson field guides. Hunters remember certain species by their songs, others by their behavior, still others by their plumage. It took me years to learn what features of each bird species were most salient for New Guineans and hence should be included in my brief description.

For example, when I described the moustached tree swift's white moustache and eye stripe, which are so striking as seen through my binoculars or in field guides, no New Guinean ever guessed the bird I was talking about. Instead, what impresses New Guineans is the silhouette, distinctive at a hundred yards: the bird's wings are so long that they cross behind its back as it sits perched, and the forked tail also appears crossed. In villages all over the New Guinea region, if I stand with my arms crossed behind my back and with my legs crossed and say nothing more, people immediately laugh, know that I'm referring to the moustached tree swift, and proceed to describe its habits and to give their name for it. As another example, I never got a response when I described the bush hen's chickenlike build and green bill. Instead, I learned to imitate the catlike wailing duet of the male and female foraging together. The result is always a laugh of recognition, a name and account of habits, and a story to the effect that the answering wails really don't come from two birds, but from a single bird's mouth and anus answering each other.

Thus, to elicit names successfully, one must learn how local hunters perceive each bird species. The worst risk is that hunters are likely to give you oversimplified information, or no information at all, if they sense that you yourself don't know much about the subject. This risk is illustrated by a tale of woe I heard from the late Ralph Bulmer, an ethnobiologist who was unusual in being not only an anthropologist but also a zoologist of professional caliber. Bulmer spent years with the Kalam people of the New Guinea Highlands, studying their understanding of birds, mammals, and plants. Out of those years came one of the most remarkable contributions to the ethnobiological literature: a book entitled *Birds of My Kalam Country*, which Bulmer coauthored with a Kalam tribesman/walking encyclopedia named Ian Saem Majnep. In that book, Saem recorded in his own words his knowledge of 137 out of the 140 bird species found by Western ornithologists in the Kalam area, while Bulmer added his own observations plus identifications of

Saem's Kalam bird names (for example, *tbwm-kab-ket-nonm* = crested berrypecker = *Paramythia montium*).

One year, after Kalam people had already told Bulmer names and descriptions for more than 1,400 species of animals and plants known to them, Bulmer began to quiz them about rocks as well. To his great surprise, they claimed to have just one word covering all rocks. In vain did Bulmer protest that the Kalam had until recently used stone tools, and so surely they must have names for different types of rocks to identify which ones made good tools. Bulmer's Kalam friends brushed aside his protests and continued to insist that they didn't classify rocks by name.

The next year, Bulmer returned to the Kalam area with a geologist friend whom he introduced to his Kalam informants. Within an hour, the geologist gave Bulmer a long list of words that the informants had volunteered for different rocks, which they classified according to texture, color, locality, hardness, and use. At that point Bulmer exploded to his Kalam friends, "How could you lie to me? After all these years that I've been working with you! You kept insisting that you didn't bother to classify rocks, and now you've embarrassed me in front of my friend!" To which the Kalam replied, "When you asked us about birds and plants, we saw that you knew a lot about them, and that you could understand what we told you. When you began asking us about rocks, it was obvious you didn't know anything about them. Why should we waste our time telling you something you couldn't possibly understand? But your friend's questions showed that he does know about rocks."

Therein lies the root of the ethnobiologist's dilemma. You have to know almost as much about the local birds as the tribesman you're interviewing if you're to succeed in learning his names for birds. It's pointless walking with a hunter through the jungle and asking him to name bird calls, when you dont know what bird species is making each call that you hear. You can't describe a bird's salient habits if you don't know its habits and know which of them appear most salient to a local hunter. Worst of all, your informants will perceive correctly that you can't grasp all the complexities of their knowledge, so they'll tell you only as much as they think you can understand. Tribesmen in New Guinea and some other parts of the world know far more about local birds than do most anthropologists interviewing them. To approach the tribesmen's knowledge takes years even for ornithologists specializing in New Guinea birds. Thus, ethnobiologists, need to emulate Bulmer's example, invest the time required to attain professional competence in a local fauna, and learn to identify birds in the way that tribesmen do. The second-best alternative is for ethnobiologists to collaborate with biologists who already have that competence.

This piece has seemingly been about a mere problem of methodology in an arcane discipline. In fact, all of us must often ask experts to explain things to us that they understand well and we don't. We have to ask questions of our doctor, car mechanic, tax accountant, house contractor, and so forth. It's usually frustrating, because few experts have the time, patience, or ability to explain things in a way that nonexperts can understand.

For instance, the starter on my 1961, VW Beetle broke down not just last month but many times before that. One mechanic after another fixed it but would not explain the problem and how I could avoid it. The mechanics undoubtedly saw that I am as ignorant about cars as Ralph Bulmer was about rocks, and that I could not understand their explanation. The bad service that I continue to get is my own fault for not practicing what I preach to ethnobiologists: I never took the trouble to study a VW manual. Similarly, consumer advocates are now urging us that if we want to get good care from our doctors, we have to be willing to spend some time reading up on our own health problems.

Thus, I see the ethnobiologist's dilemma as a metaphor for much of modern life. To them that already understand, more knowledge will be freely given. To the rest of us dolts, it's a struggle.

Questions on Meaning

1. Though local New Guinea tribesmen knew much about their local bird life, what information were they incapable of giving? Why?
2. Why were the tribesmen incapable of recognizing dead birds or of giving them the same names they gave to the live birds?
3. What did Diamond learn about his own language when he realized that the tribesmen had many words for birds and only one word for rocks, no matter what their texture or shape or mineral content?

Questions on Rhetorical Strategy and Style

1. Diamond's essay presents much interesting information about the naming practices of the New Guinea tribesmen, but he also has an important rhetorical purpose as he presents the information to his readers. What does he want his readers to see and think as they learn about the language of the tribesmen?
2. How does Diamond set up the problem of discovery of information so that the reader can follow him through his research and discoveries? Why does he end with the discussion of how few words we have for birds and how few words the tribesmen have for rocks? What does that difference say about our cultural values?

Writing Assignments

1. Investigate your own name (or names) and try to find out where you got it, what it means, and why your family chose that name for you. Write about your reaction to your name and its meaning or to some other name that you know or like.
2. Scientific classifications of animals and minerals help us to understand the natural world, but they also suggest something about the ways in which we think about it. Take some time to observe groups of people around you, perhaps students or people at the store. How would you classify them and what sort of scientific groupings could you construct? Write an essay that explains how different people would fit into these groups.
3. Choose a word or a group of words that you feel reflects a distinct cultural value (for example, high school slang). Employing Diamond's use of examples and his organizational strategy as a model, write an essay in which you try to convince your readers to reconsider their perspective.

What a Certain Visionary Once Said

Tomson Highway

Tomson Highway (1951–) was raised on the Brochet Reservation (a Cree reservation) in northern Manitoba. He attended a Catholic boarding school as a child and went to high school in Winnipeg. He graduated from the University of Western Ontario and currently lives in Toronto, where he founded the Native Earth Performing Arts Theatre. In 1986 his play, The Rez Sisters, *received two awards for best new play in Toronto's theatrical season. In 1990 he received the Toronto Arts Award for* Dry Lips Oughta Move to Kapuskasing. *In 1994 he became the first aboriginal writer to be inducted in the Order of Canada. Highway has also published a novel,* Kiss of the Fur Queen *(1997) and produced a musical,* Rose *(2000). In the following essay, which originally appeared in 1992, Highway uses descriptive language to characterize the appeal of Northern Canada.*

1   As you travel north from Winnipeg, the flatness of the prairie begins to give way. And the northern forests begin to take over, forests of spruce and pine and poplar and birch. The northern rivers and northern rapids, the waterfalls, the eskers, the northern lakes—thousands of them—with their innumerable islands encircled by golden-sand beaches and flat limestone surfaces that slide gracefully into water. As you travel farther north, the trees themselves begin to diminish in height and size. And get smaller, until, finally, you reach the barren lands. It is from these reaches that herds of caribou in the thousands come thundering down each winter. It is here that you find

trout and pickerel and pike and whitefish in profusion. If you're here in August, your eyes will be glutted with a sudden explosion of colour seldom seen in any southern Canadian landscape: fields of wild raspberries, cloudberries, blueberries, cranberries, stands of wild flowers you never believed such remote northern terrain was capable of nurturing. And the water is still so clean you can dip your hand over the side of your canoe and you can drink it. In winter, you can eat the snow, without fear. In both winter and summer, you can breathe, this is your land, your home.

Here, you can begin to remember that you are a human being. And if you take the time to listen—really listen—you can begin to hear the earth breathe. And whisper things simple men, who never suspected they were mad, can hear. Madmen who speak Cree, for one, can in fact understand the language this land speaks, in certain circles. Which would make madmen who speak Cree a privileged lot.

Then you seat yourself down on a carpet of reindeer moss and you watch the movements of the sky, filled with stars and galaxies of stars by night, streaked by endlessly shifting cloud formations by day. You watch the movements of the lake which, within one hour, can change from a surface of glass to one of waves so massive in their fury they can—and have—killed many a man. And you begin to understand that men and women can, within maybe not one hour but one day, change from a mood of reflective serenity and self-control to one of depression and despair so deep they can—and have—killed many a man.

You begin to understand that this earth we live on—once thought insensate, inanimate, dead by scientists, theologians and such—has an emotional psychological and spiritual life every bit as complex as that of the most complex, sensitive and intelligent of individuals.

And it's ours. Or is it?

A certain ancient aboriginal visionary of this country once said: "We have not inherited this land, we have merely borrowed it from our children."

If that's the case, what a loan!

Eh?

Questions on Meaning

1. Highway expresses a common sentiment about being in nature. Somehow, the thinking goes, when we are in nature we discover our essential selves. How do you feel when you are away from crowded and distracting circumstances? What makes nature spiritual? How might the earth have an "emotional psychological" life? How does this stand in opposition to a scientific orientation, as the author suggests?

2. In a way, the essay begs a certain question: If we must travel to such places to "remember that [we] are human," then are we less than human when we are living our everyday, hectic lives? How do you react to this suggestion?

3. In paragraph 3, Highway draws an analogy between "the movements of the lake" and the moods of humans. What makes them analogous?

Questions on Strategy and Style

1. The author is very careful to bring his readers along on his journey to the north. Why did he choose this strategy? What effect does it have on your experience of reading the essay? Is he trying to put you in a certain frame of mind? Why is this important?

2. How does this brief narrative resemble a poem? Consider the language and the structure of the piece as you frame your answer. If it were written as a poem, what might be different about it? Would that change its meaning in any way?

3. Notice that the "certain visionary" mentioned in the title does not come up until the very end of the essay. Why is that? Why does he not mention the visionary by name? What is the tone behind the last word in the essay?

Writing Assignments

1. Highway's essay is an example of nature writing. However, one might say that views of nature are informed by cultural perspective. As a Native writer, Highway's sensibilities will reflect a particular viewpoint. In fact, it may be fair to say that Cree people have a perspective on nature that is somewhat distinct from other tribes. If you are unfamiliar with the worldview of Native people, research it and write a brief report on what you learn.

2. Write your own narrative essay of a place that is important to you. In planning your essay, consider how you might convey to readers the significance of this place to you. What will you have to provide your readers with in order for them to understand what is special about this place? What do you want your readers to experience and why?

Anatomy of a Hangover

Donald G. Ross

In this article, readers who have not yet experienced the aftereffects of too much alcohol will be horrified, while readers who have experienced a hangover may be edified to learn about the chemical causes of their misery. As you read, note particularly the way Ross uses cause and effect, description, and process analysis. Ross's techniques are familiar to readers and writers of scientific reports, but he has toned down the technicality of science and applied it to a well-known experience.

1   Fred awakens with a pounding headache. The room seems to be spinning. Feeling nauseated and sweating profusely, he stumbles into the kitchen for a drink of water. As he glances around the room, he spots the empty bottles of red wine. "Did I really drink that much?" he asks himself. Shaking his head, he is overcome with another wave of piercing head pains and nausea. Fred is in the throws of a substantial hangover. But why do some people get hangovers while others seemingly are able to drink with abandon?

What Is a Hangover?

A hangover typically begins several hours after a person stops drinking, when the blood alcohol level is falling. Symptoms usually peak around the time it hits zero and persist for up to 24 hours. The unpleasant symptoms that commonly follow a heavy bout of drinking can range from a mild headache and upset stomach to a feeling of severe illness—raging headache, nausea, dizziness, and extreme sensitivity to light and sound (see Table 1). The specific symptoms and their intensity may vary widely—from person to person, from drinking bout to drinking bout, and with the type and amount of alcohol consumed.

In general, the more alcohol one consumes, the more likely that one will suffer a hangover. A 1993 survey found that 75 percent of the people who drank to intoxication had hangovers at least some of the time. A study of 2,160 Finnish men found that over 43.8 percent of the heaviest drinkers, those who drank about nine drinks per week, had one or more hangovers every month, compared to 6.6 percent for the rest of the study group. Yet individual differences are large. Some people have hangovers after drinking only one to three alcoholic drinks, while others drink heavily without any morning-after misery.

What Causes a Hangover?

Scientists blame hangover symptoms on several different factors. Alcohol directly affects the brain and other organs, and its withdrawal may be a culprit. Toxic compounds produced as the body processes alcohol may also be responsible. Alcoholic drinks often contain non-alcoholic, yet biologically active, components. Concurrent use of other drugs, restricted eating, and going to bed later than normal can contribute to the intensity of the hangover. Personal traits, such as temperament, personality, and family history of alcoholism, can also be cofactors. Evidence suggest that an interaction of more than one of these factors is responsible for the myriad of hangover symptoms.

Direct Effects of Alcohol

5   Since its diuretic properties increase urinary output and send drinkers on regular visits to the bathroom, alcohol commonly causes dehydration and electrolyte imbalance. Consumption of about four drinks of alcohol and water (about 250 milliliters) causes the excretion of 600 to 1,000 milliliters of urine! During a hangover, the sweating, vomiting, and diarrhea cause further fluid loss and electrolyte imbalance. Symptoms of dehydration—thirst, weakness, dryness of mucous membranes, dizziness, and lightheadedness—are also typical symptoms of a hangover.

Alcohol directly irritates and inflames the lining of the stomach and intestines. It also triggers increased production of gastric acid and increased pancreatic and intestinal secretions. Beverages with high alcohol content delay stomach emptying. And high alcohol consumption produces fatty acids in liver cells and can cause a fatty liver. An interplay of all these factors commonly causes the upper abdominal pain, nausea, and vomiting of a hangover.

Alcohol alters the body's normal metabolic processes and can cause low blood sugar levels (hypoglycemia). Alcohol-induced hypoglycemia usually occurs in diabetics, as well as alcoholics who binge drink for several days without eating. Hypoglycemia may or may not contribute to a hangover, but the two conditions have similar symptoms—headache, fatigue, weakness, and mood disturbances.

Alcohol has sedating effects that put one to sleep. But it is a disturbed sleep, and rebound effects can lead to insomnia. Drinking often takes place at night in competition with normal sleeping hours, so it reduces sleep time. Alcohol also decreases the amount of dreaming and deep sleep. You may have heard the sonorous sounds of someone snoring away the night after a bout of drinking. Alcohol relaxes the soft palate, increasing snoring and possibly causing sleep apnea.

Alcohol upsets circadian rhythms, and the effects persist into the hangover period. It alters the normal ebb and flow of body temperature, abnormally lowering it during intoxication and abnormally raising it during a hangover, thus promoting sweating the next morning. Alcohol also disrupts the nighttime release of growth hormone and the rise and fall of cortisol levels. The overall disruption of circadian rhythms is similar to "jet lag" and makes hangover symptoms worse.

10 Alcohol intoxication leads to the dilation of blood vessels, a possible cause of headaches. It also affects the activity of neurotransmitters and hormones, such as histamine, serotonin, and prostaglandins, which have been implicated in head pain. 10

Alcohol Withdrawal and Toxic Byproducts

A hangover may be a mild manifestation of alcohol withdrawal. Overlapping symptoms include nausea and vomiting, tremor, sweating, anxiety, agitation, and headache. Since consuming additional alcohol can alleviate the immediate unpleasantness of both alcohol withdrawal and hangover, they may share a common underlying mechanism. (Further alcohol use—the "hair of the dog that bit you" hangover remedy—should be avoided. Additional drinking only enhances the toxicity of the alcohol previously consumed and extends the recovery time.)

Your body gets rid of alcohol as fast as it can. The liver converts alcohol to acetaldehyde, which the enzyme aldehyde dehydrogenase (ALDH) quickly converts to a harmless substance that is used for energy or stored as fat. Acetaldehyde is highly toxic, and most people's bodies rapidly and efficiently convert it to avoid its accumulation. Despite this effort, small amounts of acetaldehyde are found in the bloodstream during intoxication.

The ability to convert acetaldehyde varies between women and men and has a strong genetic component. For nonalcoholics, the ALDH enzyme in the stomach lining of women is 40 percent less active than in men. About half the people of Asian descent have low levels of ALDH and experience flushing on the face and neck after drinking alcohol, probably due to high blood acetaldehyde levels. In alcohol aversion therapy, the medication disulfiram (Antabuse) deliberately blocks the conversion of acetaldehyde, allowing even small amounts of alcohol to trigger a highly unpleasant reaction, which includes a throbbing headache, breathing difficulties, nausea, copious vomiting, flushing, vertigo, confusion, and a drop in blood pressure.

Which Drinks Are More Likely To Cause a Hangover?

Gin and vodka are mostly pure ethanol, while brandy, whiskey, and red wine contain other biologically active compounds known as congeners. Congeners contribute to the distinctive taste, smell, and appearance of alcoholic beverages, but they have a dark side. Beverages containing congeners are more likely to cause a hangover than beverages of mostly pure ethanol. Congeners also may enhance the alcoholic beverage's intoxicating effects and worsen a subsequent hangover.

15   One congener, methanol, is a particularly vicious villain. Although it is a type of alcohol, its chemical structure differs slightly from ethanol's. When the body metabolizes methanol, it produces highly toxic compounds that in high concentrations cause blindness and even death.

The distilled spirits most frequently associated with hangovers, such as brandies and whiskeys, contain the highest concentrations of methanol. In addition, a study of red-wine consumption found that methanol persisted in the blood for several hours after ethanol was metabolized—a time period that matches the course of a hangover.

Some people suffer aftereffects from drinking red wine but not white wine or vodka. While red wine can increase serotonin and histamine levels, triggering pounding headaches in susceptible people, white wine and vodka do not affect the production of these substances.

Personal Factors

People with certain personality traits, such as neuroticism, anger, and defensiveness, seem to suffer hangovers more frequently than others. Hangovers also are associated with negative life events and feelings of guilt about drinking. People who have a personality risk for alcoholism tend to have more severe hangover symptoms and may drink in an attempt to find relief.

Treating a Hangover

So what can one do about a hangover? Innumerable folk remedies purport to prevent, shorten, or cure a hangover, but few have undergone rigorous, scientific investigation. Time is the most effective remedy—symptoms usually disappear within 8 to 24 hours. Consumption of fruits, fruit juices, or other fructose-containing foods has been reported to decrease a hangover's intensity, but this has not been well studied. Eating bland foods containing complex carbohydrates, such as toast or crackers, can combat low blood sugar levels and possibly nausea. Sleep can ease fatigue, and drinking nonalcoholic, noncaffeinated beverages can alleviate dehydration (caffeine is a diuretic and increases urine production).

20   Certain medications can provide symptom relief. Antacids may 20 relieve nausea and stomach pains. Aspirin may reduce headache and muscle aches, but it could increase stomach irritation. Acetaminophen should be avoided because alcohol metabolism enhances its toxicity to the liver. People who drink three or more alcoholic beverages per day should avoid all over-the-counter pain relievers and fever reducers. These heavy drinkers may have an increased risk of liver damage and stomach bleeding from these medicines, which contain aspirin, other

salicylates, acetaminophen (Tylenol), ibuprofen (Advil), naproxen sodium (Aleve), or ketoprofen (Orudis KT and Actron).
Prevention

As the Old Adage Says, Prevention Is the Best Medicine

A person who drinks only small, nonintoxicating amounts of alcohol is less likely to suffer a hangover than a person who drinks to get drunk. Even among intoxicated people, the ones who drink the most are the most likely to wake up in misery.

TABLE 1: SYMPTOMS OF A HANGOVER

Class of Symptoms	Type
Constitutional	Fatigue, weakness, and thirst
Pain	Headache and muscle aches
Gastrointestinal	Nausea, vomiting, and stomach pain
Sleep and biological rhythms	Decreased duration and quality of sleep
Sensory	Vertigo and sensitivity to light and sound
Cognitive	Decreased attention and concentration
Mood	Depression, anxiety, and irritability
Sympathetic hyperactivity	Tremor, sweating, and increased pulse and systolic blood pressure

Questions on Meaning

1. What chemical changes does alcohol consumption bring about in the body? What physical changes does it bring about?
2. What factors affect the severity of a hangover?
3. What should be done to cure or mitigate the symptoms of a hangover?

Questions on Rhetorical Strategy and Style

1. What aspects of drinking does Ross choose not to deal with? Why do you think he made that choice?
2. List several of the cause-effect sequences that Ross describes. For example, one sequence could be that taking aspirin for a hangover causes increased damage to the stomach.
3. Does Ross's description of alcohol's effects change your attitudes about alcohol? If you found this piece persuasive, identify the most persuasive parts. If you did not find it persuasive, identify the parts that might be used in a different and more persuasive article.

Writing Assignments

1. Use the information in Ross's article to create a pamphlet on drinking aimed at a high-school-aged audience. Try to teach, not preach.
2. Use the information in Ross's article to write a questionnaire on popular beliefs about alcohol. For example, one question might deal with effective hangover cures, another with the differential effects of alcohol on males and females. Add some questions to establish the age, gender, and drinking habits of your informants (the people who answer your questionnaire). Give the questionnaire to a group of your choosing and report the results.

Reach Out and Annoy Someone

Jonathan Rowe

Jonathan Rowe's long list of credentials includes a degree from Harvard, a law degree from the University of Pennsylvania, publications in major magazines such as The Atlantic Monthly *and* Columbia Journalism Review, *political work as a congressional staffer and with Ralph Nader, and editorial work in various contexts. Currently, he is a contributing editor of* The Washington Monthly, *in which this piece first appeared in late 2000. In this article, Rowe addresses the "second-hand smoke" of the new millennium: overheard cell-phone conversations.*

When public space turns private,
we're all stuck listening to the noise

1 In the latter 1990s, in the midst of the high tech boom, I spent a lot of time in a coffee shop in the theater district in San Francisco. It was near Union Square, the tourist hub, and I observed a scene play out there time and time again. Mom is nursing her mocha. The kids are picking at their muffins, feet dangling from their chairs. And there's Dad, pulled back slightly from the table, talking into his cell phone.

I would watch the kids' faces, vacant and a little forlorn, and wonder what happens to kids whose parents aren't there even when they are. How can we expect kids to pay attention if we are too busy to pay attention to them? Peter Breggin, the psychiatrist, says much "attention deficit disorder" is really "dad deficit disorder." Maybe he's right.

"Reach Out And Annoy Someone" by Jonathan Rowe, published in *The Washington Monthly*, November 2000.

As I sat there, I would think, too, about the disconnect between the way we talk about the economy in the U.S. and the way we actually experience it. The media were enthusing daily about the nations record "expansion," and here were these kids staring off into space. It was supposed to be a "communications revolution," and yet here, in the technological epicenter, the members of this family were avoiding one another's eyes.

With technology in particular, we can't seem to acknowledge the actual content of our economic experience; and we discuss the implications only within a narrow bandwidth of human concern. Is there a health risk? Might the thing cause cancer? That's about it with cell phones, computers, genetic engineering, and a host of other new developments. As a result, we must await the verdict of the doctors to find out whether we are permitted to have qualms or reservations. Jacob Needleman, the contemporary philosopher, says that we Americans are "metaphysically repressed," and the inability to discuss the implications of technology—except in bodily or stock market terms—is a case in point.

5   I don't discount the significance of cancer. But there is something 5 missing from a discussion that can't get beyond the most literal and utilitarian concerns. Actually, some of the problems with cell phones aren't at all squishy or abstract. If you've been clipped by a car tooling around the corner while the driver sits gabbing, cell phone in hand, then you are aware of this. The big problem, of course, is the noise. For sheer intrusiveness, cell phones rank with mega-amp car stereos and political commercials, and they are harder to escape.

We all know the drill. First the endearing beep, which is like an alarm clock going off at 5:30 a.m. Then people shout into the things, as though they are talking across the Cross Bronx Expressway. It's become a regular feature at movies and ball games, restaurants and parks. I've heard the things going off in men's room stalls. They represent more than mere annoyances. Cell phones affect life in ways that are, I suspect, beyond the capacity of the empirical mind to grasp.

Travel is an example. Thomas Carlyle once advised Anthony Trollope to use travel as a time to "sit still and label his thoughts." For centuries, travel played this quiet role. I have a hunch that the eloquence and depth of this nation's founders had partly to do with their mode of travel. Madison, Jefferson, and the others had that long ride to Philadelphia in which to sort out their thoughts and work over their sentences in their minds. There was time in which thought could expand; we can hear the echoes today in the spaciousness and considered quality of such documents as the *Federalist Papers*—a quality that political argument today rarely achieves.

In more recent times, trains have served as a link to that kind of travel. I used to look forward to Amtrak rides almost as a sanctuary. They provided precious hours in which to work or read or simply muse without the interruptions of the telephone and office. But now, cell phones have caught up with me. They have turned Amtrak into a horizontal telephone booth; on a recent trip to New York my wife and I were besieged by cell phones and their cousins, high-powered Walkmen, literally on all sides. The trip, which used to be a pleasure, has become one long headache.

I wrote the president of Amtrak to tell him this. I tried to be constructive. There is a real opportunity here for Amtrak to get ahead of the curve, I said. Why not provide "Quiet Cars" the way they provided No Smoking cars when smoking first became an issue? Amtrak could give riders a choice, which is what America is supposed to be about—and which Amtrak's main competitors, the airlines, cannot do. This seemed like a no-lose proposition. The yakkers could yak-, others could enjoy the quiet, and Amtrak could have a PR coup. (In a just world, the cell phoners would have to sit together in Noise Cars, but I was trying to be accommodating.)

10 The argument seemed pretty convincing. As the weeks passed, I 10 imagined my letter circulating at the highest levels. Perhaps I'd even be called in as a consultant. Now that I have the reply, I'm not holding my breath. But the reasons that Amtrak offered for inaction are worth a few moments, since they suggest how quickly technology invokes its own system of rationalization.

For example, the letter said that Amtrak does not want to inconvenience the "responsible" users of cell phones. That's typical; try to isolate a few aberrant users and so legitimate the rest. But cell phones are like cigarettes in this respect—they are intrusive when used normally, as intended. They beep like a seat belt warning, or play a tinny melody like a musical toilet seat. People usually shout into them. They produce secondhand noise, just as cigarettes produce secondhand smoke; and from the standpoint of the forced consumer of this noise, the only responsible use is non-use.

Then the letter turned the issue upside down. "We hesitate to restrict responsible users of cell phones," it said, "especially since many customers find train travel to be an ideal way to get work done." But that is exactly why cell phones should be restricted—because many travelers are trying to get work done. For one thing, the notion that people are busily working on cell phones is New Economy hype. I have been a coerced eavesdropper on more conversations than I could count. I have listened to executives gab about their shopping hauls and weekend conquests. I once had to endure, between Philadelphia and New York-, an extended brag from an associate sports agent regarding the important people he was meeting. It is not often that I hear anyone actually discussing work.

But more importantly, consider the assumption here. We have two people who arguably are trying to get some work done. There's the cell phone user, who wants to make noise. And there's myself (and probably numerous others), who would appreciate a little quiet. Why does the noise automatically take precedence over the quiet? Why does the polluter get first dibs on the air?

This is where the trail starts to get warm, I think. There is something about technology that enables it to take front seat in any situation it enters; which is to say, there is something in ourselves that seeks to give it this seat. A Maine essayist by the name of John Gould once noted this about the ordinary telephone. He was up on his roof one day when his wife called to him about something. "Later," he said, "Can't you see I'm working?" Later came, and this time the phone rang. Gould scrambled down the ladder in a frantic attempt to get to that phone.

15   Afterwards he reflected upon what had happened. His wife could   15
wait, he thought, but the phone rang with the authority of Mussolini in a bad mood. Most of us probably have had this experience. We've been making a purchase when the phone rang and the clerk dropped us cold and got into a long conversation on the phone. Or perhaps we had a visitor in our own office and interrupted the conversation to pick up the phone. Whatever is happening, the telephone comes first. Call waiting ratchets up the authority structure like a dictatorship that adds minions at the top. Now there are intrusions upon the intrusions; how many of us hear that click and think, "Oh, just let it ring."

What is it about these things that makes us so obedient, and so oblivious to that which lies outside them—such as actual people? I once asked a man who was bellowing into a cell phone in the coffee shop in San Francisco why he was talking so loudly. A bad connection, he said. It had not crossed his mind that anything else mattered at that moment. Like computers and television, cell phones puff people into their own psychological polar field, and the pull is strong. I've watched people complete a conversation, start to put the thing away, and then freeze. They sit staring at it, as though trying to think of someone else to call. The phone is there. It demands to be used, almost the way a cigarette demands to be smoked. Does the person own the cell phone, or is it the other way around?

And what does that suggest about where this "communications revolution" is taking us? When I was in Hong Kong a year and a half ago, it was becoming a cell-phone hell. The official statistics said there was one phone for every two people, but it often felt like two for one. They were everywhere; the table scenes in the splendid food courts in the high rise malls were San Francisco to the second or third power. At a table with four people, two or three might be talking on the phone. You'd see a couple on a date, and one was talking on the phone.

In a way I could understand the fixation. Hong Kong is crowded almost beyond belief. It makes parts of Manhattan feel like Kansas, and I suspect that a cell phone offers an escape, a kind of crack in space. It is an entrance to a realm in which you are the center of attention, the star. Access becomes a status symbol in itself. A lawyer friend of mine there described the new ritual at the start of business meetings. Everyone puts their cell phone on the conference table, next to their legal pad, almost like a gun. My power call against yours, *gweilo* (Chinese for foreigner; literally "ghost"). The smallest ones are the most expensive, and therefore have the most status.

In places like Hong Kong, moreover, most people live in cramped quarters, which means consumption must take less space consuming forms. That's all understandable. To a lesser degree, such considerations apply in places such as Washington and New York.

20 There is something lonely about a wired world. The more 20 plugged in everyone else is the more we feel we have to be there too. But then effect becomes cause. The very thing that pulls us away from live public spaces begins to make those spaces uninhabitable. It is the pollution of the aural commons, the enclosure of public space by

giant telecommunications firms, and the result is to push us all towards private space—if we can afford it.

This is technological Reaganism, a world in which personal desires are all that matters and to hell with everything else. So everything else starts to go to hell. The libertarian dogmatics of the computer crowd thus become self-fulfilling prophecies. But there's this, too. Not only are they saying, "Get out of my face." They are also saying, "I can't stop myself. I'm hooked." It is a communications revolution all right, but one that requires psychologists and anthropologists to understand. Economists just don't get it. They couch these events in the language of Locke and Smith—of rational people seeking a rational self-interest. But in reality it's the old dark stuff: the vagrant passions and attachments of the human heart.

But forgive me. I forgot. This is the longest economic expansion on record we are talking about here so we aren't supposed to get too deep. So I'll just close with a prediction. Secondhand noise is going to become a bigger issue in the next decade than secondhand smoke was in the last. It will be part of the big second wave of environmentalism—the fight against cognitive pollution, the despoiling of the aural and visual commons, whether by cell phones and walkmen or by advertising everywhere.

It's going to be a wrenching battle, but I predict at least one early victory. Quiet cars on Amtrak within five years. Meanwhile, I have my eye on a company in Israel, called NetLine Technologies, that makes small portable devices to block cell phones. Technically, they are illegal, and I doubt that more technology ultimately is the answer. But they do raise a useful question. If some people can use technology to pollute the air we share, why can't other people use technology to clean it up again?

Questions on Meaning

1. How do you feel when you hear other people's cellphone conversations in public spaces? Why?
2. In your view, what is Rowe's strongest argument against cell phones? What is his weakest? Why?

Questions on Rhetorical Strategy and Style

1. Rowe's style contains a casual blend of ease and erudition. His intent is to appeal to an educated audience who is reading for pleasure. For example, he writes, "And there's Dad, pulled back slightly from the table, talking into his cell phone." But he also writes, "I don't discount the significance of cancer." Find several other examples of the two styles.
2. This article presents an extended argument against cellphone use in public. In discussing the prevalence of cell phones on trains, Rowe argues that the rights of cellphone users to talk in public should not prevail over the rights of non-users to have peace and quiet. Write a paragraph expanding Rowe's discussion of the rights of users or non-users.

Writing Assignments

1. Observe people in a public space such as a mall or busy street. Spend an hour taking notes on those who use cell phones. Describe users' appearance, gestures, tones of voice, volume of speaking, and anything else that seems interesting about their use of the phone. Write an essay on who uses cellphones most.
2. Suppose that your state proposed a law restricting cellphone use to private spaces. What problems with this law would you foresee? What benefits? Write a paper about your thoughts on this possibility.

The Sources of Authenticity

Charles Taylor

Charles Taylor (1931–) was born in Montreal and is a graduate of McGill University and Oxford University, where he received a doctorate in philosophy in 1961. He is a Rhodes Scholar and is currently a member of the philosophy department at McGill. He has received many awards, including the Prix Leon-Gerin (1992) in recognition of his contribution to Quebec intellectual life. He is a fellow of both the Royal Society of Canada and the British Academy, and is also a member of the American Academy of Arts and Sciences. His more recent works include Source of Self: The Making of the Modern Identity *(1989) and* The Malaise of Modernity *(1991), from which the following selection is taken. Taylor's primary focus has been on the formation of human identity and in the following essay he explores, in a modern sense, the significance of being in contact with one's own essential nature.*

1   The ethic of authenticity is something relatively new and peculiar to modern culture. Born at the end of the eighteenth century, it builds on earlier forms of individualism, such as the individualism of disengaged rationality, pioneered by Descartes, where the demand is that each person think self-responsibly for him- or herself, or the political individualism of Locke, which sought to make the person and his or her will prior to social obligation. But authenticity also has been in some respects in conflict with these earlier forms. It is a child of the Romantic period, which was critical of disengaged rationality and of an atomism that didn't recognize the ties of community.

One way of describing its development is to see its starting point in the eighteenth-century notion that human beings are endowed with a moral sense, an intuitive feeling for what is right and wrong. The original point of this doctrine was to combat a rival view, that knowing right and wrong was a matter of calculating consequences, in particular those concerned with divine reward and punishment. The notion was that understanding right and wrong was not a matter of dry calculation, but was anchored in our feelings. Morality has, in a sense, a voice within.[1]

The notion of authenticity develops out of a displacement of the moral accent in this idea. On the original view, the inner voice is important because it tells us what is the right thing to do. Being in touch with our moral feelings would matter here, as a means to the end of acting rightly. What I'm calling the displacement of the moral accent comes about when being in touch takes on independent and crucial moral significance. It comes to be something we have to attain to be true and full human beings.

To see what is new in this, we have to see the analogy to earlier moral views, where being in touch with some source—God, say, or the Idea of the Good—was considered essential to full being. Only now the source we have to connect with is deep in us. This is part of the massive subjective turn of modern culture, a new form of inwardness, in which we come to think of ourselves as beings with inner depths. At first, this idea that the source is within doesn't exclude our being related to God or the Ideas; it can be considered our proper way to them. In a sense, it can be seen just as a continuation and intensification of the development inaugurated by Saint Augustine, who saw the road to God as passing through our own reflexive awareness of ourselves.

The first variants of this new view were theistic, or at least pantheist. This is illustrated by the most important philosophical writer who helped to bring about this change, Jean Jacques Rousseau. I think Rousseau is important not because he inaugurated the change; rather I would argue that his great popularity comes in part from his articulating something that was already happening in the culture. Rousseau frequently presents the issue of morality as that of our following a voice of nature within us. This voice is most often drowned out by the passions induced by our dependence on others, of which the key one is "amour propre" or pride. Our moral salvation comes from recovering authentic moral contact with ourselves. Rousseau even gives a name to the intimate contact with oneself, more fundamental than any moral view, that is a source of joy and contentment: "le sentiment de l'existence."[2]

Rousseau also articulated a closely related idea in a most influential way. This is the notion of what I want to call self-determining freedom. It is the idea that I am free when I decide for myself what concerns me, rather than being shaped by external influences. It is a standard of freedom that obviously goes beyond what has been called negative liberty, where I am free to do what I want without interference by others because that is compatible with my being shaped and influenced by society and its laws of conformity. Self-determining freedom demands that I break the hold of all such external impositions, and decide for myself alone.

I mention this here not because it is essential to authenticity. Obviously the two ideals are distinct. But they have developed together, sometimes in the works of the same authors, and their relations have been complex, sometimes at odds, sometimes closely bound together. As a result, they have often been confused, and this has been one of the sources of the deviant forms of authenticity, as I shall argue. I will return to this later.

Self-determining freedom has been an idea of immense power in our political life. In Rousseau's work it takes political form, in the notion of a social contract state founded on a general will, which precisely because it is the form of our common freedom can brook no opposition in the name of freedom. This idea has been one of the intellectual sources of modern totalitarianism, starting, one might argue, with the Jacobins. And although Kant reinterpreted this notion of freedom in purely moral terms, as autonomy, it returns to the political sphere with a vengeance with Hegel and Marx.

But to return to the ideal of authenticity: it becomes crucially important because of a development that occurs after Rousseau and that I associate with Herder—once again its major early articulator rather than its originator. Herder put forward the idea that each of us has an original way of being human. Each person has his or her own "measure" is his way of putting it.[3] This idea has entered very deep into modern consciousness. It is also new. Before the late eighteenth century no one thought that the differences between human beings had this kind of moral significance. There is a certain way of being human that is *my* way. I am called upon to live my life in this way, and not in imitation of anyone else's. But this gives a new importance to being true to myself. If I am not, I miss the point of my life, I miss what being human is for *me*.

10   This is the powerful moral ideal that has come down to us. It   10 accords crucial moral importance to a kind of contact with myself, with my own inner nature, which it sees as in danger of being lost, partly through the pressures towards outward conformity, but also because in taking an instrumental stance to myself, I may have lost the capacity to listen to this inner voice. And then it greatly increases the importance of this self-contact by introducing the principle of originality: each of our voices has something of its own to say. Not only should I not fit my life to the demands of external conformity; I can't even find the model to live by outside myself. I can find it only within.

Being true to myself means being true to my own originality, and that is something only I can articulate and discover. In articulating it, I am also defining myself. I am realizing a potentiality that is properly my own. This is the background understanding to the modern ideal of authenticity, and to the goals of self-fulfilment or self-realization in which it is usually couched. This is the background that gives moral force to the culture of authenticity, including its most degraded, absurd, or trivialized forms. It is what gives sense to the idea of "doing your own thing" or "finding your own fulfilment."

Notes

[1]   The development of this doctrine, at first in the work of Francis Hutcheson, drawing on the writings of the Earl of Shaftesbury, and its adversarial relation to Locke's theory, I have discussed at greater length in *Sources of the Self,* chapter 15.

[2]   "Le sentiment de l'existence dépouillé de toute autre affection est par lui-même un sentiment précieux de contentement et de paix qui suffiroit seul pour rendre cette existence chère el douce à qui sauroit écarter de soi toutes les impressions sensuelles et terrestres quí viennent sans cesse nous en distraire et en troubler ici bas la douceur. Mais la pluspart des hommes agités de passions continuelles connoissent peu cet état et ne l'ayant gouté qu'imparfaitement durant peu d'instans n'en conservent qu'une idée obscure et confuse qui

ne leur en fait pas sentir le charme." Rousseau, *Les Rêveries du Promeneur Solitaire,* Ve Promenade, in *Oeuvre Complètes,* vol. 1 (Paris: Gallimard, 1959), p. 1047.

3 "Jeder Mensch haat ein eigenes Mass, gleichsam eine eigne Stimmung aller seiner sinnlichen Gefühle zu einander." Herder, *Ideen,* vii. I., in *Herders Sämtliche Werke,* vol. XIII, ed. Bernard Suphan, 15 vols. (Berlin: Weidmann, 1877–1913), p. 291.

Questions on Meaning

1. According to Taylor the concept of authenticity is tied to notions of individualism, self-determination, and moral responsibility. How are these concepts connected with each other? Do you accept the notion that "human beings are endowed with a moral sense, an intuitive feeling for what is right and wrong"? Explain your position.

2. This essay discusses the above concepts in a philosophical way that many might find difficult. However, if you were to look around you, you would find more popular and accessible treatments of notions of individualism, such as those found in self-help books. Find some examples of these treatments. Why is the search for the "true self" so important to people?

3. Taylor informs us of Rousseau's idea that humans are free—that is, not "shaped by external influences." Offer examples of how this may or may not be true. Why does Taylor assume that general audiences would be interested in this issue?

Questions on Strategy and Style

1. This selection was first a part of a lecture series broadcast on Canadian Broadcasting Corporation radio. Describe a few of its qualities that bear resemblance to its original format. Think about lectures you've heard at the school you attend. What is the rhetorical purpose of lectures? What academic traditions do they reflect?

2. How does philosophical writing differ from other types of writing? What are the characteristics that make it difficult? Is it necessary for it to be so? Why or why not?

3. How would you capture the logical flow or line of reasoning in Taylor's argument? What sort of reasoning procedure does he follow. Does it fit into a particular format that you recognize?

Writing Assignments

1. In his essay Taylor seems to explain complex terms in relatively accessible fashion. Still, you might better appreciate his essay if you were to do additional background research. Write a brief report on Rousseau's definition of morality and the social contract; on Descartes on dualism; and on Locke on the Self. Reread Taylor with this knowledge in mind. How has this research affected your second reading?

2. Perhaps it is valid to suggest that the Taylor essay has some connection to the so-called nature vs. nurture debate. Write an essay dealing with your thoughts on this issue. To what extent are people endowed with certain universal qualities? How, on the other hand, are people shaped by their surroundings? Does "moral relativism" exist, as many claim?

The Ethic of Compassion
The Dalai Lama

His Holiness the Dalai Lama (1935–) was born a peasant in Taktser, Tibet under the birth name of Lhamo Dhondrub. He is the fourteenth Dalai Lama (spiritual leader of Tibet, reincarnation of the thirteenth Dalai Lama, and an incarnation of the Buddha of Compassion). He lives in Dharamsala, India. He was recognized at age two as the Dalai Lama and was enthroned on February 22, 1940. He completed the Geshe Lharampa Degree (equivalent to a Doctorate of Buddhist Philosophy) in 1959 and became head of Tibet—but was driven out by a Chinese invasion. He has worked on behalf of Tibet from India, asking the United Nations for help and working to bring Buddhist beliefs back to the country. He received the Albert Schweitzer Humanitarian Award (1987); Raoul Wallenberg Congressional Human Rights Award (1989); the Nobel Peace Prize (1989); Franklin D. Roosevelt Freedom Medal (1994); and the Hessian Peace Prize (2005). His books include Kindness, Clarity and Insight *(Snow Lion, 1984);* Compassion and the Individual *(Wisdom Publications, 1991); and* The Power of Compassion *(Harper Collins, 1995).*

Compassion is good when first considered, for it is easy to feel compassion for one who suffers. Compassion is harder to muster for wealthy and powerful people and even harder to feel when true compassion leads to a career change or an even greater life upheaval.

1 We noted earlier that all the world's major religions stress the importance of cultivating love and compassion. In the Buddhist philosophical tradition, different levels of attainment

are described. At a basic level, compassion (*nying je*) is understood mainly in terms of empathy—our ability to enter into and, to some extent, share others' suffering. But Buddhist—and perhaps others—believe that this can be developed to such a degree that not only does our compassion arise without any effort, but it is unconditional, undifferentiated, and universal in scope. A feeling of intimacy toward all other sentient beings, including of course those who would harm us, is generated, which is likened in the literature to the love a mother has for her only child.

But this sense of equanimity toward all others is not seen as an end in itself. Rather, it is seen as the springboard to a love still greater. Because our capacity for empathy is innate, and because the ability to reason is also an innate faculty, compassion shares the characteristics of consciousness itself. The potential we have to develop it is therefore stable and continuous. It is not a resource which can be used up—as water is used up when we boil it. And though it can be described in terms of activity, it is not like a physical activity which we train for, like jumping, where once we reach a certain height we can go no further. On the contrary, when we enhance our sensitivity toward others' suffering through deliberately opening ourselves up to it, it is believed that we can gradually extend out compassion to the point where the individual feels so moved by even the subtlest suffering of others that they come to have an over-whelming sense of responsibility toward those others. This causes the one who is compassionate to dedicate themselves entirely to helping others overcome both their suffering and the causes of their suffering. In Tibetan, this ultimate level of attainment is called *nying je chenmo,* literally "great compassion."

Now I am not suggesting that each individual must attain these advanced states of spiritual development in order to lead an ethically wholesome life. I have described *nying je chenmo* not because it is a precondition of ethical conduct but rather because I believe that pushing the logic of compassion to the highest level can act as a powerful inspiration. If we can just keep the aspiration to develop *nying je chenmo,* or great compassion, as an ideal, it will naturally have a significant impact on our outlook. Based on the simple recognition that, just as I do, so do all others desire to be happy and not to suffer, it will serve as a constant reminder against selfishness and partiality. It will remind us that there is little to be gained from being kind and generous because we hope to win something in return. It will remind us that actions motivated by the desire to create a good name for our-selves are still selfish, however much they may appear to be acts of kindness. It will also remind us that there is nothing exceptional about acts of charity toward those we already feel close to. And it will help us to recognize that the bias we naturally feel toward our families and friends is actually a highly unreliable thing on which to base ethi-cal conduct. If we reserve ethical conduct for those whom we feel close to, the danger is that we will neglect our responsibilities toward those outside this circle.

Why is this? So long as the individuals in question continue to meet our expectations, all is well. But should they fail to do so, some-one we consider a dear friend one day can become our sworn enemy the next. As we saw earlier, we have a tendency to react badly to all who threaten fulfillment of our cherished desires, though they may be our closest relations. For this reason, compassion and mutual respect offer a much more solid basis for our relations with others. This is also true of partnerships. If our love for someone is based largely on attraction, whether it be their looks or some other superficial charac-teristic, our feelings for that person are liable, over time, to evaporate. When they lose the quality we found alluring, or when we find our-selves no longer satisfied by it, the situation can change completely, this despite their being the same person. This is why relationships based purely on attraction are almost always unstable. On the other hand, when we begin to perfect our compassion, neither the other's appearance nor their behavior affects our underlying attitude.

Consider, too, that habitually our feelings toward others depend very much on their circumstances. Most people, when they see some-one who is handicapped, feel sympathetic toward that person. But then when they see others who are wealthier, or better educated, or better placed socially, they immediately feel envious and competitive toward them. Our negative feelings prevent us from seeing the same-ness of ourselves and all others. We forget that just like us, whether fortunate or unfortunate, distant or near, they desire to be happy and not to suffer.

The struggle is thus to overcome these feelings of partiality. Cer-tainly, developing genuine compassion for our loved ones is the obvi-ous and appropriate place to start. The impact our actions have on our close ones will generally be much greater than on others, and therefore our responsibilities toward them are greater. Yet we need to recognize that, ultimately, there are no grounds for discriminating in their favor. In this sense, we are all in the same position as a doctor confronted by ten patients suffering the same serious illness. They are each equally deserving of treatment. The reader should not suppose that what is being advocated here is a state of detached indifference, however. The further essential challenge, as we begin to extend our compassion toward all others, is to maintain the same level of intimacy as we feel toward those closest to us. In other words, what is being suggested is that we need to strive for even-handedness in our approach toward all others, a level ground into which we can plant the seed of *nying je chenmo,* of great love and compassion.

If we can begin to relate to others on the basis of such equanimity, our compassion will not depend on the fact that so and so is my husband, my wife, my relative, my friend. Rather, a feeling of closeness toward all others can be developed based on the simple recognition that, just like myself, all wish to be happy and to avoid suffering. In other words, we will start to relate to others on the basis of their sentient nature. Again, we can think of this in terms of an ideal, one which it is immensely difficult to attain. But, for myself, I find it one which is profoundly inspiring and helpful.

Let us now consider the role of compassionate love and kindheartedness in our daily lives. Does the ideal of developing it to the point where it is unconditional mean that we must abandon our own interests entirely? Not at all. In fact, it is the best way of serving them—indeed, it could even be said to constitute the wisest course for fulfilling self-interest. For if it is correct that those qualities such as love, patience, tolerance, and forgiveness are what happiness consists in, and if it is also correct that *nying je,* or compassion, as I have defined it, is both the source and the fruit of these qualities, then the more we are compassionate, the more we provide for our own happiness. Thus, any idea that concern for others, though a noble quality, is a matter for our private lives only, is simply short-sighted. Compassion belongs to every sphere of activity, including, of course, the workplace.

Here, though, I must acknowledge the existence of a perception—shared by many, it seems—that compassion is, if not actually an impediment, at least irrelevant to professional life. Personally, I would argue that not only is it relevant, but that when compassion is lacking, our activities are in danger of becoming destructive. This is because when we ignore the question of the impact our actions have on others' well-being, inevitably we end up hurting them. The ethic of compassion helps provide the necessary foundation and motivation for both restraint and the cultivation of virtue. When we begin to develop a genuine appreciation of the value of compassion, our outlook on others begins automatically to change. This alone can serve as a powerful influence on the conduct of our lives. When, for example, the temptation to deceive others arises, our compassion for them will prevent us from entertaining the idea. And when we realize that our work itself is in danger of being exploited to the detriment of others, compassion will cause us to disengage from it. So to take an imaginary case of a scientist whose research seems likely to be a source of suffering, they will recognize this and act accordingly, even if this means abandoning the project.

10   I do not deny that genuine problems can arise when we dedicate 10 ourselves to the ideal of compassion. In the case of a scientist who felt unable to continue in the direction their work was taking them, this could have profound consequences both for themselves and for their families. Likewise, those engaged in the caring professions—in medicine, counseling, social work, and so on—or even those looking after someone at home may sometimes become so exhausted by their duties that they feel overwhelmed. Constant exposure to suffering, coupled occasionally with a feeling of being taken for granted, can induce feelings of helplessness and even despair. Or it can happen that individuals may find themselves performing outwardly generous actions merely for the sake of it—simply going through the motions, as it were. Of course this is better than nothing. But when left unchecked, this can lead to insensitivity toward others' suffering. If this starts to happen, it is best to disengage for a short while and make a deliberate effort to reawaken that sensitivity. In this it can be helpful to remember that despair is never a solution. It is, rather, the ultimate failure. Therefore, as the Tibetan expression has it, even if the rope breaks nine times, we must splice it back together a tenth time. In this way, even if ultimately we do fail, at least there will be no feelings of regret. And when we combine this insight with a clear appreciation of our potential to benefit others, we find that we can begin to restore our hope and confidence.

Some people may object to this ideal on the grounds that by entering into others' suffering, we bring suffering on ourselves. To an extent, this is true. But I suggest that there is an important qualitative distinction to be made between experiencing one's own suffering and experiencing suffering in the course of sharing in others'. In the case of one's own suffering, given that it is involuntary, there is a sense of oppression: it seems to come from outside us. By contrast, sharing in someone else's suffering must at some level involve a degree of voluntariness, which itself is indicative of a certain inner strength. For this reason, the disturbance it may cause is considerably less likely to paralyze us than our own suffering.

Of course, even as an ideal, the notion of developing unconditional compassion is daunting. Most people, including myself, must struggle even to reach the point where putting others' interests on a par with our own becomes easy. We should not allow this to put us off, however. And while undoubtedly there will be obstacles on the way to developing a genuinely warm heart, there is the deep consolation of knowing that in doing so we are creating the conditions for our own happiness. As I mentioned earlier, the more we truly desire to benefit others, the greater the strength and confidence we develop and the greater the peace and happiness we experience. If this still seems unlikely, it is worth asking ourselves how else we are to do so. With violence and aggression? Of course not. With money? Perhaps up to a point, but no further. But with love, by sharing in others' suffering, by recognizing ourselves clearly in all others—especially those who are disadvantaged and those whose rights are not respected—by helping them to, be happy: yes. Through love, through kindness, through compassion we establish understanding between ourselves and others. This is how we forge unity and harmony.

Compassion and love are not mere luxuries. As the source both of inner and external peace, they are fundamental to the continued survival of our species. On the one hand, they constitute non-violence in action. On the other, they are the source of all spiritual qualities: of forgiveness, tolerance, and all the virtues. Moreover, they are the very thing that gives meaning to our activities and makes them constructive. There is nothing amazing about being highly educated; there is nothing amazing about being rich. Only when the individual has a warm heart do these attributes become worthwhile.

So to those who say that the Dalai Lama is being unrealistic in advocating this ideal of unconditional love, I urge them to experiment with it nonetheless. They will discover that when we reach beyond the confines of narrow self-interest, our hearts become filled with strength. Peace and joy become our constant companion. It breaks down barriers of every kind and in the end destroys the notion of my interest as independent from others' interest. But most important, so far as ethics is concerned, where love of one's neighbor, affection, kindness, and compassion live, we find that ethical conduct is automatic. Ethically wholesome actions arise naturally in the context of compassion.

Questions on Meaning

1. Compassion means to empathize with another, to feel that person's joy, pain, and hope. Why does the author say that feeling compassion for the disabled or the poor is easy? Why is it hard to feel sympathy for those we envy?
2. What would happen to our ordinary, selfish lives if we were to start feeling real compassion? Would we be able to use the environment and the rest of the world as we do now? What would we have to change?
3. What does the individual gain by feeling compassion? Is the kind of peace and love that are described in this essay really what people want? Why do most of us live lives that are aimed at making money and winning, rather than loving?

Questions on Rhetorical Strategy and Style

1. The tone of this essay is very gentle and kind, but the message is quite tough. How does the author warn the reader in the introduction that the essay is going to be demanding and maybe a bit disturbing?
2. The essay moves to a cause and effect structure: If one feels true compassion, the feeling may cause one to have to change one's life. The feeling, though a good one, may lead to uncomfortable results. How does this causality affect the reader of the essay? Is a reader likely to change behavior in light of this cause and effect explanation?
3. The end of the essay promises that great good can come from feeling compassion. How does the writer hope to persuade the reader that these benefits are worthwhile? Does this ending promise better things for the world if many readers are persuaded? Is it even possible?

Writing Assignments

1. A wise person once said that we should feel compassion rather than guilt, for we will act from compassion, but we will merely suffer from guilt. Think of someone you know whom you consider compassionate. Write about what that person does with life. What kind of work does the person do? What kind of entertainment and leisure activities does that person pursue?

2. Write about a world leader whom you consider compassionate. Show how this feeling is displayed in the person's actions. What would happen to world politics if everyone acted with compassion?

3. Consider a world conflict, either one occurring now or one in history. Write about how the events could be or would have been different had the parties shown more compassion and less aggression.

Luck

Mark Twain

Mark Twain is the pen name of Samuel Clemens (1835–1910), who grew up in Hannibal, Missouri, along the Mississippi River. Twain became a riverboat pilot for a few years in his mid-twenties, moving then into newspaper work and writing. The phrase "mark twain" was called out by a boatman on the riverboat who measured the water depth through which the boat was passing: mark twain meant the water was two fathoms deep, safe for passage. Twain's books include Innocents Abroad *(1869), a book of humorous travel sketches;* Roughing It *(1872), about a period he spent prospecting in the West; and the two well-known novels* The Adventures of Tom Sawyer *(1876) and* The Adventures of Huckleberry Finn *(1884).*

[Note—This is not a fancy sketch. I got it from a clergyman who was an instructor at Woolwich forty years ago, and who vouched for its truth.—M.T.]

1   It was at a banquet in London in honor of one of the two or three conspicuously illustrious English military names of this generation. For reasons which will presently appear, I will withhold his real name and titles, and call him Lieutenant General Lord Arthur Scoresby, V. C., K. C. B., etc., etc., etc. What a fascination there is in a renowned name! There sat the man, in actual flesh, whom I had heard of so many thousands of times since that day, thirty years before, when his name shot suddenly to the zenith from a Crimean battlefield, to remain forever celebrated. It was food and drink to me to look, and look, and look at that demigod; scanning, searching, not-

ing: the quietness, the reserve, the noble gravity of his countenance; the simple honesty that expressed itself all over him; the sweet unconsciousness of his greatness—unconsciousness of the hundreds of admiring eyes fastened upon him, unconsciousness of the deep, loving, sincere worship welling out of the breasts of those people and flowing toward him.

The clergyman at my left was an old acquaintance of mine—clergyman now, but had spent the first half of his life in the camp and field, and as an instructor in the military school at Woolwich. Just at the moment I have been talking about, a veiled and singular light glimmered in his eyes, and he leaned down and muttered confidentially to me—indicating the hero of the banquet with a gesture:

"Privately—he's an absolute fool."

This verdict was a great surprise to me. If its subject had been Napoleon, or Socrates, or Solomon, my astonishment could not have been greater. Two things I was well aware of: that the Reverend was a man of strict veracity, and that his judgment of men was good. Therefore I knew, beyond doubt or question, that the world was mistaken about this hero: he *was* a fool. So I meant to find out, at a convenient moment, how the Reverend, all solitary and alone, had discovered the secret.

Some days later the opportunity came, and this is what the Reverend told me.

About forty years ago I was an instructor in the military academy at Woolwich. I was present in one of the sections when young Scoresby underwent his preliminary examination. I was touched to the quick with pity; for the rest of the class answered up brightly and handsomely, while he—why, dear me, he didn't know *anything*, so to speak. He was evidently good, and sweet, and lovable, and guileless; and so it was exceedingly painful to see him stand there, as serene as a graven image, and deliver himself of answers which were veritably miraculous for stupidity and ignorance. All the compassion in me was aroused in his behalf. I said to myself, when he comes to be examined again, he will be flung over, of course; so it will be simply a harmless act of charity to ease his fall as much as I can. I took him aside, and found that he knew a little of Caesar's history; and as he didn't know anything else, I went to work and drilled him like a galley slave on a certain line of stock questions concerning Caesar which I knew would be used. If you'll believe me, he went through with flying colors on examination day! He went through on that purely superficial "cram," and got compliments too, while others, who knew a thousand times more than he, got plucked. By some strangely lucky accident—an accident not likely to happen twice in a century—he was asked no question outside of the narrow limits of his drill.

It was stupefying. Well, all through his course I stood by him, with something of the sentiment which a mother feels for a crippled child; and he always saved himself—just by miracle, apparently.

Now of course the thing that would expose him and kill him at last was mathematics. I resolved to make his death as easy as I could; so I drilled him and crammed him, and crammed him and drilled him, just on the line of questions which the examiners would be most likely to use, and then launching him on his fate. Well, sir, try to conceive of the result: to my consternation, he took the first prize! And with it he got a perfect ovation in the way of compliments.

Sleep? There was no more sleep for me for a week. My conscience tortured me day and night. What I had done I had done purely through charity, and only to ease the poor youth's fall—I never had dreamed of any such preposterous result as the thing that had happened. I felt as guilty and miserable as the creator of Frankenstein. Here was a woodenhead whom I had put in the way of glittering promotions and prodigious responsibilities, and but one thing could happen: he and his responsibilities would all go to ruin together at the first opportunity.

10 The Crimean war had just broken out. Of course there had to be 10
a war, I said to myself: we couldn't have peace and give this donkey a chance to die before he is found out. I waited for the earthquake. It came. And it made me reel when it did come. He was actually gazetted to a captaincy in a marching regiment! Better men grow old and gray in the service before they climb to a sublimity like that. And who could ever have foreseen that they would go and put such a load of responsibility on such green and inadequate shoulders? I could just barely have stood it if they had made him a cornet; but a captain— think of it! I thought my hair would turn white.

Consider what I did—I who so loved repose and inaction. I said to myself, I am responsible to the country for this, and I must go along with him and protect the country against him as far as I can. So I took my poor little capital that I had saved up through years of work and grinding economy, and went with a sigh and bought a cornetcy in his regiment, and away we went to the field.

And there—oh dear, it was awful. Blunders? Why, he never did anything *but* blunder. But, you see, nobody was in the fellow's secret—everybody had him focused wrong, and necessarily misinterpreted his performance every time—consequently they took his idiotic blunders for inspirations of genius; they did, honestly! His mildest blunders were enough to make a man in his right mind cry; and they did make me cry—and rage and rave too, privately. And the thing that kept me always in a sweat of apprehension was the fact that every fresh blunder he made increased the luster of his reputation! I kept saying to myself, he'll get so high, that when discovery does finally come, it will be like the sun falling out of the sky.

He went right along up, from grade to grade, over the dead bodies of his superiors, until at last, in the hottest moment of the battle of——down went our colonel, and my heart jumped into my mouth, for Scoresby was next in rank! Now for it, said I; we'll all land in Sheol in ten minutes, sure.

The battle was awfully hot; the allies were steadily giving way all over the field. Our regiment occupied a position that was vital; a blunder now must be destruction. At this crucial moment, what does this immortal fool do but detach the regiment from its place and order a charge over a neighboring hill where there wasn't a suggestion of an enemy! "There you go!" I said to myself; "this *is* the end at last."

And away we did go, and were over the shoulder of the hill before the insane movement could be discovered and stopped. And what did we find? An entire and unsuspected Russian army in reserve! And what happened? We were eaten up? That is necessarily what would have happened in ninety-nine cases out of a hundred. But no, those Russians argued that no single regiment would come browsing around there at such a time. It must be the entire English army, and that the sly Russian game was detected and blocked; so they turned tail, and away they went, pell-mell, over the hill and down into the field, in wild confusion, and we after them; they themselves broke the solid Russian center in the field, and tore through, and in no time there was the most tremendous rout you ever saw, and the defeat of the allies was turned into a sweeping and splendid victory! Marshal Canrobert looked on, dizzy with astonishment, admiration, and delight; and sent

15

right off for Scoresby, and hugged him, and decorated him on the field, in presence of all the armies!

And what was Scoresby's blunder that time? Merely the mistaking his right hand for his left—that was all. An order had come to him to fall back and support our right; and instead, he fell *forward* and went over the hill to the left. But the name he won that day as a marvelous military genius filled the world with his glory, and that glory will never fade while history books last.

He is just as good and sweet and lovable and unpretending as a man can be, but he doesn't know enough to come in when it rains. Now that is absolutely true. He is the supremest ass in the universe; and until half an hour ago nobody knew it but himself and me. He has been pursued, day by day and year by year, by a most phenomenal and astonishing luckiness. He has been a shining soldier in all our wars for a generation; he has littered his whole military life with blunders, and yet has never committed one that didn't make him a knight or a baronet or a lord or something. Look at his breast; why, he is just clothed in domestic and foreign decorations. Well, sir, every one of them is the record of some shouting stupidity or other; and taken together, they are proof that the very best thing in all this world that can befall a man is to be born lucky. I say again, as I said at the banquet, Scoresby's an absolute fool.

Questions on Meaning

1. The theme of this story might be stated sarcastically as "No good deed goes unpunished." List the ways in which the Reverend is punished for his good deed.
2. If you have read Tom Sawyer or Huckleberry Finn, you may find Twain's language unexpectedly formal and complex. Why is his language appropriate to the characters? Give examples to support your answer.

Questions on Rhetorical Strategy and Style

1. What is gained by Twain's putting the story of the soldier within the story of the narrator's conversation with the Reverend? (Hint: how does it affect credibility?)
2. Reread the introductory paragraph. In what ways does Twain use hyperbole (exaggeration and overstatement)? What is the effect of the hyperbole when you read the Reverend's narrative?

Writing Assignments

1. Have a little fun telling the story of someone you know who is incompetent but lucky.
2. Narrate a series of events involving you or someone you know when punishment was the result of doing a good deed.

The Perils of Indifference

Elie Wiesel

Elie Wiesel (1928–) was born in the village of Sighet in Romania to a religious Jewish family. In 1944 his life changed when his family was deported by the Nazis to Auschwitz, where his father died in 1945. After the camp was liberated by the Allied forces, Wiesel spent a few years in a French orphanage. In 1948 he entered the Sorbonne and began writing for the newspaper L'arche. *In 1954 he made the decision to write about the Holocaust, which led to the publication of his first book,* Night *(1958), followed by* Jews of Silence *(1966). In 1963 he became a U.S. citizen. In 1978 he was appointed chair of the Presidential Commission on the Holocaust, which led to the American memorial monument to the victims of Nazi oppression during World War II. In 1985 Wiesel received the Congressional Gold Medal of Achievement. The following year he received the Nobel Peace Prize. He has written numerous books dealing with the Holocaust, hatred, racism, genocide, and faith, including* Sages and Dreamers *(1991), and his memoir* All Rivers Run to the Sea *(1995). In the following speech he addresses Congress and the President about the need for vigilance in the face of evil.*

1   Mr. President, Mrs. Clinton, members of Congress, Ambassador Holbrooke, Excellencies, friends:
Fifty-four years ago to the day, a young Jewish boy from a small town in the Carpathian Mountains woke up, not far from Goethe's

beloved Weimar, in a place of eternal infamy called Buchenwald. He was finally free, but there was no joy in his heart. He thought there never would be again. Liberated a day earlier by American soldiers, he remembers their rage at what they saw. And even if he lives to be a very old man, he will always be grateful to them for that rage, and also for their compassion. Though he did not understand their language, their eyes told him what he needed to know—that they, too, would remember, and bear witness.

And now, I stand before you, Mr. President—Commander-in-Chief of the army that freed me, and tens of thousands of others—and I am filled with a profound and abiding gratitude to the American people. Gratitude is a word that I cherish. Gratitude is what defines the humanity of the human being. And I am grateful to you, Hillary, or Mrs. Clinton, for what you said, and for what you are doing for children in the world, for the homeless, for the victims of injustice, the victims of destiny and society. And I thank all of you for being here.

We are on the threshold of a new century, a new millennium. What will the legacy of this vanishing century be? How will it be remembered in the new millennium? Surely it will be judged, and judged severely, in both moral and metaphysical terms. These failures have cast a dark shadow over humanity: two World Wars, countless civil wars, the senseless chain of assassinations (Gandhi, the Kennedys, Martin Luther King, Sadat, Rabin), bloodbaths in Cambodia and Nigeria, India and Pakistan, Ireland and Rwanda, Eritrea and Ethiopia, Sarajevo and Kosovo; the inhumanity in the gulag and the tragedy of Hiroshima. And, on a different level, of course, Auschwitz and Treblinka. So much violence; so much indifference.

5   What is indifference? Etymologically, the word means "no difference." A strange and unnatural state in which the lines blur between light and darkness, dusk and dawn, crime and punishment, cruelty and compassion, good and evil. What are its courses and inescapable consequences? Is it a philosophy? Is there a philosophy of indifference conceivable? Can one possibly view indifference as a virtue? Is it necessary at times to practice it simply to keep one's sanity, live normally, enjoy a fine meal and a glass of wine, as the world around us experiences harrowing upheavals?

Of course, indifference can be tempting—more than that, seductive. It is so much easier to look away from victims. It is so much easier to avoid such rude interruptions to our work, our dreams, our hopes.

It is, after all, awkward, troublesome, to be involved in another person's pain and despair. Yet, for the person who is indifferent, his or her neighbor are of no consequence. And, therefore, their lives are meaningless. Their hidden or even visible anguish is of no interest. Indifference reduces the Other to an abstraction.

Over there, behind the black gates of Auschwitz, the most tragic of all prisoners were the "Muselmanner," as they were called. Wrapped in their torn blankets, they would sit or lie on the ground, staring vacantly into space, unaware of who or where they were—strangers to their surroundings. They no longer felt pain, hunger, thirst. They feared nothing. They felt nothing. They were dead and did not know it.

Rooted in our tradition, some of us felt that to be abandoned by humanity then was not the ultimate. We felt that to be abandoned by God was worse than to be punished by Him. Better an unjust God than an indifferent one. For us to be ignored by God was a harsher punishment than to be a victim of His anger. Man can live far from God—not outside God. God is wherever we are. Even in suffering? Even in suffering.

In a way, to be indifferent to that suffering is what makes the human being inhuman. Indifference, after all, is more dangerous than anger and hatred. Anger can at times be creative. One writes a great poem, a great symphony. One does something special for the sake of humanity because one is angry at the injustice that one witnesses. But indifference is never creative. Even hatred at times may elicit a response. You fight it. You denounce it. You disarm it.

10   Indifference elicits no response. Indifference is not a response. Indifference is not a beginning; it is an end. And, therefore, indifference is always the friend of the enemy, for it benefits the aggressor—never his victim, whose pain is magnified when he or she feels forgotten. The political prisoner in his cell, the hungry children, the homeless refugees—not to respond to their plight, not to relieve their solitude by offering them a spark of hope is to exile them from human memory. And in denying their humanity, we betray our own.

Indifference, then, is not only a sin, it is a punishment.

And this is one of the most important lessons of this outgoing century's wide-ranging experiments in good and evil.

In the place that I come from, society was composed of three simple categories: the killers, the victims, and the bystanders. During the darkest of times, inside the ghettoes and death camps—and I'm glad that Mrs. Clinton mentioned that we are now commemorating that event, that period, that we are now in the Days of Remembrance—but then, we felt abandoned, forgotten. All of us did.

And our only miserable consolation was that we believed that Auschwitz and Treblinka were closely guarded secrets; that the leaders of the free world did not know what was going on behind those black gates and barbed wire; that they had no knowledge of the war against the Jews that Hitler's armies and their accomplices waged as part of the war against the Allies. If they knew, we thought, surely those leaders would have moved heaven and earth to intervene. They would have spoken out with great outrage and conviction. They would have bombed the railways leading to Birkenau, just the railways, just once.

15 And now we knew, we learned, we discovered that the Pentagon 15
knew, the State Department knew. And the illustrious occupant of the White House then, who was a great leader—and I say it with some anguish and pain, because, today is exactly 54 years marking his death—Franklin Delano Roosevelt died on April the 12th, 1945. So he is very much present to me and to us. No doubt, he was a great leader. He mobilized the American people and the world, going into battle, bringing hundreds and thousands of valiant and brave soldiers in America to fight fascism, to fight dictatorship, to fight Hitler. And so many of the young people fell in battle. And, nevertheless, his image in Jewish history—I must say it—his image in Jewish history is flawed.

The depressing tale of the *St. Louis* is a case in point. Sixty years ago, its human cargo—nearly 1,000 Jews—was turned back to Nazi Germany. And that happened after the Kristallnacht, after the first state sponsored pogrom, with hundreds of Jewish shops destroyed, synagogues burned, thousands of people put in concentration camps. And that ship, which was already in the shores of the United States, was sent back. I don't understand. Roosevelt was a good man, with a heart. He understood those who needed help. Why didn't he allow these refugees to disembark? A thousand people—in America, the great country, the greatest democracy, the most generous of all new nations in modern history. What happened? I don't understand. Why the indifference, on the highest level, to the suffering of the victims?

But then, there were human beings who were sensitive to our tragedy. Those non-Jews, those Christians, that we call the "Righteous Gentiles," whose selfless acts of heroism saved the honor of their faith. Why were they so few? Why was there a greater effort to save SS murderers after the war than to save their victims during the war? Why did some of America's largest corporations continue to do business with Hitler's Germany until 1942? It has been suggested, and it was documented, that the Wehrmacht could not have conducted its invasion of France without oil obtained from American sources. How is one to explain their indifference?

And yet, my friends, good things have also happened in this traumatic century: the defeat of Nazism, the collapse of communism, the rebirth of Israel on its ancestral soil, the demise of apartheid, Israel's peace treaty with Egypt, the peace accord in Ireland. And let us remember the meeting, filled with drama and emotion, between Rabin and Arafat that you, Mr. President, convened in this very place. I was here and I will never forget it.

And then, of course, the joint decision of the United States and NATO to intervene in Kosovo and save those victims, those refugees, those who were uprooted by a man, whom I believe that because of his crimes, should be charged with crimes against humanity.

20 But this time, the world was not silent. This time, we do respond. 20
This time, we intervene.

Does it mean that we have learned from the past? Does it mean that society has changed? Has the human being become less indifferent and more human? Have we really learned from our experiences? Are we less insensitive to the plight of victims of ethnic cleansing and other forms of injustices in places near and far? Is today's justified intervention in Kosovo, led by you, Mr. President, a lasting warning that never again will the deportation, the terrorization of children and their parents, be allowed anywhere in the world? Will it discourage other dictators in other lands to do the same?

What about the children? Oh, we see them on television, we read about them in the papers, and we do so with a broken heart. Their fate is always the most tragic, inevitably. When adults wage war, children perish. We see their faces, their eyes. Do we hear their pleas? Do we feel their pain, their agony? Every minute one of them dies of disease, violence, famine.

Some of them—so many of them—could be saved.

And so, once again, I think of the young Jewish boy from the Carpathian Mountains. He has accompanied the old man I have become throughout these years of quest and struggle. And together we walk towards the new millennium, carried by profound fear and extraordinary hope.

Questions on Meaning

1. Wiesel defines indifference as a "strange and unnatural state." What is your definition? How can indifference be unnatural?

2. What does the author mean by "Better an unjust God than an indifferent one"? How does this relate to the way various theologies explanation why bad things happen to good people?

3. How aware were you that the United States knew about the concentration camps? Explain what you understand about that time in history.

Questions on Rhetorical Strategy and Style

1. How does the tone of Wiesel's speech acknowledge or account for the significance of the day? Why does he open with a personal recollection?

2. What is the rhetorical purpose of referring to the "new millennium [and] the legacy of this vanishing century"? What is the metaphoric significance of "vanishing" in this context?

3. The speech essentially offers an extended definition of indifference. Describe how that definition develops over the course of the occasion.

Writing Assignments

1. Wiesel refers to more recent examples of genocide, such as in Rwanda and Kosovo. Write an essay explaining what occurred in these places and why.

2. Toward the end of his speech, Wiesel asks whether we have learned from the past. "Has the human being become less indifferent and more human?" Write an essay in which you respond to this question. What is your answer?

College Pressures

William Zinsser

William Zinsser (1922–) was born in New York City. A graduate of Princeton University (1944), Zinsser has worked as a feature and editorial writer, drama editor, and film critic for The New York Herald Tribune; *a columnist for* Life, Look, *and* The New York Times; *an editor for the Book-of-the-Month Club; and an English instructor at Yale University. Zinsser's books include* Pop Goes America *(1963),* On Writing Well: An Informal Guide to Writing Nonfiction *(1976),* Writing With a Word Processor *(1983),* Writing to Learn *(1988),* Willie and Dwike *(1984), and* Spring Training *(1989). In the essay that follows, published in* Blair and Ketchum's Country Journal *magazine in 1979, Zinsser describes the pressures experienced by college students in the late 1970s that make them rigidly goal-driven and unable to explore.*

Dear Carlos: I desperately need a dean's excuse for my chem midterm which will begin in about 1 hour. All I can say is that I totally blew it this week. I've fallen incredibly, inconceivably behind.

Carlos: Help! I'm anxious to hear from you. I'll be in my room and won't leave it until I hear from you. Tomorrow is the last day for . . .

Carlos: I left town because I started bugging out again. I stayed up all night to finish a take-home make-up exam & am typing it to hand in on the 10th. It was due on the 5th. P.S. I'm going to the dentist. Pain is pretty bad.

Carlos: Probably by Friday I'll be able to get back to my studies. Right now I'm going to take a long walk. This whole thing has taken a lot out of me.

Carlos: I'm really up the proverbial creek. The problem is I really bombed the history final. Since I need that course for my major I . . .

Carlos: Here follows a tale of woe. I went home this weekend, had to help my Mom, & caught a fever so didn't have much time to study. My professor . . .

Carlos: Aargh! Trouble. Nothing original but everything's piling up at once. To be brief, my job interview . . .

Hey Carlos, good news! I've got mononucleosis.

1   Who are these wretched supplicants, scribbling notes so laden with anxiety, seeking such miracles of postponement and balm? They are men and women who belong to Branford College, one of the twelve residential colleges at Yale University, and the messages are just a few of the hundreds that they left for their dean, Carlos Hortas— often slipped under his door at 4 A.M.—last year.

But students like the ones who wrote those notes can also be found on campuses from coast to coast—especially in New England and at many other private colleges across the country that have high academic standards and highly motivated students. Nobody could doubt that the notes are real. In their urgency and their gallows humor they are authentic voices of a generation that is panicky to succeed.

My own connection with the message writers is that I am master of Branford College. I live in its Gothic quadrangle and know the students well. (We have 485 of them.) I am privy to their hopes and fears—and also to their stereo music and their piercing cries in the dead of night ("Does anybody *ca-a-are?*"). If they went to Carlos to ask how to get through tomorrow, they come to me to ask how to get through the rest of their lives.

Mainly I try to remind them that the road ahead is a long one and that it will have more unexpected turns than they think. There will be plenty of time to change jobs, change careers, change whole attitudes and approaches. They don't want to hear such liberating news. They want a map—right now—that they can follow unswervingly to career security, financial security, Social Security and, presumably, a prepaid grave.

5   What I wish for all students is some release from the clammy grip of the future. I wish them a chance to savor each segment of their

education as an experience in itself and not as a grim preparation for the next step. I wish them the right to experiment, to trip and fall, to learn that defeat is as instructive as victory and is not the end of the world.

My wish, of course, is naïve. One of the few rights that America does not proclaim is the right to fail. Achievement is the national god, venerated in our media—the million-dollar athlete, the wealthy executive—and glorified in our praise of possessions. In the presence of such a potent state religion, the young are growing up old.

I see four kinds of pressure working on college students today: economic pressure, parental pressure, peer pressure, and self-induced pressure. It is easy to look around for villains—to blame the colleges for charging too much money, the professors for assigning too much work, the parents for pushing their children too far, the students for driving themselves too hard. But there are no villains; only victims.

"In the late 1960s," one dean told me, "the typical question that I got from students was 'Why is there so much suffering in the world?' or 'How can I make a contribution?' Today it's 'Do you think it would look better for getting into law school if I did a double major in history and political science, or just majored in one of them?' " Many other deans confirmed this pattern. One said: "They're trying to find an edge—the intangible something that will look better on paper if two students are about equal."

Note the emphasis on looking better. The transcript has become a sacred document, the passport to security. How one appears on paper is more important than how one appears in person. *A* is for Admirable and *B* is for Borderline, even though, in Yale's official system of grading, *A* means "excellent" and *B* means "very good." Today, looking very good is no longer good enough, especially for students who hope to go on to law school or medical school. They know that entrance into the better schools will be an entrance into the better law firms and better medical practices where they will make a lot of money. They also know that the odds are harsh. Yale Law School, for instance, matriculates 170 students from an applicant pool of 3,700; Harvard enrolls 550 from a pool of 7,000.

10 It's all very well for those of us who write letters of recommendation for our students to stress the qualities of humanity that will make them good lawyers or doctors. And it's nice to think that admission officers are really reading our letters and looking for the extra dimension of commitment or concern. Still, it would be hard for a student not to

visualize these officers shuffling so many transcripts studded with *As* that they regard a *B* as positively shameful.

The pressure is almost as heavy on students who just want to graduate and get a job. Long gone are the days of the "gentleman's C," when students journeyed through college with a certain relaxation, sampling a wide variety of courses—music, art, philosophy, classics, anthropology, poetry, religion—that would send them out as liberally educated men and women. If I were an employer I would rather employ graduates who have this range and curiosity than those who narrowly pursued safe subjects and high grades. I know countless students whose inquiring minds exhilarate me. I like to hear the play of their ideas. I don't know if they are getting *As* or *Cs*, and I don't care. I also like them as people. The country needs them, and they will find satisfying jobs. I tell them to relax. They can't.

Nor can I blame them. They live in a brutal economy. Tuition, room, and board at most private colleges now comes to at least $7,000, not counting books and fees. This might seem to suggest that the colleges are getting rich. But they are equally battered by inflation. Tuition covers only 60 percent of what it costs to educate a student, and ordinarily the remainder comes from what colleges receive in endowments, grants, and gifts. Now the remainder keeps being swallowed by the cruel costs—higher every year—of just opening the doors. Heating oil is up. Insurance is up. Postage is up. Health-premium costs are up. Everything is up. Deficits are up. We are witnessing in America the creation of a brotherhood of paupers—colleges, parents, and students, joined by the common bond of debt.

Today it is not unusual for a student, even if he works part time at college and full time during the summer, to accrue $5,000 in loans after four years—loans that he must start to repay within one year after graduation. Exhorted at commencement to go forth into the world, he is already behind as he goes forth. How could he not feel under pressure throughout college to prepare for this day of reckoning? I have used "he," incidentally, only for brevity. Women at Yale are under no less pressure to justify their expensive education to themselves, their parents, and society. In fact, they are probably under more pressure. For although they leave college superbly equipped to bring fresh leadership to traditionally male jobs, society hasn't yet caught up with this fact.

Along with economic pressure goes parental pressure. Inevitably, the two are deeply intertwined.

15   I see many students taking pre-medical courses with joyless tenacity. They go off to their labs as if they were going to the dentist. It saddens me because I know them in other corners of their life as cheerful people.

"Do you want to go to medical school?" I ask them.

"I guess so," they say, without conviction, or "Not really."

"Then why are you going?"

"Well, my parents want me to be a doctor. They're paying all this money and . . ."

20   Poor students, poor parents. They are caught in one of the oldest webs of love and duty and guilt. The parents mean well; they are trying to steer their sons and daughters toward a secure future. But the sons and daughters want to major in history or classics or philosophy—subjects with no "practical" value. Where's the payoff on the humanities? It's not easy to persuade such loving parents that the humanities do indeed pay off. The intellectual faculties developed by studying subjects like history and classics—an ability to synthesize and relate, to weigh cause and effect, to see events in perspective—are just the faculties that make creative leaders in business or almost any general field. Still, many fathers would rather put their money on courses that point toward a specific profession—courses that are pre-law, pre-medical, pre-business, or, as I sometimes heard it put, "pre-rich."

But the pressure on students is severe. They are truly torn. One part of them feels obligated to fulfill their parents' expectations; after all, their parents are older and presumably wiser. Another part tells them that the expectations that are right for their parents are not right for them.

I know a student who wants to be an artist. She is very obviously an artist and will be a good one—she has already had several modest local exhibits. Meanwhile she is growing as a well-rounded person and taking humanistic subjects that will enrich the inner resources out of which her art will grow. But her father is strongly opposed. He thinks that an artist is a "dumb" thing to be. The student vacillates and tries to please everybody. She keeps up with her art somewhat furtively and takes some of the "dumb" courses her father wants her to take—at least they are dumb courses for her. She is a free spirit on a campus of tense students—no small achievement in itself—and she deserves to follow her muse.

Peer pressure and self-induced pressure are also intertwined, and they begin almost at the beginning of freshman year.

"I had a freshman student I'll call Linda," one dean told me, "who came in and said she was under terrible pressure because her roommate, Barbara, was much brighter and studied all the time. I couldn't tell her that Barbara had come in two hours earlier to say the same thing about Linda."

25   The story is almost funny except that it's not. It's symptomatic of all the pressures put together. When every student thinks every other student is working harder and doing better, the only solution is to study harder still. I see students going off to the library every night after dinner and coming back when it closes at midnight. I wish they would sometimes forget about their peers and go to a movie. I hear the clacking of typewriters in the hours before dawn. I see the tension in their eyes when exams are approaching and papers are due: *"Will I get everything done?"*   25

Probably they won't. They will get sick. They will get "blocked." They will sleep. They will oversleep. They will bug out. *Hey Carlos, help!*

Part of the problem is that they do more than they are expected to do. A professor will assign five-page papers. Several students will start writing ten-page papers to impress him. Then more students will write ten-page papers, and a few will raise the ante to fifteen. Pity the poor student who is still just doing the assignment.

"Once you have 20 or 30 percent of the student population deliberately overexerting," one dean points out, "it's bad for everybody. When a teacher gets more and more effort from his class, the student who is doing normal work can be perceived as not doing well. The tactic works, psychologically."

Why can't the professor just cut back and not accept longer papers? He can, and he probably will. But by then the term will be half over and the damage done. Grade fever is highly contagious and not easily reversed. Besides, the professor's main concern is with his course. He knows his students only in relation to the course and doesn't know that they are also overexerting in their other courses. Nor is it really his business. He didn't sign up for dealing with the student as a whole person and with all the emotional baggage the student brought along from home. That's what deans, masters, chaplains, and psychiatrists are for.

30   To some extent this is nothing new: a certain number of professors have always been self-contained islands of scholarship and shyness, more comfortable with books than with people. But the new pauperism has widened the gap still further, for professors who actually like to spend time with students don't have as much time to spend. They also are overexerting. If they are young, they are busy trying to publish in order not to perish, hanging by their finger nails onto a shrinking profession. If they are old and tenured, they are buried under the duties of administering departments—as departmental chairmen or members of committees—that have been thinned out by the budgetary axe.

Ultimately it will be the students' own business to break the circles in which they are trapped. They are too young to be prisoners of their parents' dreams and their classmates' fears. They must be jolted into believing in themselves as unique men and women who have the power to shape their own future.

"Violence is being done to the undergraduate experience," says Carlos Hortas. "College should be open-ended: at the end it should open many, many roads. Instead, students are choosing their goal in advance, and their choices narrow as they go along. It's almost as if they think that the country has been codified in the type of jobs that exist—that they've got to fit into certain slots. Therefore, fit into the best-paying slot.

"They ought to take chances. Not taking chances will lead to a life of colorless mediocrity. They'll be comfortable. But something in the spirit will be missing."

I have painted too drab a portrait of today's students, making them seem a solemn lot. That is only half of their story; if they were so dreary I wouldn't so thoroughly enjoy their company. The other half is that they are easy to like. They are quick to laugh and to offer friendship. They are not introverts. They are unusually kind and are more considerate of one another than any student generation I have known.

35   Nor are they so obsessed with their studies that they avoid sports and extracurricular activities. On the contrary, they juggle their crowded hours to play on a variety of teams, perform with musical and dramatic groups, and write for campus publications. But this in turn is one more cause of anxiety. There are too many choices. Academically,

they have 1,300 courses to select from; outside class they have to decide how much spare time they can spare and how to spend it.

This means that they engage in fewer extracurricular pursuits than their predecessors did. If they want to row on the crew and play in the symphony they will eliminate one; in the '60s they would have done both. They also tend to choose activities that are self-limiting. Drama, for instance, is flourishing in all twelve of Yale's residential colleges as it never has before. Students hurl themselves into these productions—as actors, directors, carpenters, and technicians—with a dedication to create the best possible play, knowing that the day will come when the run will end and they can get back to their studies.

They also can't afford to be the willing slave of organizations like the *Yale Daily News*. Last spring at the one-hundredth anniversary banquet of that paper—whose past chairmen include such once and future kings as Potter Stewart, Kingman Brewster, and William F. Buckley, Jr.—much was made of the fact that the editorial staff used to be small and totally committed and that "Newsies" routinely worked fifty hours a week. In effect they belonged to a club; Newsies is how they defined themselves at Yale. Today's student will write one or two articles a week, when he can, and he defines himself as a student. I've never heard the word Newsie except at the banquet.

If I have described the modern undergraduate primarily as a driven creature who is largely ignoring the blithe spirit inside who keeps trying to come out and play, it's because that's where the crunch is, not only at Yale but throughout American education. It's why I think we should all be worried about the values that are nurturing a generation so fearful of risk and so goal-obsessed at such an early age.

I tell students that there is no one "right" way to get ahead—that each of them is a different person, starting from a different point and bound for a different destination. I tell them that change is a tonic and that all the slots are not codified nor the frontiers closed. One of my ways of telling them is to invite men and women who have achieved success outside the academic world to come and talk informally with my students during the year. They are heads of companies or ad agencies, editors of magazines, politicians, public officials, television magnates, labor leaders, business executives, Broadway producers, artists, writers, economists, photographers, scientists, historians—a mixed bag of achievers.

40   I ask them to say a few words about how they got started. The students assume that they started in their present profession and knew all along that it was what they wanted to do. Luckily for me, most of them got into their field by a circuitous route, to their surprise, after many detours. The students are startled. They can hardly conceive of a career that was not pre-planned. They can hardly imagine allowing the hand of God or chance to nudge them down some unforseen trail.   40

Questions on Meaning

1. Why does Zinsser identify "achievement" as the "national god"? What is his wish for students? Who does he say is responsible for getting students out of their achievement trap?
2. In this 1979 essay, Zinsser expresses the opinion that female students are under more pressure than male students. Do you believe that is the case today?

Questions on Rhetorical Strategy and Style

1. In the second paragraph after the notes to Carlos, Zinsser identifies students who are "panicky to succeed" as often being students at "New England and other private colleges that have high academic standards and highly motivated students." How do you react to this comment? Do you feel that Zinsser becomes more inclusive as he continues the essay, or does he maintain this somewhat elitist perspective?
2. How does Zinsser use the writing strategy of classification and division to describe the various pressures students face? How do these pressures compare to the pressures students feel today? Using his divisions, how would you classify the pressures you feel at school?
3. How does Zinsser compare and contrast the outlook of students in the 1960s to students in the late 1970s? How would you compare and contrast the outlook of students today to those he describes?

Writing Assignments

1. Find where Zinsser uses an example of an artistic student to illustrate parental pressure. How well do you relate to the trials and tribulations of an artistic student at Yale in the late 1970s? What are the characteristics of a student who would best reflect the pressures *you* feel?
2. Reread paragraph 11 ("The pressure is almost as heavy . . .") and paragraph 20 ("Poor students, poor parents.") and compare and contrast how you are approaching your college years to the approach Zinsser would like to see students take. Explain why you feel you are headed in the right direction or not.

3. It is not difficult for students to get caught up in competing with their peers in terms of time spent studying, pages of reports, and, of course, grades. Describe the peer pressures you have felt at college. How have they affected the way you study and your feelings of accomplishment?

4. In the 1960s, students used to joke that they would like to collect Social Security upon graduation and work a few years extra when they reached retirement age so they could enjoy life while they were young. Write an essay about what you would do if you were given a living allowance and told to take a few years off after college *without penalty on your resume.* Would you take courses you couldn't because of requirements in your major, perform volunteer work, travel, live alone in a cabin and read, help your family at home, wait tables at a resort? How do you think this spontaneous, experimental time would affect your outlook on life? What "unforeseen trails" do you think you might be "nudged down"?

Is There a There in Cyberspace?

John Perry Barlow

John Perry Barlow, former Wyoming rancher, one-time song-writer for the Grateful Dead, cofounder of the Electronic Frontier Foundation, and board member of the WELL (Whole Earth 'Lectronic Link), often speaks and writes about computer communication. This essay, which appeared in the Utne Reader *(March/April 1995), explores the differences and similarities between a small town in Wyoming, the "nomadic City of the Deadheads," and cyberspace.*

1   I am often asked how I went from pushing cows around a remote Wyoming ranch to my present occupation (which *The Wall Street Journal* recently described as "cyber-space cadet"). I haven't got a short answer, but I suppose I came to the virtual world looking for community.

Unlike most modern Americans, I grew up in an actual place, an entirely nonintentional community called Pinedale, Wyoming. As I struggled for nearly a generation to keep my ranch in the family, I was motivated by the belief that such places were the spiritual home of humanity. But I knew their future was not promising.

At the dawn of the 20th century, over 40 percent of the American workforce lived off the land. The majority of us lived in towns like Pinedale. Now fewer than 1 percent of us extract a living from the soil. We just became too productive for our own good.

Of course, the population followed the jobs. Farming and ranching communities are now home to a demographically insignificant percentage of Americans, the vast majority of whom live not in ranch houses but in more or less identical split-level "ranch homes" in more or less identical suburban "communities." Generica.

From John Perry Barlow, "Is There a There in Cyberspace?"

5   In my view, these are neither communities nor homes. I believe   5
the combination of television and suburban population patterns is
simply toxic to the soul. I see much evidence in contemporary America to support this view.

Meanwhile, back at the ranch, doom impended. And, as I
watched community in Pinedale growing ill from the same economic
forces that were killing my family's ranch, the Bar Cross, satellite
dishes brought the cultural infection of television. I started looking
around for evidence that community in America would not perish
altogether.

I took some heart in the mysterious nomadic City of the Deadheads, the virtually physical town that follows the Grateful Dead
around the country. The Deadheads lacked place, touching down
briefly wherever the band happened to be playing, and they lacked
continuity in time, since they had to suffer a new diaspora every time
the band moved on or went home. But they had many of the other
necessary elements of community, including a culture, a religion of
sorts (which, though it lacked dogma, had most of the other, more
nurturing aspects of spiritual practice), a sense of necessity, and, most
importantly, shared adversity.

I wanted to know more about the flavor of their interaction, what
they thought and felt, but since I wrote Dead songs (including "Esti-
mated Prophet" and "Cassidy"), I was a minor icon to the Deadheads,
and was thus inhibited, in some socially Heisenbergian way, from getting a clear view of what really went on among them.

Then, in 1987, I heard about a "place" where Deadheads gathered
where I could move among them without distorting too much the
field of observation. Better, this was a place I could visit without leaving Wyoming. It was a shared computer in Sausalito, California, called
the Whole Earth 'Lectronic Link, or WELL. After a lot of struggling
with modems, serial cables, init strings, and other computer arcana
that seemed utterly out of phase with such notions as Deadheads and
small towns, I found myself looking at the glowing yellow word
"Login:" beyond which lay my future.

10   "Inside" the WELL were Deadheads in community. There were   10
thousands of them there, gossiping, complaining (mostly about the
Grateful Dead), comforting and harassing each other, bartering, engaging in religion (or at least exchanging their totemic set lists), beginning and ending love affairs, praying for one another's sick kids.

There was, it seemed, everything one might find going on in a small town, save dragging Main Street and making out on the back roads.

I was delighted. I felt I had found the new locale of human community—never mind that the whole thing was being conducted in mere words by minds from whom the bodies had been amputated. Never mind that all these people were deaf, dumb, and blind as paramecia or that their town had neither seasons nor sunsets nor smells.

Surely all these deficiencies would be remedied by richer, faster communications media. The featureless log-in handles would gradually acquire video faces (and thus expressions), shaded 3-D body puppets (and thus body language). This "space," which I recognized at once to be a primitive form of the cyberspace William Gibson predicted in his sci-fi novel *Neuromancer,* was still without apparent dimensions or vistas. But virtual reality would change all that in time.

Meanwhile, the commons, or something like it, had been rediscovered. Once again, people from the 'burbs had a place where they could encounter their friends as my fellow Pinedalians did at the post office and the Wrangler Cafe. They had a place where their hearts could remain as the companies they worked for shuffled their bodies around America. They could put down roots that could not be ripped out by forces of economic history. They had a collective stake. They had a community.

It is seven years now since I discovered the WELL. In that time, I cofounded an organization, the Electronic Frontier Foundation, dedicated to protecting its interests and those of other virtual communities like it from raids by physical government. I've spent countless hours typing away at its residents, and I've watched the larger context that contains it, the Internet, grow at such an explosive rate that, by 2004, every human on the planet will have an e-mail address unless the growth curve flattens (which it will).

15   My enthusiasm for virtuality has cooled. In fact, unless one counts   15
interaction with the rather too large society of those with whom I exchange electronic mail, I don't spend much time engaging in virtual community at all. Many of the near-term benefits I anticipated from it seem to remain as far in the future as they did when I first logged in. Perhaps they always will.

Pinedale works, more or less, as it is, but a lot is still missing from the communities of cyberspace, whether they be places like the

WELL, the fractious newsgroups of USENET, the silent "auditoriums" of America Online, or even enclaves on the promising World Wide Web.

What is missing? Well, to quote Ranjit Makkuni of Xerox Corporation's Palo Alto Research Center, "the *prāna* is missing," *prāna* being the Hindu term for both breath and spirit. I think he is right about this and that perhaps the central question of the virtual age is whether or not *prāna* can somehow be made to fit through any disembodied medium.

Prāna is, to my mind, the literally vital element in the holy and unseen ecology of relationship, the dense mesh of invisible life, on whose surface carbon-based life floats like a thin film. It is at the heart of the fundamental and profound difference between information and experience. Jaron Lanier has said that "information is alienated experience," and, that being true, *prāna* is part of what is removed when you create such easily transmissible replicas of experience as, say, the evening news.

Obviously a great many other, less spiritual, things are also missing entirely, like body language, sex, death, tone of voice, clothing, beauty (or homeliness), weather, violence, vegetation, wildlife, pets, architecture, music, smells, sunlight, and that ol' harvest moon. In short, most of the things that make my life real to me.

20 Present, but in far less abundance than in the physical world, which I call "meat space," are women, children, old people, poor people, and the genuinely blind. Also mostly missing are the illiterate and the continent of Africa. There is not much human diversity in cyberspace, which is populated, as near as I can tell, by white males under 50 with plenty of computer terminal time, great typing skills, high math SATS, strongly held opinions on just about everything, and an excruciating face-to-face shyness, especially with the opposite sex.

But diversity is as essential to healthy community as it is to healthy ecosystems (which are, in my view, different from communities only in unimportant aspects).

I believe that the principal reason for the almost universal failure of the intentional communities of the '60s and '70s was a lack of diversity in their members. It was a rare commune with any old people in it, or people who were fundamentally out of philosophical agreement with the majority.

Indeed, it is the usual problem when we try to build something that can only be grown. Natural systems, such as human communities, are simply too complex to design by the engineering principles we insist on applying to them. Like Dr. Frankenstein, Western civilization is now finding its rational skills inadequate to the task of creating and caring for life. We would do better to return to a kind of agricultural mind-set in which we humbly try to re-create the conditions from which life has sprung before. And leave the rest to God.

Given that it has been built so far almost entirely by people with engineering degrees, it is not so surprising that cyberspace has the kind of overdesigned quality that leaves out all kinds of elements nature would have provided invisibly.

25 Also missing from both the communes of the '60s and from cyberspace are a couple of elements that I believe are very important, if not essential, to the formation and preservation of real community: an absence of alternatives and a sense of genuine adversity, generally shared. What about these? 25

It is hard to argue that anyone would find losing a modem literally hard to survive, while many have remained in small towns, have tolerated their intolerances and created entertainment to enliven their culturally arid lives simply because it seemed there was no choice but to stay. There are many investments—spiritual, material, and temporal— one is willing to put into a home one cannot leave. Communities are often the beneficiaries of these involuntary investments.

But when the going gets rough in cyberspace, it is even easier to move than it is in the 'burbs, where, given the fact that the average American moves some 12 times in his or her life, moving appears to be pretty easy. You can not only find another bulletin board service (BBS) or newsgroup to hang out in, you can, with very little effort, start your own.

And then there is the bond of joint suffering. Most community is a cultural stockade erected against a common enemy that can take many forms. In Pinedale, we bore together, with an understanding needing little expression, the fact that Upper Green River Valley is the coldest spot, as measured by annual mean temperature, in the lower 48 states. We knew that if somebody was stopped on the road most winter nights, he would probably die there, so the fact that we might loathe him was not sufficient reason to drive on past his broken pickup.

By the same token, the Deadheads have the Drug Enforcement Administration, which strives to give them 20-year prison terms without parole for distributing the fairly harmless sacrament of their faith. They have an additional bond in the fact that when their Microbuses die, as they often do, no one but another Deadhead is likely to stop to help them.

30   But what are the shared adversities of cyberspace? Lousy user interfaces? The flames of harsh invective? Dumb jokes? Surely these can all be survived without the sanctuary provided by fellow sufferers.

One is always free to yank the jack, as I have mostly done. For me, the physical world offers far more opportunity for *prāna*-rich connections with my fellow creatures. Even for someone whose body is in a state of perpetual motion, I feel I can generally find more community among the still-embodied.

Finally, there is that shyness factor. Not only are we trying to build community here among people who have never experienced any in my sense of the term, we are trying to build community among people who, in their lives, have rarely used the word *we* in a heartfelt way. It is a vast club, and many of the members—following Groucho Marx—wouldn't want to join a club that would have them.

And yet . . .

How quickly physical community continues to deteriorate. Even Pinedale, which seems to have survived the plague of ranch failures, feels increasingly cut off from itself. Many of the ranches are now owned by corporate types who fly their Gulfstreams in to fish and are rarely around during the many months when the creeks are frozen over and neighbors are needed. They have kept the ranches alive financially, but they actively discourage their managers from the interdependence my former colleagues and I require. They keep agriculture on life support, still alive but lacking a functional heart.

35   And the town has been inundated with suburbanites who flee here, bringing all their terrors and suspicions with them. They spend their evenings as they did in Orange County, watching television or socializing in hermetic little enclaves of fundamentalist Christianity that seem to separate them from us and even, given their sectarian animosities, from one another. The town remains. The community is largely a wraith of nostalgia.

So where else can we look for the connection we need to prevent our plunging further into the condition of separateness Nietzsche called sin? What is there to do but to dive further into the bramble bush of information that, in its broadcast forms, has done so much to tear us apart?

Cyberspace, for all its current deficiencies and failed promises, is not without some very real solace already.

Some months ago, the great love of my life, a vivid young woman with whom I intended to spend the rest of it, dropped dead of undiagnosed viral cardiomyopathy two days short of her 30th birthday. I felt as if my own heart had been as shredded as hers.

We had lived together in New York City. Except for my daughters, no one from Pinedale had met her. I needed a community to wrap around myself against colder winds than fortune had ever blown at me before. And without looking, I found I had one in the virtual world.

40 On the WELL, there was a topic announcing her death in one of 40 the conferences to which I posted the eulogy I had read over her before burying her in her own small town of Nanaimo, British Columbia. It seemed to strike a chord among the disembodied living on the Net. People copied it and sent it to one another. Over the next several months I received almost a megabyte of electronic mail from all over the planet, mostly from folks whose faces I have never seen and probably never will.

They told me of their own tragedies and what they had done to survive them. As humans have since words were first uttered, we shared the second most common human experience, death, with an openheartedness that would have caused grave uneasiness in physical America, where the whole topic is so cloaked in denial as to be considered obscene. Those strangers, who had no arms to put around my shoulders, no eyes to weep with mine, nevertheless saw me through. As neighbors do.

I have no idea how far we will plunge into this strange place. Unlike previous frontiers, this one has no end. It is so dissatisfying in so many ways that I suspect we will be more restless in our search for home here than in all our previous explorations. And that is one reason why I think we may find it after all. If home is where the heart is, then there is already some part of home to be found in cyberspace.

So . . . does virtual community work or not? Should we all go off to cyberspace or should we resist it as a demonic form of symbolic abstraction? Does it supplant the real or is there, in it, reality itself?

Like so many true things, this one doesn't resolve itself to a black or a white. Nor is it gray. It is, along with the rest of life, black/white. Both/neither. I'm not being equivocal or wishy-washy here. We have to get over our Manichean sense that everything is either good or bad, and the border of cyberspace seems to me a good place to leave that old set of filters.

45 But really it doesn't matter. We are going there whether we want 45 to or not. In five years, everyone who is reading these words will have an e-mail address, other than the determined Luddites who also eschew the telephone and electricity.

When we are all together in cyberspace we will see what the human spirit, and the basic desire to connect, can create there. I am convinced that the result will be more benign if we go there open-minded, open-hearted, and excited with the adventure than if we are dragged into exile.

And we must remember that going to cyberspace, unlike previous great emigrations to the frontier, hardly requires us to leave where we have been. Many will find, as I have, a much richer appreciation of physical reality for having spent so much time in virtuality.

Despite its current (and perhaps in some areas permanent) insufficiencies, we should go to cyberspace with hope. Groundless hope, like unconditional love, may be the only kind that counts.

Questions on Meaning

1. Is there a *there* in cyberspace? What is the thesis of Barlow's essay?
2. Without looking at the essay, write a definition of "community." Next, reread the essay and list the many elements or characteristics of a "community" that Barlow gives.
3. Explain the difference between a "nonintentional" and an "intentional" community.

Questions on Rhetorical Strategy and Style

1. Barlow develops his argument with abundant comparison and contrast. See how many different topics you can find that he compares and contrasts—from his occupations to American society at the beginning and end of the 20th century to Pinedale and Deadheads. Describe the effectiveness of these comparisons and contrasts in embellishing his discussion about communities.
2. How does Barlow's tone change from the paragraph before the break in the essay through the first two paragraphs after the break? Why? How does his tone shift again by the end of the essay?

Writing Assignments

1. Think about your physical "community"—the people you live with, the campus environment, the city or town in which your college is located, etc. Using the elements or characteristics of a "community" that Barlow presents (see question 2), determine the strengths and weaknesses of your physical "community." If you have a virtual "community," compare and contrast it to your physical "community." Which "community" is more fulfilling? Why?
2. Barlow is not the first person to attack television as causing the erosion of "community." Do you agree that television is "toxic to the soul"? Write an essay arguing that television either does or does not bring a "cultural infection" to a community. Argue both from your own experience and from researching television viewing trends.
3. Barlow emphasizes that "shared adversity" and "joint suffering" are critical elements of a strong "community." Write an essay about an adverse experience you have had that formed a bond with your "community" or with another person(s). Perhaps you

have experienced a natural disaster in which your neighborhood worked together to take care of each other, or maybe you have been hospitalized for an operation or serious injury and developed a special relationship with your nurses. How did the "community" or bond develop? What other elements of a "community" were present? What effect did the experience have on you and the "community" or other person(s)?

The Gender Blur

Deborah Blum

Deborah Blum (1954–) was born in Urbana, Illinois to an entomologist and a legal scholar. Educated in journalism at the University of Georgia (B.A.) and the University of Wisconsin (M.A.), she has worked as a reporter for several newspapers in Georgia and Florida, and as a science writer for the Sacramento, California Bee. *Currently, Blum is professor of journalism at the University of Wisconsin. Her first book,* The Monkey Wars, *explored the issue of medical and psychological experimentation on primates. Lauded for its balanced approach, the book grew out of a Pulitzer Prize-winning series she had written on the subject in 1992. Her work has also earned her other awards, among them a Westinghouse Award from the American Academy of Arts and Sciences and a Clarion Award for Investigative Reporting, both in 1992; and a National Award for Non-Deadline Reporting from the Society of Professional Journalists in 1996. In 1997 she co-edited* A Field Guide for Science Writers. *Her most recent book,* Sex on the Brain: The Biological Differences Between Men and Women *(1997), explores the roles of biology and environment in determining gender. In this selection, based on that book, Blum describes how imprecise biological determiners of sex can be. Using extensive examples of indeterminate sexual identity, Blum raises questions about the rigid classification of male and female in the human race.*

¹ I was raised in one of those university-based, liberal elite families that politicians like to ridicule. In my childhood, every human being—regardless of gender—was exactly alike under the skin, and I mean exactly, barring his or her different opportunities. My parents wasted no opportunity to bring this point home. One Christmas, I received a Barbie doll and a softball glove. Another brought a green enamel stove, which baked tiny cakes by the heat of a lightbulb, and also a set of steel-tipped darts and competition-quality dartboard. Did I mention the year of the chemistry set and the ballerina doll? ¹

It wasn't until I became a parent—I should say, a parent of two boys—that I realized I had been fed a line and swallowed it like a sucker (barring the part about opportunities, which I still believe). This dawned on me during my older son's dinosaur phase, which began when he was about 2 1/2. Oh, he loved dinosaurs, all right, but only the blood-swilling carnivores. Plant-eaters were wimps and losers, and he refused to wear a T-shirt marred by a picture of a stegosaur. I looked down at him one day, as he was snarling around my feet and doing his toddler best to gnaw off my right leg, and I thought: This goes a lot deeper than culture.

Raising children tends to bring on this kind of politically incorrect reaction. Another friend came to the same conclusion watching a son determinedly bite his breakfast toast into the shape of a pistol he hoped would blow away—or at least terrify—his younger brother. Once you get past the guilt part—Did I do this? Should I have bought him that plastic allosaur with the oversized teeth?—such revelations can lead you to consider the far more interesting field of gender biology, where the questions take a different shape: Does love of carnage begin in culture or genetics, and which drives which? Do the gender roles of our culture reflect an underlying biology, and, in turn, does the way we behave influence that biology?

The point I'm leading up to—through the example of my son's innocent love of predatory dinosaurs—is actually one of the most straightforward in this debate. One of the reasons we're so fascinated by childhood behaviors is that, as the old saying goes, the child becomes the man (or woman, of course.) Most girls don't spend their preschool years snarling around the house and pretending to chew off their companion's legs. And they—mostly—don't grow up to be as aggressive as men. Do the ways that we amplify those early differences in childhood shape the adults we become? Absolutely. But it's worth exploring the starting place—the faint signal that somehow gets amplified.

"There's plenty of room in society to influence sex differences," says Marc Breedlove, a behavioral endocrinologist at the University of California at Berkeley and a pioneer in defining how hormones can help build sexually different nervous systems. "Yes, we're born with predispositions, but it's society that amplifies them, exaggerates them. I believe that—except for the sex differences in aggression. Those [differences] are too massive to be explained simply by society."

Aggression does allow a straightforward look at the issue. Consider the following statistics: Crime reports in both the United States and Europe record between 10 and 15 robberies committed by men for every one by a woman. At one point, people argued that this was explained by size difference. Women weren't big enough to intimidate, but that would change, they predicted, with the availability of compact weapons. But just as little girls don't routinely make weapons out of toast, women—even criminal ones—don't seem drawn to weaponry in the same way that men are. Almost twice as many male thieves and robbers use guns as their female counterparts do.

Or you can look at more personal crimes: domestic partner murders. Three-fourths of men use guns in those killings; 50 percent of women do. Here's more from the domestic front: In conflicts in which a woman killed a man, he tended to be the one who had started the fight—in 51.8 percent of the cases, to be exact. When the man was the killer, he again was the likely first aggressor, and by an even more dramatic margin. In fights in which women died, they had started the argument only 12.5 percent of the time.

Enough. You can parade endless similar statistics but the point is this: Males are more aggressive, not just among humans but among almost all species on earth. Male chimpanzees, for instance, declare war on neighboring troops, and one of their strategies is a warning strike: They kill females and infants to terrorize and intimidate. In terms of simple, reproductive genetics, it's an advantage of males to be aggressive: You can muscle you way into dominance, winning more sexual encounters, more offspring, more genetic future. For the female—especially in a species like ours, with time for just one successful pregnancy a year—what's the genetic advantage in brawling?

Thus the issue becomes not whether there is a biologically influenced sex difference in aggression—the answer being a solid, technical

"You betcha"—but rather how rigid that difference is. The best science, in my opinion, tends to align with basic common sense. We all know that there are extraordinarily gentle men and murderous women. Sex differences are always generalizations: They refer to a behavior, with some evolutionary rationale behind it. They never define, entirely, an individual. And that fact alone should tell us that there's always—even in the most biologically dominated traits—some flexibility, an instinctive ability to respond, for better and worse, to the world around us.

10   This is true even with physical characteristics that we've often assumed are nailed down by genetics. Scientists now believe height, for instance, is only about 90 percent heritable. A person's genes might code for a six-foot-tall body, but malnutrition could literally cut that short. And there's also some evidence, in girls anyway, that children with stressful childhoods tend to become shorter adults. So while some factors are predetermined, there's evidence that the prototypical male/female body design can be readily altered.

It's a given that humans, like most other species—bananas, spiders, sharks, ducks, any rabbit you pull out of a hat—rely on two sexes for reproduction. So basic is that requirement that we have chromosomes whose primary purpose is to deliver the genes that order up a male or a female. All other chromosomes are numbered, but we label the sex chromosomes with the letters X and Y. We get one each from our mother and our father, and the basic combinations are these: XX makes female, XY makes male.

There are two important—and little known—points about these chromosomal matches. One is that even with this apparently precise system, there's nothing precise—or guaranteed—about the physical construction of male and female. The other point makes that possible. It appears that sex doesn't matter in the early stages of embryonic development. We are unisex at the point of conception.

If you examine an embryo at about six weeks, you see that it has the ability to develop in either direction. The fledgling embryo has two sets of ducts—Wolffian for male, Muellerian for female—an either/or structure, held in readiness for further development. If testosterone and other androgens are released by hormone-producing cells, then the Wolffian ducts develop into the channel that connects penis to testes, and the female ducts wither away.

Without testosterone, the embryo takes on a female form; the male ducts vanish and the Muellerian ducts expand into oviducts, uterus, and vagina. In other words, in humans, anyway (the opposite is true in birds), the female is the default sex. Back in the 1950s, the famed biologist Alfred Jost showed that if you castrate a male rabbit fetus, choking off testosterone, you produce a completely feminized rabbit.

15   We don't do these experiments in humans—for obvious reasons—but there are naturally occurring instances that prove the same point. For instance: In the fetal testes are a group of cells called Leydig cells, that make testosterone. In rare cases, the fetus doesn't make enough of these cells (a defect known as Leydig cell hypoplasia). In this circumstance we see the limited power of the XY chromosome. These boys have the right chromosomes and the right genes to be boys; they just don't grow a penis. Obstetricians and parents often think they see a baby girl, and these children are routinely raised as daughters. Usually, the "mistake" is caught about the time of puberty, when menstruation doesn't start. A doctor's examination shows the child to be internally male; there are usually small testes, often tucked with the abdomen. As the researchers put it, if the condition had been known from the beginning, "the sisters would have been born as brothers."   15

Just to emphasize how tricky all this body-building can get, there's a peculiar genetic defect that seems to be clustered by heredity in a small group of villages in the Dominican Republic. The result of the defect is a failure to produce an enzyme that concentrates testosterone, specifically for building genitals. One obscure little enzyme only, but here's what happens without it: You get a boy with undescended testes and a penis so short and stubby that it resembles an oversized clitoris.

In the mountain villages of this Caribbean nation, people are used to it. The children are usually raised as "conditional" girls. At puberty, the secondary tide of androgens rises and is apparently enough to finish the construction project. The scrotum suddenly descends, the phallus grows, and the child develops a distinctly male body—narrow hips, muscular build, and even slight beard growth. At that point, the family shifts the child over from daughter to son. The dresses are thrown out. He begins to wear male clothes and starts dating girls. People in the Dominican Republic are so familiar with this condition that there's a colloquial name for it: *guevedoces*, meaning "eggs (or testes) at 12."

It's the comfort level with this slip-slide of sexual identity that's so remarkable and, I imagine, so comforting to the children involved. I'm positive that the sexual transition of these children is less traumatic than the abrupt awareness of the "sisters who would have been brothers." There's a message of tolerance there, well worth repeating, and there are some other key lessons too.

These defects are rare and don't alter the basic male-female division of our species. They do emphasize how fragile those divisions can be. Biology allows flexibility, room to change, to vary and grow. With that comes room for error as well. That it's possible to live with these genetic defects, that they don't merely kill us off, is a reminder that we, male and female alike, exist on a continuum of biological possibilities that can overlap and sustain either sex.

20 Marc Breedlove points out that the most difficult task may be separating how the brain responds to hormones from how the brain responds to the *results* of hormones. Which brings us back, briefly, below the belt: In this context, the penis is just a result, the product of androgens at work before birth. "And after birth," says Breedlove, "virtually everyone who interacts with that individual will note that he has a penis, and will, in many instances, behave differently than if the individual was a female."

Do the ways that we amplify physical and behavioral differences in childhood shape who we become as adults? Absolutely. But to understand that, you have to understand the differences themselves—their beginning and the very real biochemistry that may lie behind them.

Here is a good place to focus on testosterone—a hormone that is both well-studied and generally underrated. First, however, I want to acknowledge that there are many other hormones and neurotransmitters that appear to influence behavior. Preliminary work shows that fetal boys are a little more active than fetal girls. It's pretty difficult to argue socialization at that point. There's a strong suspicion that testosterone may create the difference.

And there are a couple of relevant animal models to emphasize the point. Back in the 1960s, Robert Goy, a psychologist at the University of Wisconsin at Madison, first documented that young male monkeys play much more roughly than young females. Goy went on to show that if you manipulate testosterone level—raising it in females, damping it down in males—you can reverse those effects, creating sweet little male monkeys and rowdy young females.

Is testosterone the only factor at work here? I don't think so. But clearly we can argue a strong influence, and, interestingly, studies have found that girls with congenital adrenal hypoplasia—who run high in testosterone—tend to be far more fascinated by trucks and toy weaponry than most little girls are. They lean toward rough-and-tumble play, too. As it turns out, the strongest influence on this "abnormal" behavior is not parental disapproval, but the company of other little girls, who tone them down and direct them toward more routine girl games.

25   And that reinforces an early point: If there is indeed a biology to sex differences, we amplify it. At some point—when it is still up for debate—we gain a sense of our gender, and with it a sense of "gender-appropriate" behavior.   25

Some scientists argue for some evidence of gender awareness in infancy, perhaps by the age of 12 months. The consensus seems to be that full-blown "I'm a girl" or "I'm a boy" instincts arrive between the ages of 2 and 3. Research shows that if a family operates in a very traditional, Beaver Cleaver kind of environment, filled with awareness of and association with "proper" gender behaviors, the "boys do trucks, girls do dolls" attitude seems to come very early. If a child grows up in a less traditional family, with an emphasis on partnership and sharing—"We all do the dishes, Joshua"—children maintain a more flexible sense of gender roles until about age 6.

In this period, too, relationships between boys and girls tend to fall into remarkably strict lines. Interviews with children find that 3-year-olds say that about half their friendships are with the opposite sex. By the age of 5, that drops to 20 percent. By 7, almost no boys or girls have, or will admit to having, best friends of the opposite sex. They still hang out on the same playground, play on the same soccer teams. They may be friendly, but the real friendships tend to be boy-to-boy or girl-to-girl.

There's some interesting science that suggests that the space between boys and girls is a normal part of development; there are periods during which children may thrive and learn from hanging out with peers of the same sex. Do we, as parents, as a culture at large, reinforce such separations? Is the pope Catholic? One of my favorite studies looked at little boys who asked for toys. If they asked for a heavily armed action figure, they got the soldier about 70 percent of the time. If they asked for a "girl" toy, like a baby doll or a Barbie, their parents purchased it maybe 40 percent of the time. Name a child who won't figure out to work *that* system.

How does all this fit together—toys and testosterone, biology and behavior, the development of the child into the adult, the way that men and women relate to one another?

30   Let me make a cautious statement about testosterone: It not only   30 has some body-building functions, it influences some behaviors as well. Let's make that a little less cautious: These behaviors include rowdy play, sex drive, competitiveness, and an in-your-face attitude. Males tend to have a higher baseline of testosterone than females—in our species, about seven to ten times as much—and therefore you would predict (correctly, I think) that all of those behaviors would be more generally found in men than in women.

But testosterone is also one of my favorite examples of how responsive biology is, how attuned it is to the way we live our lives. Testosterone, it turns out, rises in response to competition and threat. In the days of our ancestors, this might have been hand-to-hand combat or high-risk hunting endeavors. Today, scientists have measured testosterone rise in athletes preparing for a game, in chess players awaiting a match, in spectators following a soccer competition.

If a person—or even just a person's favored team—wins, testosterone continues to rise. It falls with a loss. (This also makes sense in an evolutionary perspective. If one was being clobbered with a club, it would be extremely unhelpful to have a hormone urging one to battle on.) Testosterone also rises in the competitive world of dating, settles down with a stable and supportive relationship, climbs again if the relationship starts to falter.

It's been known for years that men in high-stress professions—say, police work or corporate law—have higher testosterone levels than men in the ministry. It turns out that women in the same kind of strong-attitude professions have higher testosterone than women who choose to stay home. What I like about this is the chicken-or-egg aspect. If you argue that testosterone influenced the behavior of those women, which came first? Did they have high testosterone and choose the law? Or did they choose the law, and the competitive environment ratcheted them up on the androgen scale? Or could both be at work?

And, returning to children for a moment, there's an ongoing study by Pennsylvania researchers, tracking that question in adolescent girls, who are being encouraged by their parents to engage in competitive activities that were once for boys only. As they do so, the researchers are monitoring, regularly, two hormones: testosterone and cortisol, a stress hormone. Will these hormones rise in response to this new, more traditionally male environment? What if more girls choose the competitive path; more boys choose the other? Will female testosterone levels rise, male levels fall? Will that wonderful, unpredictable, flexible biology that we've been given allow a shift, so that one day, we will literally be far more alike?

35   We may not have answers to all those questions, but we can ask them, and we can expect that the answers will come someday, because science clearly shows us that such possibilities exist. In this most important sense, sex differences offer us a paradox. It is only through exploring and understanding what makes us different that we can begin to understand what binds us together.

Questions on Meaning

1. According to Blum, why are males naturally more aggressive than females? What evidence does she offer to support this conclusion?
2. What does Blum mean when she says that "the female is the default sex" in humans? How do the examples she provides explain the importance of understanding this biological fact?
3. Blum and the experts she cites emphasize the significance of culture and environment "amplifying" biological differences. What biologically determined behaviors are often amplified in male and female children? How are those behaviors amplified?

Questions on Rhetorical Strategy and Style

1. Effective classification demands that each part of an identified group share the same features. How does Blum's analysis call into question the classifications "male" and "female"? What generally accepted features of each group does she question?
2. Blum employs several examples to illustrate her point. Choose two of those examples and explain how they work with the scientific data to underscore the imprecision of sex determiners in humans.
3. What is the impact of Blum's opening her essay with the story of her own childhood and her son's? How do you react as a reader to those stories? What would be the effect on the essay by beginning with a more scientific discussion?

Writing Assignments

1. Think about your own childhood: In what ways did your family reinforce traditionally accepted sex roles? To what extent were you free to exhibit behaviors of the opposite sex? Write an essay in which you use these examples to support or challenge Blum's conclusions.
2. Although Blum does not discuss the political implications of her work, it is clear that sex roles are important to many political discussions. Find articles in magazines and newspapers on sex-discrimination, "family values," the feminist movement, the promise-keepers movement, and other sex-related issues. What groups are more likely to embrace a biological explanation of sex roles? What groups emphasize cultural influences? To what extent do any of these groups use scientific evidence to support their positions?

Camping for Their Lives

Scott Bransford

Educated at the University of California-Berkeley School of Journalism (class of 2011), Scott Bransford is a native of California's Central Valley. He was a correspondent for the Sacramento Business Journal *from 2005 to 2009, and is currently an independent journalist and writer. Bransford has written for the* High Country News, New America Media, *and* Utne Reader; *his blog can be found at http://scottbransford.blogspot.com/. His interest in environmental and social justice issues is evident in the following selection, which was nominated for 2009* Utne Independent Press Awards *for general excellence and environmental coverage. In it, Bransford explores the growing phenomenon of tent cities, profiling residents and advocating for more progressive governmental responses to the issue of affordable housing.*

1   Marie and Francisco Caro needed a home after they got married, but like many people in California's Central Valley, they didn't have enough money to sign a lease or take out a mortgage.

They were tired of sleeping on separate beds in crowded shelters, so they found a slice of land alongside the Union Pacific Railroad tracks in downtown Fresno. The soil was sandy and dry, prone to rising up into clouds when the autumn winds came. All around, farm equipment factories and warehouses loomed out of the dust, their walls coarse and sun-bleached like desert mountainsides.

Even a strong person could wither in a place like this, but if they wanted to build a home, nobody was likely to stop them. So Marie

Reprinted from *High Country News*, March 16, 2009, by permission of the author.

and Francisco gathered scrap wood and took their chances. They raised their tarp roof high like a steeple, then walled off the world with office cubicle dividers. Thieves stayed outside and so did the wind, and the sound of the passing freight trains softened.

When I visited the Caros in January, a fire burned in a repurposed oil barrel, warming the cool air, and fresh-cut Christmas tree boughs hung on the walls for decoration.

5   While Francisco chopped wood, Marie confided that she wants to live somewhere else. All she needs is a modest place with a sink and a gas stove, she said, maybe even a television. But until times change, she said, she'll be happy in her self-made abode, cooking on top of the oil barrel, making meals with whatever food God brings.

"He gives us bread," said Marie, a Fresno native who quit school in the 10th grade, ashamed of a learning disability that got in the way of her reading. "I'm just waiting for my home."

From the well-kept interior of the Caros' place, one can hardly see the jagged rows of tents and shanties on the vacant land around them. About 200 people—primarily poor whites and migrant workers from Mexico—have built informal habitats along the railroad tracks.

There are many names for this fledgling city, where Old Glory flies from improvised flagpoles and trash heaps rise and fall with the wavering population. To some it's Little Tijuana, but most people call it Taco Flat.

Just to the south, under a freeway overpass, there's another camp of roughly equal size called New Jack City where most of the residents are black. Even more makeshift dwellings are scattered throughout the neighborhood nearby.

10 Fresno, which the Brookings Institution ranked in 2005 as the American city with the greatest concentration of poverty, is far from the only place where people are resorting to life in makeshift abodes. Similar encampments are proliferating throughout the West, everywhere from the industrial hub of Ontario, California, to the struggling casino district of Reno, Nevada, and the upscale suburbs of Washington state.

In any other country, these threadbare villages would be called slums, but in the United States, the preferred term is *tent city*, a label that implies that they are just a temporary phenomenon. Many journalists, eager to prove that the country is entering the next Great Depression, blame the emergence of these shantytowns on the economic downturn, calling them products of foreclosures and layoffs.

While there's some truth to this notion, the fact is that these roving, ramshackle neighborhoods were part of the American cityscape long before the stock market nosedived, and they are unlikely to disappear when prosperity returns. The recent decades of real estate speculation and tough-love social policies have cut thousands of people out of the mainstream markets for work and housing, and the existing network of shelters for the homeless is overburdened and outdated.

People such as the Caros are part of a vanguard that has been in crisis for years, building squatter settlements as a do-or-die alternative to the places that rejected them. This parallel nation, with a population now numbering at least 2,000 in Fresno alone, was born during the boom times, and it is bound to flourish as the economy falters.

"The chickens are coming home to roost," says Larry Haynes, executive director of Mercy House, an organization based in Southern California that serves homeless people. "What this speaks of is an absolute crisis of affordability and accessibility."

15   Against a backdrop of faded industrial buildings and rusty water   15
towers, Taco Flat looks like a relic of a bygone era. These rough-and-ready dwellings, untouched by the luxuries of electricity, sewage lines, and cable connections, seem like an aberration in a country that has grown accustomed to newness.

Much of the shock value of tent cities comes from the fact that they force one to do a bit of time travel, revisiting an atmosphere of social disorder that seems more fitting to a Gold Rush-era squatter camp, and a level of destitution that recalls the Hoovervilles of the 1930s. Even tent city residents themselves feel trapped in circular trajectories of history, doomed to lives shaped by the threat of lawlessness and the ever-looming peril of relocation.

Frankie Lynch, one of the self-proclaimed mayors of Taco Flat, has ancestors who fled Oklahoma during the Dust Bowl years, only to discover a new kind of poverty in the farmworker camps of California's Central Valley. Now he's drifting, too, unable to find the construction work that used to pay his bills.

"It's just going back to the same thing," says Lynch, 50. "I remember my grandparents and my dad talking about labor camps, and going town to town to work."

Crime is a concern here—according to county estimates, 41 percent of the homeless population has been incarcerated at some point—but the greatest fear for most Taco Flat residents is that they've lost their place in mainstream society, whether as a result of mental or physical illness, of past mistakes, or of the whims of global capitalism.

In better times, they might have weathered their troubles, getting by with work in factories, call centers, or construction sites. But those jobs are gone, and many people wonder if they will ever come back.

Tent cities have much in common with the squatter camps of the Great Depression, but to simply call them Hoovervilles is to ignore their complexity. To truly understand them, one must look at current trends in the developing world, where informal urbanism—a form of "slum" development that takes place outside the conventions of city planning—is now the predominant mode of city-making.

Informal urbanism, characterized by unauthorized occupation of land, makeshift construction, and lack of public utilities, is how many burgeoning nations meet their housing needs. It thrives in places like Fresno, where poverty is endemic and there is a wide gap between rich and poor.

Rahul Mehrotra, an associate professor in the urban studies and planning department at the Massachusetts Institute of Technology, says there's a kinship between Taco Flat and the squatter settlements of Mumbai, India, where he runs an architectural firm.

"It's really a reflection of the government's inability to provide housing affordably across society," Mehrotra says. Informal urbanism also thrives wherever people face exclusion from the mainstream markets for work and shelter, he adds, whether they are excluded for ethnic, economic, or political reasons.

This can be seen in Taco Flat's large contingent of undocumented workers, who left their homes in Latin America to find work on the Central Valley's farms and construction sites. As borders tighten and the threat of immigration raids lingers, the act of signing a lease has become more risky, prompting many to forgo formal housing altogether. Undocumented workers are also plagued by low wages, which aren't keeping pace with the rising costs of housing. This hardship has only been exacerbated by jobs disappearing in the Central Valley, where an ongoing drought is turning some of the world's most fertile farmland into a desert.

The situation has left Mexican workers like Juan Garcia, 21, suspended between two countries. In neither country is there a guarantee of a livelihood, and home is all too often an abstraction. At least in Garcia's native state of Colima, there are always the comforts of family.

"It's better in Mexico," Garcia says. "I'm going back."

In Fresno and other struggling cities, which perpetually strive to boost tax revenues with development, tent cities are often seen as symbols of criminality and dereliction, glaring setbacks to neighborhood revitalization efforts. That perception is common wherever informal urbanism exists, Mehrotra says, and it often leaves squatter camps on the brink of ruin.

"You are always on the edge of demolition," he says. This hit home in Fresno a few years ago, when workers began raiding encampments throughout the city, tearing down makeshift homes and destroying personal property. The city of Fresno and the California Department of Transportation conducted these sweeps in the name of public health, citing citizen complaints about open-air defecation.

30 Yet the raids did nothing to stop tent cities from forming, and 30 they ultimately led to lawsuits. In October 2006, residents who lost their homes in the raids filed a class-action suit against the city of Fresno and the state of California. A U.S. district judge ordered the defendants to pay $2.3 million in damages.

Two hundred miles south of Fresno, there's also been a battle over tent cities in the Inland Empire, an industrial stronghold that stretches out into the deserts east of Los Angeles. Flying into Ontario International Airport, one can see the nucleus of this struggle, in a neighborhood less than a mile from the tarmac.

There, on a stretch of vacant land surrounded by aging homes and abandoned orchards, tents are arranged in neat rows. This used to be one of Southern California's largest squatter settlements, an unruly village of tarp and scrap wood that grew until some 400 residents called it home. People moved here from as far away as Florida, recalls Brent Schultz, Ontario's director of housing and neighborhood revitalization.

Local officials were disturbed to find out that Ontario was becoming a magnet for the dispossessed, Schultz says. Rather than simply bulldoze the makeshift neighborhood. Ontario officials embarked on a $100,000 campaign to discipline and punish squatters, setting up a formal camp where tarp dwellings became symbols of order.

In the spring of last year, police and code enforcement officers issued color-coded bracelets to distinguish Ontario residents from newcomers, then gradually banished the out-of-towners. Then they demolished the shanties and set up an official camp with a chain-link fence and guard shack. Residents were issued IDs and a strict set of rules: no coming and going after 10 p.m., no pets, no children or visitors, no drugs, and no alcohol. About 120 people stuck around, but many left to escape the regimentation. As of July, the population was about 60.

35   "It's like a prison," says Melody Woolsey, 40, who has lived in 35 both versions of the encampment. Schultz, on the other hand, considers the camp one of Ontario's greatest success stories. Some of the camp's residents agree: They say it's a bit like a gated community on a modest scale, a rare haven where one can live affordably without fear of robbery or violence.

"Some people come up here and say it looks like a concentration camp, but they don't live here," says Robert, 51, an unemployed factory technician. "They're only looking at it from the outside. I look at it that it's a secure community."

Yet the neighborhood is filled with angry people who were excluded from the camp and left to take shelter in cars or in other vacant lots, often under threat of police citations. Many of these outcasts see the camp as a symbol of injustice, a cynical and inauthentic gesture of compassion.

For people throughout the American West, the very concept of home is changing, adjusting downward to a reality in which buying cheap land, picking out a subdivision lot, or even renting an apartment has become nothing more than a fancy daydream. That's a painful realization for a region steeped in myths of plenty. But in these hard times, tent cities increasingly are the last province of hope for having a place of one's own.

Tent cities like Taco Flat are communities like any other, and if they are neglected, they will be lost to crime, addiction, and illness. Yet whenever officials act to destroy or stifle them with punitive regulations, they not only wipe out the pride of residents struggling to survive, they also jettison a spirit of self-reliance and innovation that could be harnessed to help meet the housing needs of the future.

40   The promise of tent cities begins with their architecture. Makeshift 40 dwellings may not be the dream homes of yesteryear, but they are

simple, affordable, and sustainable in their use of salvaged materials. With imaginative designers, they could help solve the present housing crisis, a faster alternative to the process of building shelters and low-income apartment complexes.

That possibility is already taking shape in Portland, Oregon, where activists have carved out a space for improvised dwellings in Dignity Village, a community that can house up to 60 people. Founded in 2000 and now approved by the city, it's considered a model by housing advocates worldwide.

Beyond the check-in desk in the village's security post, residents find a balance between the human needs for safety and personal freedom. Most are required to do at least 10 hours of community service a week—helping build or remodel homes, for example—but otherwise they set their own schedules.

"This isn't a flophouse," says Joe Palinkas, 55. "This is a community place. You support the village by taking care of yourself as if you were on your own."

Tent cities also could become a locus for action and dialogue, a place where outreach workers, social service agencies, and everyday citizens can reach out to society's most vulnerable members.

45   Leaders in California's Central Valley might do well to take inspiration from Dignity Village. Instead, planners still see tent cities as obstacles to revitalization. Fresno and Madera counties recently adopted a 10-year plan to end homelessness, and Gregory Barfield, the area's newly appointed homelessness czar, says tent cities aren't part of the picture.

"A Dignity Village for us is not the best course of action," says Barfield. "We've got to find out a way to move forward with housing people."

But such talk means little to Taco Flat residents like Arthur Barela, 45, who lost his job when the Central Valley's farms began to dry out. For him, the only real home is the one he has made with his blankets, his tent, and his tarp. He still has the strength to keep his place clean, but his frame is nearly skeletal.

"Hopefully, things don't get chaotic and things don't get out of hand," says Barela, kneeling before his tent as if in prayer. "Sometimes hunger can make a person do crazy things."

Questions on Meaning

1. How are the tent cities in the United States like those in developing countries? What do these similarities suggest about the United States economy and social system?
2. What are the reasons that residents offer for resorting to living in tent cities? How do these reasons help to explain the recent growth of these communities?
3. What did Ontario, California officials hope to achieve by demolishing the existing tent city and constructing a new one? How do the various reactions of residents reflect the complex nature of this decision?

Questions on Rhetorical Strategy and Style

1. List several terms used to describe the communities Bransford discusses in this article. How do the terms reflect attitudes and beliefs about the people who live in these communities?
2. Why does Bransford use people like the Caros, Frankie Lynch, and Juan Garcia as representatives of Taco Flat? How does this strategy lead the reader to Bransford's desired conclusion about the place?
3. What features of Dignity Village provide points of contrast with the established tent city in Ontario, California? How does Bransford use these contrasts to support his position?

Writing Assignments

1. Bransford claims that when officials try to eliminate or over-regulate tent cities, "they not only wipe out the pride of residents struggling to survive, they also jettison a spirit of self-reliance and innovation that could be harnessed to help meet the housing needs of the future." Based on your reading of this article, respond to this statement in a brief essay.
2. Visit the web site for Dignity Village (http://www.dignityvillage. org/), and read several articles about the place. Then write a profile of the community, focusing on its goals, its practices, its impact on the wider community, and anything else that you consider relevant. Do you think that Dignity Village is a reasonable solution to the problem of homelessness?

The Imitation Economy
Drake Bennett

Drake Bennett was born in New York City and graduated from Harvard University with a degree in American History and Literature in 1999. His work has appeared in a number of magazines, including The New York Times Magazine, Wired, Business Week, *and* Slate.com. *From 2002 to 2005, Bennett wrote for* The American Prospect, *a publication self-described as "an authoritative magazine of liberal ideas, committed to a just society, an enriched democracy, and effective liberal politics." He is currently a staff writer for the* Boston Globe's *Ideas section, where the following essay appeared. In it, Bennett critiques the American love affair with innovation, citing a number of authorities who challenge the conventional wisdom that innovation is the key to success. It is often imitation, these authorities claim, that spurs economic growth and social development.*

1   Two weeks after it went on sale, the iPad is still the toast of the tech world, with its image gracing magazine covers, market analysts speculating about whether it will transform the worlds of publishing and entertainment, and consumers buying the gadget at a healthy clip. This at a cost of at least $500 each, at a time when Americans are still cautious about large nonessential purchases, and for a device that remains difficult to succinctly describe, much less figure out the purpose of.

   It's early yet, but it looks like another success for a company that, more than any other consumer brand, is synonymous with the new. Apple has forged a unique and lucrative reputation for creating irresistible, intuitive objects of techno-desire, shaping along the way how

Reprinted by permission from *The Boston Globe*, April 18, 2010.

we work, communicate, and procrastinate, and the look and feel of the electronic gadgetry that increasingly fills our lives.

Apple's success, in short, is a testament to the allure and the power of innovation. And there are other examples wherever we care to look. Global businesses from Ford to Hewlett-Packard to Google are built on innovation. At the most basic level, innovators have made modern life what it is—conquering diseases, automating work, shrinking distance, putting vast stores of information at our fingertips. Innovative artists have given us cubism and hip-hop. Innovative social scientists and politicians have given us the earned-income tax credit and the charter school. Inventors have given us the antibiotic and the air bag, the plow and the Predator drone.

Little wonder, then, that politicians and business gurus alike sing the praises of innovation. President Obama, like President Bush before him, often talks of its value, pointing to the $100 billion in last year's stimulus plan devoted to innovation projects like high-tech classrooms, high-speed rail, and a smart electricity grid, and describing the international race to develop reliable clean energy sources as a battle for control of the global economy. In business, failing to innovate is widely seen as a death sentence.

5 "Out there in some garage is an entrepreneur who's forging a bullet with your company's name on it," Gary Hamel, a leading business strategy writer and consultant, has written. "You've got one option now—to shoot first. You've got to out-innovate the innovators." 5

But invaluable though innovation may be, our relentless focus on it may be obscuring the value of its much-maligned relative, imitation. Imitation has always had a faintly disreputable ring to it—presidents do not normally give speeches extolling the virtues of the copycat. But where innovation brings new things into the world, imitation spreads them; where innovators break the old mold, imitators perfect the new one; and while innovators can win big, imitators often win bigger. Indeed, what looks like innovation is often actually artful imitation—tech-savvy observers see Apple's real genius not in how it creates new technologies (which it rarely does) but in how it synthesizes and packages existing ones.

The last decade has seen an explosion of copying in its various forms. Technology has made it easier to do everything from rip off a song to replicate the design of an engine, and rising powers like China and India are home to burgeoning industries dedicated to creating low-cost alternatives to cutting-edge, brand-name products, whether they're cars, computers, or drugs. At the same time, researchers in the fields of biology, business, and economics are looking in detail at how and why and when copying works.

What some are finding is that it is a strategy that works much better than we think—whether for businesses, people, or animals competing in the wild. At its best, copying spreads knowledge and speeds the process by which insights and inventions are honed, eliminating dead-end approaches and saving time, effort, and money.

"We hear so much about innovation, I don't know how many hundreds if not thousands of books, articles, and so forth," says Oded Shenkar, a professor at Ohio State's Fisher College of Business and author of the forthcoming book *Copycats: How Smart Companies Use Imitation to Gain a Strategic Edge*, "but imitation is at least as important as innovation if you really want to grow efficiently and make a profit."

10   And while we may dismiss imitation as the easy road—especially   10
when compared to the path-breaking of the innovator—there is an art to copying well. Researchers modeling the dynamics of social systems have found that how one copies, and when, can be crucial, making the difference between overtaking one's competitors and being written off as a pale, imitating also-ran.

"This is not just something that should happen, it's something you have to know how to do," says Shenkar. "What's true for innovation is true for imitation: You've got to get it right."

Shenkar traces our innovation fetish back to the late 18th century. Before that—for most of Western history, in other words—copying was valued just as highly as creation, and sometimes more. "In the Roman Empire, where imitation was used to align the diverse cultures and institutions of the far-flung empire under a single umbrella, it served as the official pedagogy," he writes in his book. Centuries later, Adam Smith wrote that imitation should be given "the status of a creative art." But the Romantic Age, with its celebration of the sui generis and the solitary genius—philosophers like Rousseau, poets like Shelley, and scientist-inventors like Humphry Davy—began to change that. Copying came to be seen as disreputable, as a refuge for the unimaginative.

The innovation bias is particularly strong in the United States, Shenkar argues. Partly this is thanks to a national mythology centered on the pioneer and the self-made man, partly because so many of the most transformative inventions of the 20th century—from the airplane to the television to the personal computer—were indeed hatched here.

But transformative innovations don't come along very often. And while it's important to foster them, it may not be realistic to think that a business, or any other enterprise, is going to be fueled solely by innovation. Often, the best one can hope for is incremental improvement, and the building blocks can come from many sources.

15   "If you're a big, tired firm, don't put lipstick on the pig, just be   15
the pig. Accept yourself for what you are," says Jonathan Zittrain, an internet law scholar at Harvard Law School.

The other danger for innovators is that they themselves often reap only a fraction of the benefits of their creations, as imitators crowd in after. In 2005, the management scholar Constantinos Markides and the economist Paul Geroski wrote a book laying out the advantages of what they called the "fast second," the company that gets to a market just after the pioneer and can capitalize on the first mover's mistakes and limitations.

Shenkar is quick to emphasize that his argument is limited to legal copying—he's not making the case for actually stealing intellectual property. Still, he sees embarrassment about copycatting stifling open discussion among managers—and management scholars—about the details and techniques of imitation.

"What I've found from many interviews is that there were many executives who were reluctant to even use what I call the 'i word,' to admit that they were engaged in imitation," he says.

That means when companies copy they often do it clumsily. Shenkar offers the example of the legacy airlines in the United States and their response to the low-cost threat of Southwest Airlines. Most set up copycat airlines of their own: United with TED, Continental with CALite, Delta with Song. All quickly failed.

20   The problem, Shenkar argues, is that in their scramble to copy   20
Southwest, the bigger airlines failed to see the ways that central pillars of Southwest's strategy—lower pay, short point-to-point flights, a fleet of identical smaller planes—were incompatible with the union contracts, hub-and-spoke route structures, and larger craft the traditional carriers were saddled with.

Copying isn't just a business strategy, of course. We all do it: Human beings, by nature, are incorrigible mimics. From birth, we learn by aping the sounds we hear (a recent German study found that newborns' crying already echoes their parents' speech cadences, suggesting they start imitating while still in the womb), along with the facial expressions and gestures we see, the opinions and customs and biases we are exposed to. Neuroscientists researching brain cells called mirror neurons in monkeys hypothesize that higher human emotions like empathy and moral outrage might stem from a hard-wired instinct to imitate the bodily reactions—and through them the emotions—of those around us.

"Imitation is natural to man from childhood," Aristotle wrote, "one of his advantages over the lower animals being this, that he is the most imitative creature in the world, and learns at first by imitation."

Today there is a large body of literature exploring, at the broadest level, how copying works, whether among individuals or groups, in human societies or in the wild. The researchers are biologists, psychologists, economists, political scientists, anthropologists, mathematicians, computer programmers, and others, and their work involves both field studies (looking at monkeys or birds or fish or people) and complex computer simulations of social networks.

This research has yielded its own evidence of the particular power of imitation. In a provocative new paper from the journal *Science*, a team of researchers reports evidence that copying is the best survival strategy in a variety of social settings, including some traditionally seen as inhospitable to it. The finding emerged from a tournament set up by the behavioral biologists Kevin Laland and Luke Rendell of the University of St. Andrews. They invited scholars to submit "social learning strategies" that would compete against each other, for a prize of 10,000 euros, in a computer simulation of 100 individuals trying to survive in a dynamic environment.

25   The winner turned out to be a pure copier. Rather than take the   25
time to decipher the environment, it instructed individuals to simply copy what others were doing and see how that worked. Indeed, all the best-performing strategies relied heavily on what network researchers call "social learning."

"The really striking thing that comes out of the tournament is that there's an extraordinarily broad number of circumstances in which it pays to copy," says Laland.

The trick, it turned out, was getting the timing right. During times of relative stasis, the winning algorithm exploited the information it had. But when the payoffs changed, it began to copy what others were doing, looking for a more effective new strategy. Interestingly, much of the most successful innovation in the simulation actually resulted from mistaken copying—one individual stumbling onto a new and better solution by incorrectly imitating someone else. We can see this dynamic at work, Laland suggests, in real-world examples like the discovery of penicillin, where a mistake in basic lab protocol by the biologist Alexander Fleming gave the world antibiotics.

The best copycats, the tournament suggests, are those that sample widely, and ruthlessly compare the available options against each other. And the best copycats, like the best innovators, aren't afraid to junk the current model for something new.

All of which would suggest that individuals and institutions in uncertain environments—whether they're citizens of nations in political turmoil, animals facing a changing habitat, or long-dominant firms unsettled by the Internet—should diligently apply themselves to copying everything they see.

30 Some social learning researchers, however, remain skeptical of 30 the tournament and what it says about the value of copying. Luc-Alain Giraldeau, a specialist in animal social learning behavior at the Université du Québec à Montréal, submitted several strategies to the tournament, none of which did particularly well. While he's intrigued by the results, he suspects that they will not apply to the real world.

Copying, he points out, can be catastrophic—the history of market bubbles is testament to that. The human susceptibility to social cues means people often will follow their peers even when it leads to absurd results: In a well known study from the 1950s by the psychologist Solomon Asch, subjects gave the wrong answer in an extremely easy visual test when put in a group where everyone else did the same.

Shenkar argues that the best imitators don't lose sight of this. In his book, he examines what he sees as the master imitators of the business world—among them Wal-Mart, McDonald's, Ryanair, Samsung, and, yes, Apple—and distills from them the habits of highly successful copycats. The advice is largely common sense—keeping an open mind, not being fooled by appearances, and paying attention to the details of execution—but some of it runs counter to deeply ingrained instincts.

For example, while it's tempting to copy direct competitors, especially when they're doing well, it's often more helpful to look for models in far-flung fields: It's ground less likely to have been mined by competitors, but where unfamiliar ideas have already been tested. Shenkar points to how the toy firm Ohio Art has borrowed from the automotive industry and how the medical supply firm Cardinal Health copied the methods of food distributors, but there are plenty of examples beyond the business world: Today weapons designers imitate video game designers, traffic engineers borrow from particle physics, mechanical engineers copy the intricacies of plant structure, architects mimic airplane design, and psychologists use techniques perfected by magicians to design research studies.

It's also important, though, to remember that just because someone successful does something doesn't mean it should be copied. After all, the practice may be a result rather than a cause of that success, or totally incidental to it. Bringing a ping-pong table into the office and encouraging employees to wear jeans won't create a successful tech company any more than moving into a garret apartment and contracting tuberculosis will make someone a brilliant poet.

35   "You have to look further, and make sure you understand why 35 something was successful, and whether its success applies," Shenkar says. And if it does, he argues, you rip it off as quickly as you can.

Questions on Meaning

1. Why is imitation often more desirable than innovation, according to Bennett?

2. How does Bennett account for the celebration of imitation in the Roman Empire, and for its loss of favor in the Romantic era and in the United States? What does his conclusion suggest about the impact of culture on innovation/imitation?

3. What do experts identify as the key features of successful imitation? What pitfalls should imitators avoid?

Questions on Rhetorical Strategy and Style

1. How does Bennett employ the example of Apple to illustrate the value of both innovation and imitation?

2. Appeal to authority is a key feature of persuasive writing. Identify the authorities that Bennett cites, and explain how they support his argument.

3. How does Bennett address positions contrary to his? Do you find his handling of opposing views effective? Why, or why not?

Writing Assignments

1. Oded Shenkar argues that United States culture is built on "a mythology centered on the pioneer and the self-made man." Using examples from American history—explorers, inventors, entrepreneurs, writers—write an essay in response to Shenkar's claim.

2. Bennett refers to the iPad as "a device that remains difficult to succinctly describe, much less figure out the purpose of." Read/view promotional materials on the iPad, talk with a salesperson at an Apple store, and interview people who have used the device. Then write a description of the device, focusing on its features, its purpose, and the extent to which it is, indeed, innovative.

Cyberspace: If You Don't Love It, Leave It

Esther Dyson

Ester Dyson (1951–) was born in Zurich, Switzerland. An authority on information technologies, Dyson is often termed a "futurist." A graduate of Harvard University (B.A. 1972), she reported for Forbes *and worked as a security analyst before becoming president of EDventure Holdings, where she also edits the newsletter* Release 1.0. *She also has been chairperson of the Electronic Frontier Foundation (an industry-funded advocacy organization). Dyson has been published in* Harvard Business Review, The New York Times, *and* Wired. *In this essay, which appeared in* The New York Times Magazine *(July 1995), Dyson defines and delimits the virtual real estate of cyberspace.*

1 Something in the American psyche loves new frontiers. We hanker after wide-open spaces; we like to explore; we like to remake rules instead of follow them. But in this age of political correctness and other intrusions on our national cult of independence, it's hard to find a place where you can go and be yourself without worrying about the neighbors.

There is such a place: cyberspace. Lost in the furor over porn on the Net is the exhilarating sense of freedom that this new frontier once promised—and still does in some quarters. Formerly a playground for computer nerds and techies, cyberspace now embraces every conceivable constituency: schoolchildren, flirtatious singles, Hungarian-Americans, accountants—along with pederasts and porn fans. Can they all get along? Or will our fear of kids surfing for cyberporn behind their bedroom doors provoke a crackdown?

The first order of business is to grasp what cyberspace is. It might help to leave behind metaphors of highways and frontiers and to think instead of real estate. Real estate, remember, is an intellectual, legal, artificial environment constructed *on top of* land. Real estate recognizes the difference between parkland and shopping mall, between red-light zone and school district, between church, state and drugstore.

In the same way, you could think of cyberspace as a giant and unbounded world of virtual real estate. Some property is privately owned and rented out; other property is common land; some places are suitable for children, and others are best avoided by all but the kinkiest citizens. Unfortunately, it's those places that are now capturing the popular imagination: places that offer bomb-making instructions, pornography, advice on how to procure stolen credit cards. They make cyberspace sound like a nasty place. Good citizens jump to a conclusion: Better regulate it.

The most recent manifestation of this impulse is the Exon-Coats Amendment, a well-meaning but misguided bill drafted by Senators Jim Exon, Democrat of Nebraska, and Daniel R. Coats, Republican of Indiana, to make cyberspace "safer" for children. Part of the telecommunications reform bill passed by the Senate and awaiting consideration by the House, the amendment would outlaw making "indecent communication" available to anyone under 18. Then there's the Amateur Action bulletin board case, in which the owners of a porn service in Milpitas, Calif., were convicted in a Tennessee court of violating "community standards" after a local postal inspector requested that the material be transmitted to him.

Regardless of how many laws or lawsuits are launched, regulation won't work.

Aside from being unconstitutional, using censorship to counter indecency and other troubling "speech" fundamentally misinterprets the nature of cyberspace. Cyberspace isn't a frontier where wicked people can grab unsuspecting children, nor is it a giant television system that can beam offensive messages at unwilling viewers. In this kind of real estate, users have to *choose* where they visit, what they see, what they do. It's optional, and it's much easier to bypass a place on the Net than it is to avoid walking past an unsavory block of stores on the way to your local 7-11.

Put plainly, cyberspace is a voluntary destination—in reality, many destinations. You don't just get "onto the net"; you have to go someplace in particular. That means that people can choose where to go and what to see. Yes, community standards should be enforced, but those standards should be set by cyberspace communities themselves, not by the courts or by politicians in Washington. What we need isn't Government control over all these electronic communities: We need self-rule.

What makes cyberspace so alluring is precisely the way in which it's *different* from shopping malls, television, highways and other terrestrial jurisdictions. But let's define the territory:

10   First, there are private E-mail conversations, akin to the conversations you have over the telephone or voice mail. These are private and consensual and require no regulation at all.

Second, there are information and entertainment services, where people can download anything from legal texts and lists of "great new restaurants" to game software or dirty pictures. These places are like bookstores, malls and movie houses—places where you go to buy something. The customer needs to request an item or sign up for a subscription; stuff (especially pornography) is not sent out to people who don't ask for it. Some of these services are free or included as part of a broader service like Compuserve or America Online; others charge and may bill their customers directly.

Third, there are "real" communities—groups of people who communicate among themselves. In real-estate terms, they're like bars or restaurants or bathhouses. Each active participant contributes to a general conversation, generally through posted messages. Other participants may simply listen or watch. Some are supervised by a moderator; others are more like bulletin boards—anyone is free to post anything. Many of these services started out unmoderated but are now imposing rules to keep out unwanted advertising, extraneous discussions or increasingly rude participants. Without a moderator, the decibel level often gets too high.

Ultimately, it's the rules that determine the success of such places. Some of the rules are determined by the supplier of content—some of the rules concern prices and membership fees. The rules may be simple: "Only high-quality content about oil-industry liability and pollution legislation: $120 an hour." Or: "This forum is unmoderated, and restricted to information about copyright issues. People who insist on posting advertising or unrelated material will be asked to desist (and may eventually be barred)." Or: "Only children 8 to 12, on school-related topics and only clean words. The moderator will decide what's acceptable."

Cyberspace communities evolve just the way terrestrial communities do: people with like-minded interests band together. Every cyberspace community has its own character. Overall, the communities on Compuserve tend to be more techy or professional; those on America Online, affluent young singles; Prodigy, family oriented. Then there are independents like Echo, a hip, downtown New York service, or Women's Wire, targeted to women who want to avoid the male culture prevalent elsewhere on the Net. There's SurfWatch, a new program allowing access only to locations deemed suitable for children. On the Internet itself, there are lots of passionate noncommercial discussion groups on topics ranging from Hungarian politics (Hungary-Online) to copyright law.

15   And yes, there are also porn-oriented services, where people share 15
dirty pictures and communicate with one another about all kinds of practices, often anonymously. Whether these services encourage the fantasies they depict is subject to debate—the same debate that has raged about pornography in other media. But the point is that no one is forcing this stuff on anybody.

What's unique about cyberspace is that it liberates us from the tyranny of government, where everyone lives by the rule of the majority. In a democracy, minority groups and minority preferences tend to get squeezed out, whether they are minorities of race and culture or minorities of individual taste. Cyberspace allows communities of any size and kind to flourish; in cyberspace, communities are chosen by the users, not forced on them by accidents of geography. This freedom gives the rules that preside in cyberspace a moral authority that rules in terrestrial environments don't have. Most people are stuck in the country of their birth, but if you don't like the rules of a cyberspace community, you can just sign off. Love it or leave it. Likewise, if parents don't like the rules of a given cyberspace community, they can restrict their children's access to it.

What's likely to happen in cyberspace is the formation of new communities, free of the constraints that cause conflict on earth. Instead of a global village, which is a nice dream but impossible to manage, we'll have invented another world of self-contained communities that cater to their own members' inclinations without interfering with anyone else's. The possibility of a real market-style evolution of governance is at hand. In cyberspace, we'll be able to test and evolve rules governing what needs to be governed—intellectual property, content and access control, rules about privacy and free speech. Some communities will allow anyone in; others will restrict access to members who qualify on one basis or another. Those communities that prove self-sustaining will prosper (and perhaps grow and split into subsets with ever-more-particular interests and identities). Those that can't survive—either because people lose interest or get scared off—will simply wither away.

In the near future, explorers in cyberspace will need to get better at defining and identifying their communities. They will need to put in place—and accept—their own local governments, just as the owners of expensive real estate often prefer to have their own security guards rather than call in the police. But they will rarely need help from any terrestrial government.

Of course, terrestrial governments may not agree. What to do, for instance, about pornography? The answer is labeling—not banning—questionable material. In order to avoid censorship and lower the political temperature, it makes sense for cyberspace participants themselves to agree on a scheme for questionable items, so that people or automatic filters can avoid them. In other words, posting pornography in "alt.sex.bestiality" would be O.K.; it's easy enough for software manufacturers to build an automatic filter that would prevent you—or your child—from ever seeing that item on a menu. (It's as if all the items were wrapped, with labels on the wrapper.) Someone who posted the same material under the title "Kid-Fun" could be sued for mislabeling.

20   Without a lot of fanfare, private enterprises and local groups are   20
already producing a variety of labeling and ranking services, along with kid-oriented sites like Kidlink, EdWeb and Kids' Space. People differ in their tastes and values and can find services or reviewers on the Net that suit them in the same way they select books and magazines. Or they can wander freely if they prefer, making up their own itinerary.

In the end, our society needs to grow up. Growing up means understanding that there are no perfect answers, no all-purpose solutions, no government-sanctioned safe havens. We haven't created a perfect society on earth and we won't have one in cyberspace either. But at least we can have individual choice—and individual responsibility.

Questions on Meaning

1. What are the two reasons why Dyson believes that regulation of cyberspace will not work? What other reasons can you think of?
2. Dyson mentions a number of topics on which one can find information on the Internet. What topic area creates the greatest controversy?

Questions on Rhetorical Strategy and Style

1. What analogy does Dyson use to explain cyberspace? How effective do you find that analogy compared with the "information highway" metaphor that is frequently used when discussing the Internet and electronic communication?
2. How does Dyson use step-by-step analysis to define the scope of cyberspace? How might you revise her groupings?
3. Dyson bases her argument on her opinion and her familiarity with cyberspace. How convincing do you find her arguments? Would it have helped if she had included statistics, or comments by experts, or rebuttals by individuals who disagree with her position?

Writing Assignments

1. Investigate initiatives to control information or access to information on the Internet—particularly pornographic material. Have efforts been made to label—not ban—questionable material, as Dyson suggests? Compare and contrast the effectiveness of various schemes, such as the use of "filters."
2. What has your experience been "surfing the 'net' " with regard to "questionable" sites? Do you think it is accurate to belittle concerns over pornography or bomb-making or credit-card fraud information because one can choose where to go? Describe a time when you stumbled onto a site that shocked you. What did you do? Were you concerned that you might be leaving an electronic trail, that you might find yourself receiving unwanted paper or electronic mail related to that topic, that your address might be passed on (or sold) to other purveyors of that type of material? How did that experience affect your opinion about the need for controls over information on the Internet?

3. "Love it or leave it," Dyson says about cyberspace. Unlike "real life," where one's identity is known, the anonymity of the Internet permits people to casually come and go. Write an essay about the anonymous atmosphere of Internet communities, where participants are identified by secret codes (e-mail addresses), and where it is easy to masquerade. Explain why you feel this is healthy or unhealthy for human relations. Compare and contrast Internet relationships with conventional, face-to-face relationships.

The Ways We Lie

Stephanie Ericsson

Stephanie Ericsson (1953–) was born in Dallas, Texas. She now lives in Minneapolis where she writes essays and books, and she travels to speak to groups about grief and loss. Her husband died when she was two months pregnant with her first child, an experience which prompted her to compose Companion Through the Darkness: Inner Dialogues on Grief *(Harper, 1993). She is also a screenwriter and advertising copywriter. Her books include* Shamefaced: The Road to Recovery *(1985) and* Women of AA: Recovering Together *(1985), both written after a bout with substance abuse;* Companion Through the Darkness: Inner Dialogues on Grief *(Harper, 1993); and* Companion into the Dawn: Inner Dialogues.

Lies can be defined in many ways, and these various types of lies have different effects on people. Ericsson takes the reader from the polite white lie that can preserve relationships to the destructive deceptions that destroy self, others, and even culture.

1   The bank called today and I told them my deposit was in the mail, even though I hadn't written a check yet. It'd been a rough day. The baby I'm pregnant with decided to do aerobics on my lungs for two hours, our three-year-old daughter painted the living-room couch with lipstick, the IRS put me on hold for an hour, and I was late to a business meeting because I was tired.

I told my client that traffic had been bad. When my partner came home, his haggard face told me his day hadn't gone any better than mine, so when he asked, "How was your day?" I said, "Oh, fine," knowing that one more straw might break his back. A friend called and wanted to take me to lunch. I said I was busy. Four lies in the course of a day, none of which I felt the least bit guilty about.

We lie. We all do. We exaggerate, we minimize, we avoid confrontation, we spare people's feelings, we conveniently forget, we keep secrets, we justify lying to the big-guy institutions. Like most people, I indulge in small falsehoods and still think of myself as an honest person. Sure I lie, but it doesn't hurt anything. Or does it?

I once tried going a whole week without telling a lie, and it was paralyzing. I discovered that telling the truth all the time is nearly impossible. It means living with some serious consequences: The bank charges me $60 in overdraft fees, my partner keels over when I tell him about my travails, my client fires me for telling her I didn't feel like being on time, and my friend takes it personally when I say I'm not hungry. There must be some merit to lying.

But if I justify lying, what makes me any different from slick politicians or the corporate robbers who raided the S & L industry? Saying it's okay to lie one way and not another is hedging. I cannot seem to escape the voice deep inside me that tells me: When someone lies, someone loses.

What far-reaching consequences will I, or others, pay as a result of my lie? Will someone's trust be destroyed? Will someone else pay *my* penance because I ducked out? We must consider the *meaning of our actions.* Deception, lies, capital crimes, and misdemeanors all carry meanings. *Webster's* definition of *lie* is specific:

1. a false statement or action especially made with the intent to deceive;
2. anything that gives or is meant to give a false impression.

A definition like this implies that there are many, many ways to tell a lie. Here are just a few.

The White Lie

A man who won't lie to a woman has very little consideration for her feelings.

—Bergen Evans

The white lie assumes that the truth will cause more damage than a simple, harmless untruth. Telling a friend he looks great when he looks like hell can be based on a decision that the friend needs a compliment more than a frank opinion. But, in effect, it is the liar deciding what is best for the lied to. Ultimately, it is a vote of no confidence. It is an act of subtle arrogance for anyone to decide what is best for someone else.

Yet not all circumstances are quite so cut-and-dried. Take, for instance, the sergeant in Vietnam who knew one of his men was killed in action but listed him as missing so that the man's family would receive indefinite compensation instead of the lump-sum pittance the military gives widows and children. His intent was honorable. Yet for twenty years this family kept their hopes alive, unable to move on to a new life.

Façades

> Et tu, Brute?
> —Caesar

10   We all put up façades to one degree or another. When I put on a suit   10
to go to see a client, I feel as though I am putting on another face, obeying the expectation that serious businesspeople wear suits rather than sweatpants. But I'm a writer. Normally, I get up, get the kid off to school, and sit at my computer in my pajamas until four in the afternoon. When I answer the phone, the caller thinks I'm wearing a suit (though the UPS man knows better).

But façades can be destructive because they are used to seduce others into an illusion. For instance, I recently realized that a former friend was a liar. He presented himself with all the right looks and the right words and offered lots of new consciousness theories, fabulous books to read, and fascinating insights. Then I did some business with him, and the time came for him to pay me. He turned out to be all talk and no walk. I heard a plethora of reasonable excuses, including in-depth descriptions of the big break around the corner. In six months of work, I saw less than a hundred bucks. When I confronted him, he raised both eyebrows and tried to convince me that I'd heard him wrong, that he'd made no commitment to me. A simple investigation into his past revealed a crowded graveyard of disenchanted former friends.

Ignoring the Plain Facts

> Well, you must understand that Father Porter is only human.
> —A Massachusetts priest

In the '60s, the Catholic Church in Massachusetts began hearing complaints that Father James Porter was sexually molesting children. Rather than relieving him of his duties, the ecclesiastical authorities simply moved him from one parish to another between 1960 and 1967, actually providing him with a fresh supply of unsuspecting families and innocent children to abuse. After treatment in 1967 for pedophilia, he went back to work, this time in Minnesota. The new diocese was aware of Father Porter's obsession with children, but they needed priests and recklessly believed treatment had cured him. More children were abused until he was relieved of his duties a year later. By his own admission, Porter may have abused as many as a hundred children.

Ignoring the facts may not in and of itself be a form of lying, but consider the context of this situation. If a lie is *a false action done with the intent to deceive,* then the Catholic Church's conscious covering for Porter created irreparable consequences. The church became a co-perpetrator with Porter.

Deflecting

When you have no basis for an argument, abuse the plaintiff.
—Cicero

I've discovered that I can keep anyone from seeing the true me by being selectively blatant. I set a precedent of being up-front about intimate issues, but I never bring up the things I truly want to hide; I just let people assume I'm revealing everything. It's an effective way of hiding.

15 Any good liar knows that the way to perpetuate an untruth is to deflect attention from it. When Clarence Thomas exploded with accusations that the Senate hearings were a "high-tech lynching," he simply switched the focus from a highly charged subject to a radioactive subject. Rather than defending himself, he took the offensive and accused the country of racism. It was a brilliant maneuver. Racism is now politically incorrect in official circles—unlike sexual harassment, which still rewards those who can get away with it.

Some of the most skilled deflectors are passive-aggressive people who, when accused of inappropriate behavior, refuse to respond to the accusations. This you-don't-exist stance infuriates the accuser, who, understandably, screams something obscene out of frustration. The trap is sprung and the act of deflection successful, because now the passive-aggressive person can indignantly say, "Who can talk to someone as unreasonable as you?" The real issue is forgotten and the sins of the original victim become the focus. Feeling guilty of name-calling, the victim is fully tamed and crawls into a hole, ashamed. I have watched this fighting technique work thousands of times in disputes between men and women, and what I've learned is that the real culprit is not necessarily the one who swears the loudest.

Omission

> The cruelest lies are often told in silence.
> —R. L. Stevenson

Omission involves telling most of the truth minus one or two key facts whose absence changes the story completely. You break a pair of glasses that are guaranteed under normal use and get a new pair, without mentioning that the first pair broke during a rowdy game of basketball. Who hasn't tried something like that? But what about omission of information that could make a difference in how a person lives his or her life?

For instance, one day I found out that rabbinical legends tell of another woman in the Garden of Eden before Eve. I was stunned. The omission of the Sumerian goddess Lilith from Genesis—as well as her demonization by ancient misogynists as an embodiment of female evil—felt like spiritual robbery. I felt like I'd just found out my mother was really my stepmother. To take seriously the tradition that Adam was created out of the same mud as his equal counterpart, Lilith, redefines all of Judeo-Christian history.

Some renegade Catholic feminists introduced me to a view of Lilith that had been suppressed during the many centuries when this strong goddess was seen only as a spirit of evil. Lilith was a proud goddess who defied Adam's need to control her, attempted negotiations, and when this failed, said adios and left the Garden of Eden.

20 This omission of Lilith from the Bible was a patriarchal strategy 20 to keep women weak. Omitting the strong-woman archetype of Lilith from Western religions and starting the story with Eve the Rib has helped keep Christian and Jewish women believing they were the lesser sex for thousands of years.

Stereotypes and Clichés

> Where opinion does not exist, the status quo becomes stereotyped
> and all originality is discouraged.
>
> —Bertrand Russell

Stereotype and cliché serve a purpose as a form of shorthand. Our need for vast amounts of information in nanoseconds has made the stereotype vital to modern communication. Unfortunately, it often shuts down original thinking, giving those hungry for the truth a candy bar of misinformation instead of a balanced meal. The stereotype explains a situation with just enough truth to seem unquestionable.

All the "isms"—racism, sexism, ageism, et al.—are founded on and fueled by the stereotype and the cliché, which are lies of exaggeration, omission, and ignorance. They are always dangerous. They take a single tree and make it a landscape. They destroy curiosity. They close minds and separate people. The single mother on welfare is assumed to be cheating. Any black male could tell you how much of his identity is obliterated daily by stereotypes. Fat people, ugly people, beautiful people, old people, large-breasted women, short men, the mentally ill, and the homeless all could tell you how much more they are like us than we want to think. I once admitted to a group of people that I had a mouth like a truck driver. Much to my surprise, a man stood up and said, "I'm a truck driver, and I never cuss." Needless to say, I was humbled.

Groupthink

> Who is more foolish, the child afraid of the dark, or the man afraid
> of the light?
>
> —Maurice Freehill

Irving Janis, in *Victims of Group Think,* defines this sort of lie as a psychological phenomenon within decision-making groups in which loyalty to the group has become more important than any other value, with the result that dissent and the appraisal of alternatives are suppressed. If you've ever worked on a committee or in a corporation, you've encountered groupthink. It requires a combination of other forms of lying—ignoring facts, selective memory, omission, and denial, to name a few.

The textbook example of groupthink came on December 7, 1941. From as early as the fall of 1941, the warnings came in, one after another, that Japan was preparing for a massive military operation. The navy command in Hawaii assumed Pearl Harbor was invulnerable—the Japanese weren't stupid enough to attack the United States' most important base. On the other hand, racist stereotypes said the Japanese weren't smart enough to invent a torpedo effective in less than 60 feet of water (the fleet was docked in 30 feet); after all, US technology hadn't been able to do it.

25   On Friday, December 5, normal weekend leave was granted to all   25
the commanders at Pearl Harbor, even though the Japanese consulate in Hawaii was busy burning papers. Within the tight, good-ole-boy cohesiveness of the US command in Hawaii, the myth of invulnerability stayed well entrenched. No one in the group considered the alternatives. The rest is history.

Out-and-Out Lies

> The only form of lying that is beyond reproach is lying for its own sake.
>
> —Oscar Wilde

Of all the ways to lie, I like this one the best, probably because I get tired of trying to figure out the real meanings behind things. At least I can trust the bald-faced lie. I once asked my five-year-old nephew, "Who broke the fence?" (I had seen him do it.) He answered, "The murderers." Who could argue?

At least when this sort of lie is told it can be easily confronted. As the person who is lied to, I know where I stand. The bald-faced lie doesn't toy with my perceptions—it argues with them. It doesn't try to refashion reality, it tries to refute it. *Read my lips*. . . . No sleight of hand. No guessing. If this were the only form of lying, there would be no such things as floating anxiety or the adult-children-of-alcoholics movement.

Dismissal

> Pay no attention to that man behind the curtain! I am the Great Oz!
> —The Wizard of Oz

Dismissal is perhaps the slipperiest of all lies. Dismissing feelings, perceptions, or even the raw facts of a situation ranks as a kind of lie that can do as much damage to a person as any other kind of lie.

The roots of many mental disorders can be traced back to the dismissal of reality. Imagine that a person is told from the time she is a tot that her perceptions are inaccurate. "*Mommy, I'm scared.*" "No you're not, darling." "*I don't like that man next door, he makes me feel icky.*" "Johnny, that's a terrible thing to say, of course you like him. You go over there right now and be nice to him."

30   I've often mused over the idea that madness is actually a sane   30
reaction to an insane world. Psychologist R. D. Laing supports this hypothesis in *Sanity, Madness and the Family,* an account of his investigation into the families of schizophrenics. The common thread that ran through all of the families he studied was a deliberate, staunch dismissal of the patient's perceptions from a very early age. Each of the patients started out with an accurate grasp of reality, which, through meticulous and methodical dismissal, was demolished until the only reality the patient could trust was catatonia.

Dismissal runs the gamut. Mild dismissal can be quite handy for forgiving the foibles of others in our day-to-day lives. Toddlers who have just learned to manipulate their parents' attention sometimes are dismissed out of necessity. Absolute attention from the parents would require so much energy that no one would get to eat dinner. But we must be careful and attentive about how far we take our "necessary" dismissals. Dismissal is a dangerous tool, because it's nothing less than a lie.

Delusion

> We lie loudest when we lie to ourselves.
> —Eric Hoffer

I could write the book on this one. Delusion, a cousin of dismissal, is the tendency to see excuses as facts. It's a powerful lying tool because it filters out information that contradicts what we want to believe. Alcoholics who believe that the problems in their lives are legitimate reasons for drinking rather than results of the drinking offer the classic example of deluded thinking. Delusion uses the mind's ability to see things in myriad ways to support what it wants to be the truth.

But delusion is also a survival mechanism we all use. If we were to fully contemplate the consequences of our stockpiles of nuclear weapons or global warming, we could hardly function on a day-to-day level. We don't want to incorporate that much reality into our lives because to do so would be paralyzing.

Delusion acts as an adhesive to keep the status quo intact. It shamelessly employs dismissal, omission, and amnesia, among other sorts of lies. Its most cunning defense is that it cannot see itself.

> The liar's punishment . . . is that he cannot believe anyone else.
> —George Bernard Shaw

35   These are only a few of the ways we lie. Or are lied to. As I said 35 earlier, it's not easy to entirely eliminate lies from our lives. No matter how pious we may try to be, we will still embellish, hedge, and omit to lubricate the daily machinery of living. But there is a world of difference between telling functional lies and living a lie. Martin Buber once said, "The lie is the spirit committing treason against itself." Our acceptance of lies becomes a cultural cancer that eventually shrouds and reorders reality until moral garbage becomes as invisible to us as water is to a fish.

How much do we tolerate before we become sick and tired of being sick and tired? When will we stand up and declare our *right* to trust? When do we stop accepting that the real truth is in the fine print? Whose lips do we read this year when we vote for president? When will we stop being so reticent about making judgments? When do we stop turning over our personal power and responsibility to liars?

Maybe if I don't tell the bank the check's in the mail I'll be less tolerant of the lies told me every day. A country song I once heard said it all for me: "You've got to stand for something or you'll fall for anything."

Questions on Meaning

1. Ericsson argues that lying is more than words, that people can lie with their clothes, their actions, and even their possessions. Explain why we can be dishonest even without speaking.
2. Are some lies all right? What happens when the author tries to go for a period without telling any lies at all? What are the results of being too honest?
3. Self-deception can be dangerous. What happens when people tell themselves lies about their own lives and the lives of others? What psychological results and social results come from self-deception?

Questions on Rhetorical Strategy and Style

1. The essay moves from "good" lies to harmless lies to truly harmful lies. How does this order help to make the major arguments of the essay? Why does the essay define different kinds of behavior as lies?
2. The pattern of this essay is basically a list of definitions, all set out in short passages. Why does this approach make for quick and easy reading? What advantages are there for busy readers?
3. The final section of the essay is about delusions. Why does the author place this definition last? What effect does this ending have on the importance of the whole essay?

Writing Assignments

1. Think about a time when you had to tell a "white lie." What were the circumstances? What were the results? What might have happened if you had told the truth? Write about the experience.
2. Mark Twain once said that unlike Abe Lincoln who "could not tell a lie," Twain could tell a lie but sometimes chose not to lie. Imagine a person who truly cannot tell a lie, and describe the kinds of social situations that would result from this. Write about this imaginary person.
3. Choose a character in a story, novel, TV show, or movie who is self-deluded. Write about that person's behavior and the results of that behavior. Then analyze the dangers of self-deluded behavior.

The Human Cost of an Illiterate Society

Jonathan Kozol

*Jonathan Kozol (1936–) was born in Boston and gradu-
ated from Harvard University. He has taught at Yale University, Trinity College, and the University of Massachusetts
at Amherst as well as several public schools. He is well
known for his writing on social and educational issues,
often calling for educational reform and more realistic examination of societal problems. His books include* Death
at an Early Age *(1967),* Free Schools *(1972),* On Being
a Teacher *(1981),* Illiterate America *(1985),* Rachel and
Her Children: Homeless Families in America *(1986),
and* Savage Inequalities: Children in America's Schools
(1991). The following selection is an excerpt from Illiterate America. *Kozol does not explore the causes of illiteracy
in this selection, as he does elsewhere in this book, but instead looks at a wide range of effects, or costs, of illiteracy,
both for society and the individual. Before beginning to
read, think for a moment about what it might mean to be
illiterate. Try to imagine how many ways your life would
be different if you couldn't read. Regardless of how imaginative you are, you are likely to be shocked by all the ways
illiteracy affects an illiterate person and society as a whole.*

PRECAUTIONS. READ BEFORE USING.
Poison: Contains sodium hydroxide (caustic soda-lye).
Corrosive: Causes severe eye and skin damage, may cause blindness.
Harmful or fatal if swallowed.
If swallowed, give large quantities of milk or water.

Do not induce vomiting.
Important: Keep water out of can at all times to prevent contents from violently erupting . . .

—warning on a can of Drano

1   Questions of literacy, in Socrates' belief, must at length be judged as matters of morality. Socrates could not have had in mind the moral compromise peculiar to a nation like our own. Some of our Founding Fathers did, however, have this question in their minds. One of the wisest of those Founding Fathers (one who may not have been most compassionate but surely was more prescient than some of his peers) recognized the special dangers that illiteracy would pose to basic equity in the political construction that he helped to shape.

"A people who mean to be their own governors," James Madison wrote, "must arm themselves with the power knowledge gives. A popular government without popular information or the means of acquiring it, is but a prologue to a farce or a tragedy, or perhaps both."

Tragedy looms larger than farce in the United States today. Illiterate citizens seldom vote. Those who do are forced to cast a vote of questionable worth. They cannot make informed decisions based on serious print information. Sometimes they can be alerted to their interests by aggressive voter education. More frequently, they vote for a face, a smile, or a style, not for a mind or character or body of beliefs.

The number of illiterate adults exceeds by 16 million the entire vote cast for the winner in the 1980 presidential contest. If even one third of all illiterates could vote, and read enough and do sufficient math to vote in their self-interest, Ronald Reagan would not likely have been chosen president. There is, of course, no way to know for sure. We do know this: Democracy is a mendacious term when used by those who are prepared to countenance the forced exclusion of one third of our electorate. So long as 60 million people are denied significant participation, the government is neither of, nor for, nor by, the people. It is a government, at best, of those two thirds whose wealth, skin color, or parental privilege allows them opportunity to profit from the provocation and instruction of the written word.

5   The undermining of democracy in the United States is one "expense" that sensitive Americans can easily deplore because it represents a contradiction that endangers citizens of all political positions. The human price is not so obvious at first.

Since I first immersed myself within this work I have often had the following dream: I find that I am in a railroad station or a large department store within a city that is utterly unknown to me and where I cannot understand the printed words. None of the signs or symbols is familiar. Everything looks strange: like mirror writing of some kind. Gradually I understand that I am in the Soviet Union. All the letters on the walls around me are Cyrillic. I look for my pocket dictionary but I find that it has been mislaid. Where have I left it? Then I recall that I forgot to bring it with me when I packed my bags in Boston. I struggle to remember the name of my hotel. I try to ask somebody for directions. One person stops and looks at me in a peculiar way. I lose the nerve to ask. At last I reach into my wallet for an ID card. The card is missing. Have I lost it? Then I remember that my card was confiscated for some reason, many years before. Around this point, I wake up in a panic.

This panic is not so different from the misery that millions of adult illiterates experience each day within the course of their routine existence in the U.S.A.

Illiterates cannot read the menu in a restaurant.

They cannot read the cost of items on the menu in the *window* of the restaurant before they enter.

Illiterates cannot read the letters that their children bring home from their teachers. They cannot study school department circulars that tell them of the courses that their children must be taking if they hope to pass the SAT exams. They cannot help with homework. They cannot write a letter to the teacher. They are afraid to visit in the classroom. They do not want to humiliate their child or themselves.

Illiterates cannot read instructions on a bottle of prescription medicine. They cannot find out when a medicine is past the year of safe consumption; nor can they read of allergenic risks, warnings to diabetics, or the potential sedative effect of certain kinds of nonprescription pills. They cannot observe preventive health care admonitions. They cannot read about "the seven warning signs of cancer" or the indications of blood-sugar fluctuations or the risks of eating certain foods that aggravate the likelihood of cardiac arrest.

Illiterates live, in more than literal ways, an uninsured existence. They cannot understand the written details on a health insurance form. They cannot read the waivers that they sign preceding surgical procedures. Several women I have known in Boston have entered a slum hospital with the intention of obtaining a tubal ligation and have emerged a few days later after having been subjected to a hysterectomy. Unaware of their rights, incognizant of jargon, intimidated by the unfamiliar air of fear and atmosphere of ether that so many of us find oppressive in the confines even of the most attractive and expensive medical facilities, they have signed their names to documents they could not read and which nobody, in the hectic situation that prevails so often in those overcrowded hospitals that serve the urban poor, had even bothered to explain.

Childbirth might seem to be the last inalienable right of any female citizen within a civilized society. Illiterate mothers, as we shall see, already have been cheated of the power to protect their progeny against the likelihood of demolition in deficient public schools and, as a result, against the verbal servitude within which they themselves exist. Surgical denial of the right to bear that child in the first place represents an ultimate denial, an unspeakable metaphor, a final darkness that denies even the twilight gleamings of our own humanity. What greater violation of our biological, our biblical, our spiritual humanity could possibly exist than that which takes place nightly, perhaps hourly these days, within such over-burdened and benighted institutions as the Boston City Hospital? Illiteracy has many costs; few are so irreversible as this.

Even the roof above one's head, the gas or other fuel for heating that protects the residents of northern city slums against the threat of illness in the winter months become uncertain guarantees. Illiterates cannot read the lease that they must sign to live in an apartment which, too often, they cannot afford. They cannot manage check accounts and therefore seldom pay for anything by mail. Hours and entire days of difficult travel (and the cost of bus or other public transit) must be added to the real cost of whatever they consume. Loss of interest on the check accounts they do not have, and could not manage if they did, must be regarded as another of the excess costs paid by the citizen who is excluded from the common instruments of commerce in a numerate society.

15 "I couldn't understand the bills," a woman in Washington, D.C., 15 reports, "and then I couldn't write the checks to pay them. We signed things we didn't know what they were."

Illiterates cannot read the notices that they receive from welfare offices or from the IRS. They must depend on word-of-mouth instruction from the welfare worker—or from other persons whom they have good reason to mistrust. They do not know what rights they have, what deadlines and requirements they face, what options they might choose to exercise. They are half-citizens. Their rights exist in print but not in fact.

Illiterates cannot look up numbers in a telephone directory. Even if they can find the names of friends, few possess the sorting skills to make use of the yellow pages; categories are bewildering and trade names are beyond decoding capabilities for millions of nonreaders. Even the emergency numbers listed on the first page of the phone book—"Ambulance," "Police," and "Fire"—are too frequently beyond the recognition of nonreaders.

Many illiterates cannot read the admonition on a pack of cigarettes. Neither the Surgeon General's warning nor its reproduction on the package can alert them to the risks. Although most people learn by word of mouth that smoking is related to a number of grave physical disorders, they do not get the chance to read the detailed stories which can document this danger with the vividness that turns concern into determination to resist. They can see the handsome cowboy or the slim Virginia lady lighting up a filter cigarette; they cannot heed the words that tell them that this product is (not "may be") dangerous to their health. Sixty million men and women are condemned to be the unalerted, high-risk candidates for cancer.

Illiterates do not buy "no-name" products in the supermarkets. They must depend on photographs or the familiar logos that are printed on the packages of brand-name groceries. The poorest people, therefore, are denied the benefits of the least costly products.

20 Illiterates depend almost entirely upon label recognition. Many 20 labels, however, are not easy to distinguish. Dozens of different kinds of Campbell's soup appear identical to the nonreaders The purchaser who cannot read and does not dare to ask for help, out of the fear of being stigmatized (a fear which is unfortunately realistic), frequently comes home with something which she never wanted and her family never tasted.

Illiterates cannot read instructions on a pack of frozen food. Packages sometimes provide an illustration to explain the cooking preparations; but illustrations are of little help to someone who must "boil water, drop the food—*within* its plastic wrapper—in the boiling water, wait for it to simmer, instantly remove."

Even when labels are seemingly clear, they may be easily mistaken. A woman in Detroit brought home a gallon of Crisco for her children's dinner. She thought that she had bought the chicken that was pictured on the label. She had enough Crisco now to last a year—but no more money to go back and buy the food for dinner.

Recipes provided on the packages of certain staples sometimes tempt a semiliterate person to prepare a meal her children have not tasted. The longing to vary the uniform and often starchy content of low-budget meals provided to the family that relies on food stamps commonly leads to ruinous results. Scarce funds have been wasted and the food must be thrown out. The same applies to distribution of food-surplus produce in emergency conditions. Government inducements to poor people to "explore the ways" by which to make a tasty meal from tasteless noodles, surplus cheese, and powdered milk are useless to nonreaders. Intended as benevolent advice, such recommendations mock reality and foster deeper feelings of resentment and of inability to cope. (Those, on the other hand, who cautiously refrain from "innovative" recipes in preparation of their children's meals must suffer the opprobrium of "laziness," "lack of imagination. . . .")

Illiterates cannot travel freely. When they attempt to do so, they encounter risks that few of us can dream of. They cannot read traffic signs and, while they often learn to recognize and to decipher symbols, they cannot manage street names which they haven't seen before. The same is true for bus and subway stops. While ingenuity can sometimes help a man or woman to discern directions from familiar landmarks, buildings, cemeteries, churches, and the like, most illiterates are virtually immobilized. They seldom wander past the streets and neighborhoods they know. Geographical paralysis becomes a bitter metaphor for their entire existence. They are immobilized in almost every sense we can imagine. They can't move up. They can't move out. They cannot see beyond. Illiterates may take an oral test for drivers' permits in most sections of America. It is a questionable concession. Where will they go? How will they get there? How will they get home? Could it be that some of us might like it better if they stayed where they belong?

25 Travel is only one of many instances of circumscribed existence. 25
Choice, in almost all its facets, is diminished in the life of an illiterate adult. Even the printed TV schedule, which provides most people with the luxury of preselection, does not belong within the arsenal of options in illiterate existence. One consequence is that the viewer watches only what appears at moments when he happens to have time to turn the switch. Another consequence, a lot more common, is that the TV set remains in operation night and day. Whatever the program offered at the hour when he walks into the room will be the nutriment

that he accepts and swallows. Thus, to passivity, is added frequency—indeed, almost uninterrupted continuity. Freedom to select is no more possible here than in the choice of home or surgery or food.

"You don't choose," said one illiterate woman. "You take your wishes from somebody else." Whether in perusal of a menu, selection of highways, purchase of groceries, or determination of affordable enjoyment, illiterate Americans must trust somebody else: a friend, a relative, a stranger on the street, a grocery clerk, a TV copywriter.

"All of our mail we get, it's hard for her to read. Settin' down and writing a letter, she can't do it. Like if we get a bill . . . we take it over to my sister-in-law . . . My sister-in-law reads it."

Billing agencies harass poor people for the payment of the bills for purchases that might have taken place six months before. Utility companies offer an agreement for a staggered payment schedule on a bill past due. "You have to trust them," one man said. Precisely for this reason, you end up by trusting no one and suspecting everyone of possible deceit. A submerged sense of distrust becomes the corollary to a constant need to trust. "They are cheating me . . . I have been tricked . . . I do not know . . ."

Not knowing: This is a familiar theme. Not knowing the right word for the right thing at the right time is one form of subjugation. Not knowing the world that lies concealed behind those words is a more terrifying feeling. The longitude and latitude of one's existence are beyond all easy apprehension. Even the hard, cold stars within the firmament above one's head begin to mock the possibilities for self-location. Where am I? Where did I come from? Where will I go?

30 "I've lost a lot of jobs," one man explains. "Today, even if you're 30 a janitor, there's still reading and writing . . . They leave a note saying, 'Go to room so-and-so . . .' You can't do it. You can't read it. You don't know."

"The hardest thing about it is that I've been places where I didn't know where I was. You don't know where you are . . . You're lost."

"Like I said: I have two kids. What do I do if one of my kids starts choking? I go running to the phone . . . I can't look up the hospital phone number. That's if we're at home. Out on the street, I can't read the sign. I get to a pay phone. 'Okay, tell us where you are. We'll send an ambulance.' I look at the street sign. Right there, I can't tell you what it says. I'd have to spell it out, letter for letter. By that time, one of my kids would be dead . . . These are the kinds of fears you go with, every single day . . ."

"Reading directions, I suffer with. I work with chemicals . . . That's scary to begin with . . . "

"You sit down. They throw the menu in front of you. Where do you go from there? Nine times out of ten you say, 'Go ahead. Pick out something for the both of us.' I've eaten some weird things, let me tell you!"

35   Menus. Chemicals. A child choking while his mother searches for a word she does not know to find assistance that will come too late. Another mother speaks about the inability to help her kids to read: "I can't read to them. Of course that's leaving them out of something they should have. Oh, it matters. You believe it matters! I ordered all these books. The kids belong to a book club. Donny wanted me to read a book to him. I told Donny: 'I can't read,' He said: 'Mommy, you sit down. I'll read it to you.' I tried it one day, reading from the pictures. Donny looked at me. He said, 'Mommy, that's not right.' He's only five. He knew I couldn't read . . .'"

A landlord tells a woman that her lease allows him to evict her if her baby cries and causes inconvenience to her neighbors. The consequence of challenging his words conveys a danger which appears, unlikely as it seems, even more alarming than the danger of eviction. Once she admits that she can't read, in the desire to maneuver for the time in which to call a friend, she will have defined herself in terms of an explicit impotence that she cannot endure. Capitulation in this case is preferable to self-humiliation. Resisting the definition of oneself in terms of what one cannot do, what others take for granted, represents a need so great that other imperatives (even one so urgent as the need to keep one's home in winter's cold) evaporate and fall away in face of fear. Even the loss of home and shelter, in this case, is not so terrifying as the loss of self.

"I come out of school. I was sixteen. They had their meetings. The directors meet. They said that I was wasting their school paper. I was wasting pencils . . ."

Another illiterate, looking back, believes she was not worthy of her teacher's time. She believes that it was wrong of her to take up space within her school. She believes that it was right to leave in order that somebody more deserving could receive her place.

Children choke. Their mother chokes another way: on more than chicken bones.

40   People eat what others order, know what others tell them, struggle not to see themselves as they believe the world perceives them. A

man in California speaks about his own loss of identity, of self-location, definition:

"I stood at the bottom of the ramp. My car had broke down on the freeway. There was a phone. I asked for the police. They was nice. They said to tell them where I was. I looked up at the signs. There was one that I had seen before. I read it to them: ONE WAY STREET. They thought it was a joke. I told them I couldn't read. There was other signs above the ramp. They told me to try. I looked around for somebody to help. All the cars was going by real fast. I couldn't make them understand that I was lost. The cop was nice. He told me: 'Try once more,' I did my best. I couldn't read. I only knew the sign above my head. The cop was trying to be nice. He knew that I was trapped. 'I can't send out a car to you if you can't tell me where you are.' I felt afraid. I nearly cried. I'm forty-eight years old. I only said: 'I'm on a one-way street . . .'"

The legal problems and the courtroom complications that confront illiterate adults have been discussed above. The anguish that may underlie such matters was brought home to me this year while I was working on this book. I have spoken, in the introduction, of a sudden phone call from one of my former students, now in prison for a criminal offense. Stephen is not a boy today. He is twenty-eight years old. He called to ask me to assist him in his trial, which comes up next fall. He will be on trial for murder. He has just knifed and killed a man who first enticed him to his home, then cheated him, and then insulted him—as "an illiterate subhuman."

Stephen now faces twenty years to life. Stephen's mother was illiterate. His grandparents were illiterate as well. What parental curse did not destroy was killed off finally by the schools. Silent violence is repaid with interest. It will cost us $25,000 yearly to maintain this broken soul in prison. But what is the price that has been paid by Stephen's victim? What is the price that will be paid by Stephen?

Perhaps we might slow down a moment here and look at the realities described above. This is the nation that we live in. This is a society that most of us did not create but which our President and other leaders have been willing to sustain by virtue of malign neglect. Do we possess the character and courage to address a problem which so many nations, poorer than our own, have found it natural to correct?

45 The answers to these questions represent a reasonable test of our 45
belief in the democracy to which we have been asked in public school to swear allegiance.

Questions on Meaning

1. Define what Kozol means by "human cost." You might start your thinking by considering how this cost is different from the literal monetary costs that are also described at different points in the essay.
2. Kozol relates illiteracy to the concept of subjugation. Brainstorm what your think he means by this. Who are the subjugators? What is their motivation for subjugating illiterate people?
3. In a sentence or two, express the primary theme of this essay.

Questions on Rhetorical Strategy and Style

1. One characteristic of Kozol's style is passages that link concrete examples with larger abstractions or generalizations. For example, in paragraph 24, in the context of the difficulties of an illiterate person traveling, Kozol writes, "Geographical paralysis becomes a bitter metaphor for their entire existence. They are immobilized in almost every sense we can imagine." Another example occurs in paragraphs 12 and 13, where Kozol speaks of women given a hysterectomy without being informed of the meaning of this surgery as "a final darkness that denies even the twilight gleamings of our own humanity." Analyze this passage and explain why Kozol calls this the "ultimate denial."
2. Kozol frequently uses description as a rhetorical device for developing the essay. Read back through the essay and identify at least three examples of illiterate people whose problem Kozol describes in detail. How does each of these examples contribute to the effectiveness of the essay overall?
3. How successful is Kozol in building his argument about the costs of illiteracy? What specific characteristics of the essay contribute to your evaluation?

Writing Assignments

1. To better understand the difficulty illiterates face in many types of communication, use your imagination to solve the following problem. You are the director of a new program at your college or university for teaching reading at no cost to adult illiterates in the community. You have funding to hire teachers and pay for classrooms and materials, but very little money left over to publicize the

program. How do you inform illiterates in the community about your reading classes? How do you give them basic information such as where to come and what times and how to get there? Brainstorm with others to reach the most effective solution that overcomes the problems of communication.

2. Kozol says our political leaders sustain the problem of illiteracy through "malign neglect." What does he mean by this phrase? Why is this neglect "malign"? Consider other social problems, such as homelessness or lack of good health care for people in poverty. Do you see "malign neglect" with these problems too? Write an essay in which you explore the reasons why leaders might be neglectful in these ways.

3. In paragraph 3 Kozol states that illiterate persons can only "cast a vote of questionable worth" because their decision is not based on "serious print information" but on "a face, a smile, or a style." Some social critics would say the same is true of many people who can read: that they vote based on television images and sound bytes rather than careful reading of the issues. If true, this only heightens the resulting national tragedy to which Kozol refers. What do you think about this idea? Do most people take the time to study the issues in depth before voting? Ask a few other people about how much they read before the last election. Think about what you learn from their comments, and formulate your own thesis about what really happens in an election and what you think *should* happen. Write a persuasive essay that develops your thesis.

I Think, Therefore IM

Jennifer Lee

Jennifer Lee (1976–) was born in New York City. She grad-
uated from Harvard University in 1999 with a degree in
mathematics and economics. While at Harvard she spent a
year at Beijing University on a fellowship studying interna-
tional relations. Lee has received a scholarship from the
Asian American Journalism Association and has interned at
The Boston Globe, The New York Times, Newsday, The
Wall Street Journal, *and* The Washington Post. *She joined*
the staff of The New York Times *in 2001 as a technology*
reporter and began writing for the Metro section the next
year. The following selection on instant-messaging language
originally appeared in the Times *in September 2002.*

1   Each September Jacqueline Harding prepares a classroom presentation on the common writing mistakes she sees in her students'
work.

Ms. Harding, an eighth-grade English teacher at Viking Middle
School in Guernee, Ill., scribbles the words that have plagued generations of school children across her whiteboard:

There. Their. They're.
Your. You're.
To. Too. Two.
Its. It's.

This September, she has added a new list: u, r, ur, b4, wuz, cuz, 2.

When she asked her students how many of them used shortcuts
like them in their writing, Ms. Harding said, she was not surprised
when most of them raised their hands. This, after all, is their online

lingua franca: English adapted for the spitfire conversational style of Internet instant messaging.

Ms. Harding, who has seen such shortcuts creep into student papers over the last two years, said she gave her students a warning: "If I see this in your assignments, I will take points off."

5 "Kids should know the difference," said Ms. Harding, who decided to address this issue head-on this year. "They should know where to draw the line between formal writing and conversational writing."

As more and more teenagers socialize online, middle school and high school teachers like Ms. Harding are increasingly seeing a breezy form of Internet English jump from e-mail into schoolwork. To their dismay, teachers say that papers are being written with shortened words, improper capitalization and punctuation, and characters like &, $ and @.

Teachers have deducted points, drawn red circles and tsk-tsked at their classes. Yet the errant forms continue. "It stops being funny after you repeat yourself a couple of times," Ms. Harding said.

But teenagers, whose social life can rely as much these days on text communication as the spoken word, say that they use instant-messaging shorthand without thinking about it. They write to one another as much as they write in school, or more.

"You are so used to abbreviating things, you just start doing it unconsciously on schoolwork and reports and other things," said Eve Brecker, 15, a student at Montclair High School in New Jersey.

10 Ms. Brecker once handed in a midterm exam riddled with instant-messaging shorthand. "I had an hour to write an essay on *Romeo and Juliet*," she said. "I just wanted to finish before my time was up. I was writing fast and carelessly. I spelled 'you' 'u.'" She got a C.

Even terms that cannot be expressed verbally are making their way into papers. Melanie Weaver was stunned by some of the term papers she received from a 10th-grade class she recently taught as part of an internship. "They would be trying to make a point in a paper, they would put a smiley face in the end," said Ms. Weaver, who teaches at Alvernia College in Reading, PA. "If they were presenting an argument and they needed to present an opposite view, they would put a frown."

As Trisha Fogarty, a sixth-grade teacher at Houlton Southside School in Houlton, Maine, puts it, today's students are "Generation Text."

Almost 60 percent of the online population under age 17 uses instant messaging, according to Nielsen/NetRatings. In addition to cellphone text messaging, Weblogs and e-mail, it has become a popular means of flirting, setting up dates, asking for help with homework and keeping in contact with distant friends. The abbreviations are a natural outgrowth of this rapid-fire style of communication.

"They have a social life that centers around typed communication," said Judith S. Donath, a professor at the Massachusetts Institute of Technology's Media Lab who has studied electronic communication. "They have a writing style that has been nurtured in a teenage social milieu."

15   Some teachers see the creeping abbreviations as part of a continuing assault of technology on formal written English. Others take it more lightly, saying that it is just part of the larger arc of language evolution.

"To them it's not wrong," said Ms. Harding, who is 28. "It's acceptable because it's in their culture. It's hard enough to teach them the art of formal writing. Now we've got to overcome this new instant-messaging language."

Ms. Harding noted that in some cases the shorthand isn't even shorter. "I understand 'cuz,' but what's with the 'wuz'? It's the same amount of letters as 'was,' so what's the point?" she said.

Deborah Bova, who teaches eighth-grade English at Raymond Park Middle School in Indianapolis, thought her eyesight was failing several years ago when she saw the sentence "B4 we perform, ppl have 2 practice" on a student assignment.

"I thought, 'My God, what is this?' " Ms. Bova said. "Have they lost their minds?"

20   The student was summoned to the board to translate the sentence into standard English: "Before we perform, people have to practice." She realized that the students thought she was out of touch. "It was like 'Get with it, Bova,' " she said. Ms. Bova had a student type up a reference list of translations for common instant-messaging expressions. She posted a copy on the bulletin board by her desk and took another one home to use while grading.

Students are sometimes unrepentant.

"They were astonished when I began to point these things out to them," said Henry Assetto, a social studies teacher at Twin Valley High School in Elverson, Pa. "Because I am a history teacher, they did not think a history teacher would be checking up on their grammar or their spelling," said Mr. Assetto, who has been teaching for 34 years.

But Montana Hodgen, 16, another Montclair student, said she was so accustomed to instant-messaging abbreviations that she often read right past them. She proofread a paper last year only to get it returned with the messaging abbreviations circled in red.

"I was so used to reading what my friends wrote to me on Instant Messenger that I didn't even realize that there was something wrong," she said. She said her ability to separate formal and informal English declined the more she used instant messages. "Three years ago, if I had seen that, I would have been 'What is that?'"

25 The spelling checker doesn't always help either, students say. For one, Microsoft Word's squiggly red spell-check lines don't appear beneath single letters and numbers such as u, r, c, 2 and 4. Nor do they catch words which have numbers in them such as "l8r" and "b4" by default.

Teenagers have essentially developed an unconscious "accent" in their typing, Professor Donath said. "They have gotten facile at typing and they are not paying attention."

Teenagers have long pushed the boundaries of spoken language, introducing words that then become passe with adult adoption. Now teenagers are taking charge and pushing the boundaries of written language. For them, expressions like "oic" (oh I see), "nm" (not much), "jk" (just kidding) and "lol" (laughing out loud), "brb" (be right back), "ttyl" (talk to you later) are as standard as conventional English.

"There is no official English language," said Jesse Sheidlower, the North American editor of the *Oxford English Dictionary.* "Language is spread not because anyone dictates any one thing to happen. The decisions are made by the language and the people who use the language."

Some teachers find the new writing style alarming. "First of all, it's very rude, and it's very careless," said Lois Moran, a middle school English teacher at St. Nicholas School in Jersey City.

30 "They should be careful to write properly and not to put these little codes in that they are in such a habit of writing to each other," said Ms. Moran, who has lectured her eighth-grade class on such mistakes.

Others say that the instant-messaging style might simply be a fad, something that students will grow out of. Or they see it as an opportunity to teach students about the evolution of language.

"I turn it into a very positive teachable moment for kids in the class," said Erika V. Karres, an assistant professor at the University of North Carolina at Chapel Hill who trains student teachers. She shows students how English has evolved since Shakespeare's time. "Imagine Langston Hughes's writing in quick texting instead of 'Langston writing,' " she said. "It makes teaching and learning so exciting."

Other teachers encourage students to use messaging shorthand to spark their thinking processes. "When my children are writing first drafts, I don't care how they spell anything, as long as they are writing," said Ms. Fogarty, the sixth-grade teacher from Houlton, Maine. "If this lingo gets their thoughts and ideas onto paper quicker, the more power to them." But during editing and revising, she expects her students to switch to standard English.

Ms. Bova shares the view that instant-messaging language can help free up their creativity. With the help of students, she does not even need the cheat sheet to read the shorthand anymore.

35   "I think it's a plus," she said. "And I would say that with a + sign."   35

Questions on Meaning

1. What are the social and technological conditions that have shaped cyberlingo vocabulary and its uses?
2. What does the term "lingua franca" mean? How does it capture the full significance of the text messaging style of young people?
3. Why, in your opinion, are adults frequently appalled when students use an informal or unconventional style in their writing?

Questions on Rhetorical Strategy and Style

1. Why does Lee open her article with the words Ms. Harding puts on the board each September? What is she trying to suggest to her readers?
2. How does the article adhere to the conventions of the newspaper journalism? Does the writer remain balanced and objective? Explain how.
3. Why does the writer quote the editor of the *Oxford English Dictionary?*

Writing Assignments

1. Why do teachers often seem fussy, and even offended, by their students' use of language? Why are they so insistent about the conventions of standard, edited English? Write an essay that explains to your teachers your experience trying to learn these conventions, and why your language is necessary to your sense of identity.
2. Try the exercise used by Erika Karres, the teacher at the University of North Carolina. Take a poem or any piece of writing and translate it into a quick text version. How does the meaning of it change?